The Mind and Its Depths

The Mind and Its Depths

Richard Wollheim

Harvard University Press
Cambridge, Massachusetts
London, England
1993

This book is printed on acid-free paper, and its binding materials
have been chosen for strength and durability.

Library of Congress Cataloging-in-Publication Data

Wollheim, Richard, 1923–
    The mind and its depths / Richard Wollheim.
        p.   cm.
    Includes bibliographical references and index.
    ISBN 0-674-57611-X (alk. paper)
      1. Philosophy of mind. 2. Arts—Psychological aspects.
    3. Psychoanalysis. 4. Psychology and philosophy.   I. Title.
BD418.3.W65   1993
128'.2—dc20
92-12738
        CIP

For Aline and Isaiah Berlin

Contents

Preface

This book is in more ways than one a sequel to *On Art and the Mind*. In that volume I collected all those miscellaneous philosophical writings of mine up to 1972 which I thought worth preserving. Here I do the same for the years 1975–1989. 'Worth preserving' is not an epithet of high praise. What has led me to collect the pieces I have is that they bring together ideas often kept apart. They do so generally to make a fairly simple point.

Another common feature of both volumes is that the writings they contain originated not as articles in professional journals but as something more occasional: as special lectures, or papers read to a conference, or essays commissioned for an anthology, or tributes honouring a friend. This accounts for the tone of much of the writing and for certain turns of phrase, which I have not changed, and it has also had the consequence that, though all but two of the pieces in the present volume have been previously published, none is any longer readily accessible.

In this volume, as with its predecessor, the writings span the philosophy of mind, aesthetics, and the theory of psychoanalysis. What this means in the case of the present collection is that it must be seen against the background of two books of mine in which I set out as systematically as I could what I thought philosophically about the mind and the art of painting. These are *The Thread of Life* and *Painting as an Art*. Both books began as courses of public lectures: the William James Lectures in Philosophy, delivered at Harvard in early 1981, and the Andrew W. Mellon Lectures in the Fine Arts, delivered at the National Gallery of Art in Washington in the autumn of 1984. In both works, but particularly the earlier one, I wanted to express my views with as little reference as possible to the views of others. This very evidently dissatisfied the reviewers, though I am sure that it earned the gratitude of many readers. It cannot be a correct literary principle that, for us to understand any one book, we are always required first to have read five others. Of course, understanding is a matter of degree.

In reprinting these writings of mine I have done some revision, which has been exclusively in the interests of sense, clarity, and decisiveness. I have not aimed at consistency. A number of issues recur several times in the course of these pages, but I am insufficiently confident on which occasion it was that I came closest to the truth to bring what I said at different times into uniformity. So I have left the area of the target sprayed with shot, and I hope my readers can see better than I can where I have missed.

The recurrent topics are the nature of expression, in and out of art: the tendency of early or infantile thought to represent itself as something bodily, or what I call the corporealization of thought, which in turn provides the precondition of the wish and of omnipotence; the relationship of pictures and language, an area where of recent years the waters have been severely muddied; and an issue that most philosophers profess to find far less serious than I do, and that is whether there really is such a thing as morality, or whether it is a dream, or perhaps a nightmare. It seems to me natural to think that art is more deeply rooted in human nature than morality, and I am surprised that philosophers make little of the fact that, though good art is more likeable than bad art, virtuous people do not enjoy this same advantage over those to whom we are drawn primarily for their charm, or their gaiety, or their sweetness of nature, or their outrageousness.

I have retained those notes in which at the time I thanked friends and colleagues for their help with individual lectures or essays. But there are many others whom this leaves unthanked. Many are aware of how much I owe them. During those years when the pieces collected here were being written, I learnt most from, and owe most to, (in alphabetical order) Malcolm Budd, Myles Burnyeat, Jerry Cohen, Donald Davidson, Bill Hart, Jim Hopkins, Antonia Phillips, Hanna Segal, Barry Stroud, David Wiggins, and Bernard Williams. For advice on what to include and what not to, I must thank Karen Pilkington, and for help with the preparation of the various manuscripts and typescripts that this book absorbed, I am grateful to Yulia Motofuji, Jerry Robinson, Catherine Taylor, and, once again, Katherine Backhouse, to whom I now owe three decades of thanks.

I dedicate this book to two old friends, whose company over many years, in many circumstances, has meant so much to me.

I The Sheep and the Ceremony

1. In the third book of the *Analects* of Confucius we read of the Master teaching a return to the purity and sincerity of the ancient ceremonies. He deplores superstition and the mere outward observance of forms. Then Tzu-kung, one of the disciples, asks about the monthly ceremony at which the new moon is announced to the Ancestors. Would it not be better, he queries, if the practice of sacrificing a sheep were done away with? Confucius reproves him gently. He calls him by his familiar name. "Ssu," he says, "You care for the sheep. I care for the ceremony."

In this lecture, delivered in honour of Sir Leslie Stephen, humanitarian, agnostic, distinguished historian of Utilitarianism, I shall not speak in favour of animal sacrifice, nor have I come to defend traditional religion. My lecture will not undertake to criticize Utilitarianism, except indirectly, and then only in what I regard as an implausible form. The story which I have brought to your attention, and from which I have drawn the title of this lecture, I first read three years ago, travelling in a train. The story was quoted out of context. It made a great impression on me, though I couldn't tell why, and, perhaps for this reason, more of one. A variety of thoughts associated themselves to the passage, and, if this lecture has a single theme, it is the exploration of those thoughts, or at least such of them as can justify themselves as relevant.

In the course of composing this lecture I have been reading two other lectures, both by close friends, one also delivered in honour of Sir Leslie Stephen, and what I say here, whether it shows or not, owes much to them. One is "Truth, Invention, and the Meaning of Life" by David Wiggins:[1] the other is Stuart Hampshire's "Morality and Pessimism."[2] One citation must serve for many.

2. The ceremony of announcing the new moon, which the amiable Confucius wished to see observed with full punctiliousness, may be used to

represent a whole class of actions, without which human life would be very different both from what it is and from what we may presume it to have been throughout culture. There are various ways in which such actions might be characterized, and I shall say of them that they have the following properties: They are felt to be obligatory, though not necessarily unconditionally so, and certainly not by all; they admit of being well done or being badly done, or at any rate of being variably done; they, like all actions, have consequences, but they are not to be done for, nor do they derive their value from, these consequences; the value that they have is best thought of as their capacity to give value or meaning to a life—to the life, that is, of the person who performs them. Amongst these actions are to be numbered those actions we call rituals, and I shall, in this lecture, borrow the term 'ritual' so as to say that the incident of the sheep and the ceremony raises the question of ritual and its place in the conduct of life.

Of ritual the first or prime thing to ask is, How do such actions give significance to a human life?, or, How do such actions have significance themselves? Two distinct questions, but they ask much the same thing: and they ask much the same thing, just because one of the reasons for thinking of the value that ritualistic actions give to a human life as 'significance' is that the value they give and the value they have is one and the same. They pass on what they possess: as a word does to a sentence. Of course, the significance that such an action has, and hands on, is not one that it has, or can hand on, in isolation. A ritualistic action has significance relative to, on the one hand, a set of further actions and, on the other hand, a given life or, rather, a life of a given kind: where what these actions have in common is that they may combine to give value to a life of just that kind. So that if I, after this lecture, still unconverted to the way of life that Confucius wanted to preserve, were to cry off the dinner to which I have been invited, and go out into the fens, and buy a sheep, tie it up, and hack it to death, that action, so far from endowing my life with meaning, would be a senseless piece of butchery. And here we have another reason why 'significance' is used in connection with the value of ritualistic actions, for it is in a similar way that the value of a word is relative to, on the one hand, a set of further words and, on the other hand, a community of speakers—in brief, a language.

If, then, we ask how ritualistic actions gain or give significance, a natural starting point for this inquiry is a traditional dilemma. Aristotle posed the dilemma for the human agent: medieval philosophers posed it for the divine Lawgiver. It arises in this way: A certain set of actions is preferred, a certain set of rules is ordained. Does the agent prefer the actions he prefers because they are right, or are these actions right just because he prefers them? Does God ordain the rules He ordains because they are right, or are these rules right just because God ordains them? The first alternative in each case, which makes value primary and explains desire in terms of it, leads towards realism and encourages an objectivist view of value. The second alternative, which reverses the ordering and derives value from desire, leads away from realism and encourages a voluntarist view of value. Objectivism, voluntarism—which is correct, or closer to correctness?

It has been argued, and to my mind to good effect, that voluntarism, at any rate as it has just been laid out, deriving the value of a given action from the desire to do it, falls into incoherence. It falls into incoherence because it ignores a crucial requirement that any thesis in the psychology of moral action must respect. A thesis telling us how a moral agent acts is required at the same time to make sense of his action: it must render it intelligible. And, if it is to do this, the thesis must attribute to the agent a body of thoughts and feelings which, in the first place, are perfectly comprehensible in themselves and, secondly, are fully adequate to lead the agent to do the action in question. Voluntarism fails to meet this requirement because—well, what does it do? It tells us of an agent and of an action, and that the action is of no value in the agent's eyes, yet he desires to do it: or, to spell it out, the action is *as yet* of no value in the agent's eyes. And voluntarism must be saying this, for, according to voluntarism, just what will make the action valuable for the agent is his desire to do it. Why then does the agent desire to do the action? We are owed an answer to this question, but it looks as though voluntarism has denied itself the capacity to give an answer that does not reinvite the question.

But, it will be said in defence of voluntarism, is it not an obvious truth of human psychology that there are actions we desire to do, and our desire arises for no good reason? And might not ritual be of this character?

Human psychology is scattered with theses that are obvious yet not true, and it may very well be that, like the innocence of childhood, the frivolity of adulthood is a pleasing myth that has to be given up, and on closely related grounds. But, even if the thesis is true, it is not calculated to save voluntarism. For we are talking, remember, of actions that enhance human life or invest it with meaning, and is it convincing to think of them as actions which, initially, in the life of the species, and then again in the life of each individual, originate in blind or unmotivated desire?

Should we then abandon voluntarism, embrace the alternative, or objectivist, view of the matter, and find ourselves moving towards realism about value?

That may be the correct direction to go in, but it seems to me premature and certainly not the conclusion to which the preceding discussion has forced us. This is because I have so far considered voluntarism only in a very simple-minded form. The view that desire precedes value, or that value derives from desire, does not require us to believe that the value of any given action arises out of the desire to do that action. It is surely in the spirit of voluntarism, if not true to the letter of those who have advocated it, that the value of an action should be thought to derive from desires taken generally. By which I mean that the desires that give value to an action might, but also might not, include the desire to do that action, and certainly are not limited to that one desire. So to the traditional gentleman of China (as even the best translators are constrained to call him) it may very well seem that the sacrifice of the sheep at the ceremony of the new moon is a meaningful thing to do, something which will impart value to his life, and yet it might be that, up till the moment it struck him this way, he had no desire to do it: indeed it might not even have occurred to him as a thing to do. Nevertheless, the ritual would not have struck him as of value, nor would it have been so, had his desires, more broadly considered, been different—or so a less simple-minded voluntarism might maintain.

To do justice to this kind of voluntarism something has to be said about the relationship in which, according to it, an action stands to those desires from which it acquires meaningfulness. All we can say at the moment is something negative: that it is not, as simple-minded voluntarism canvasses, the relationship of being the object of those desires. Fortunately, we do have at our disposal a model or exemplar for this relationship, and we should draw upon it if we want to see how a ritualistic action can acquire meaningfulness from desires taken broadly.

But, before doing so, I am reminded by the phrase just used, 'desires taken broadly', and its double meaning, that I owe at any rate to those who aren't used to the linguistic habits of philosophers an apology. For the practice has grown up of using the word 'desire' so as to cover a far broader range of mental conditions than it actually does. The practice is indefensible, and I shall drop it.

3. The model I claim we have for thinking about how a ritualistic action may derive meaning from a multiplicity of mental conditions is provided by the phenomenon of expressiveness in art. For the expressiveness of a work of art derives from the human mind, yet it would be absurd to think that it derives entirely from—indeed, though the mental source may include, it can also exclude—the bare desire to make just that very work of art. So what is the mental source of expressiveness?

Let us take a step back. The broad characteristics of art, including expressiveness, originate outside art: even if, for each characteristic, the original phenomenon, or prototype, is unrecognizable under the elaboration that art expends upon it. The prototype for expressiveness, or the one I want to consider in this lecture, for there may be more than one, is what, borrowing a term from Symbolist theory, I call 'correspondance', 'correspondence'. It is this: We look out over a landscape—say, an estuary at low tide with the channels of water making their way outward to the sea; or a high meadow, with tiny stacks of hay, lit up like pinpricks by the bright sun; or an expanse of heath at dusk, moorland cottages, the bark of silver birches against the darkness of the pond, tall granite boulders—and, as we are looking, before we realize what is happening to us, a mental state, simple or complex, sets itself up within us. Two features of this experience are to be noted. In the first place, the mental state isn't a mere association to the perception—as a colour might be associated, merely associated, to the thought of a number, in which case the association will share the mind with the original thought, alternatively distract the mind from it. In the present case, the mental state integrates with the perception: and for this a parallel might be with the association of a colour to the sound of a vowel, where there is not mere association, there is also condensation. And, secondly, the effect of the mental state integrating with the perception is that the mental state conditions how we perceive the landscape or what we perceive it as. Much as, though a colour could not affect how we think of a number, or could not saturate our thought, we could come to hear, say, the vowel *U* as green. The result of such an interlock between mental state and perception might be put, most generally, by saying that the landscape becomes emblematic of the mental state: it becomes emblematic of melancholy, or serenity, or mania. On occasions, things may go beyond that, and the perceiver attributes to the landscape the property of being in or having the mental state. So, seeing the heath at sunset as emblematic of serenity, he says that it is serene.

Even now, still at the stage of correspondence, we discern a connection that is to become more significant as we move from correspondence to expressiveness itself. This is the connection with metaphor. For, if we say that the heath at sunset is serene, that is metaphor. Indeed of recent years it has been claimed by a distinguished philosopher of art[3] that it is a necessary condition of expression that, when an object expresses a mental state, the predicate corresponding to that mental state is metaphorically true of the object. In this unqualified form the claim cannot be made good. Counter-examples spring to mind: A painting that expresses anxiety is not metaphorically anxious. However, rather than pursue the counter-examples, which may or may not be systematically explicable, it is worth making a more general point, which is also more significant: and that is that expressiveness and metaphor have a common origin in the human mind. To look at this, let us stay a minute longer with correspondence.

We perceive (let us say) the estuary as emblematic of melancholy; we even (for this is a case where we may do this) say that the estuary is melancholy: and we do this because of the chance coming together of two distinct factors—an internal disposition, and an external fact. The internal disposition is the capacity to project inner states upon outer reality, and the external fact is the look of the estuary, and they come together in that the look of the estuary is such as to excite the perceiver to project on to it his inner sense of loss and devastation, and the coming together was chance because the estuary was not designed to do this. Sometimes in extreme states, such as paranoia, or in that artificial neurosis which the psycho-analytic process cultivates called the transference, projection occurs without any consonance from the outer world. Such cases however are of no present interest since they provide no clue to expressiveness. Of great significance however is another feature of projection, which is rooted in the functions it serves. Over a widely varying range of conditions, from the benign to the pathological, the function of projection is to help the individual to achieve, or to restore, or to impose, internal order, and it follows from this that it is rare for mental states to be projected one by one, or singly. Characteristically a multiplicity of internal states is projected, and along with these states their structure is also projected. A landscape corresponds not to this or that mental state but to what may be called a constellation of mental states. And this feature of projection persists as we move from correspondence to our real topic: expressiveness.

The move is effected as attention turns from works of nature to works of art: from the case where the match between inner state and outer reality, which enables projection, is chance or fortuitous, to the case where the match has been contrived and the projection is therefore controlled. Across the arts the artist sees to it that the object he makes has a certain look, that—to appropriate a word, just for its generality—it has a certain surface—a visual surface, an auditory surface, a narrative surface—and this look, this surface, has been chosen just so as to bring down upon the work of art the projection of some specific mental constellation. The work of art becomes, like the work of nature, emblematic of certain mental states, but the difference between the two—and this is where expressiveness comes in—is that with art this is an objective, it is no longer merely a subjective, matter. With the work of nature there is no question of projection being correct or incorrect. With the work of art a standard of correctness emerges. The standard of correctness is set by the artist's intention, and it legislates as follows: If, or to the extent to which, the artist's intention is fulfilled, this intention fixes what the spectator ought to project on to the surface: to the extent that the artist's intention is unfulfilled, there is nothing that ought to be projected, only something that is supposed to be projected, and the intention fixes this.

It is the emergence of a standard of correctness for projection that in turn makes criticism possible. Indeed it necessitates criticism. For the task of criticism is nothing other than to retrieve the artist's intention, to reconstruct the creative process.[4] If this sounds heretical in certain quarters, where the view is taken that criticism is at liberty to project on to a work of art whatever it wishes, or whatever it finds original or suggestive or provocative, and in this liberty lies the vitality of art, it is insufficiently appreciated that, in taking this view, critics, or friends of criticism, cut off the branch on which they sit. For the view in effect cancels the status of art and relegates art to the status of nature.

A crucial question that arises at this stage is whether the artist can ever express mental states that are not or have not been his own. Now, if to express certain mental states is to excite the spectator to project those states on to a work created, then it might seem that the answer is Yes, the artist can express what isn't in him. I am however quite convinced that, except in highly artificial cases, which arise only peripherally, and are of no real aesthetic interest, this answer is wrong. To see this, what we need to do is to remind ourselves of certain facts of the case we are talking about. To begin with: What the artist's work expresses is not the same as what the work represents, narrates, depicts; it is not the subject-matter, but rather the attitudes, emotions, feelings, encouraged towards the subject-matter. And, when we further remind ourselves that these varied mental states are highly complex, highly structured, highly elusive, it will seem little wonder that a work of art's expressive content must first have been in the artist's mind before it can arrive upon the work's surface.

4. Of course, the parallel proposed between ritual and art, between the expressiveness of art and the value of ritual, cannot be used to show that ritual actually has a value. All it shows, all it is supposed to show, is that, if ritual has a value, then this value could accrue from mental states or collections of mental states taken broadly: it does not have to originate locally, or in a single desire. However I can foresee an objection, and this is that, if voluntarism is reconstructed in this way, it doesn't answer the question it sets out to answer. It only pushes it a stage further back. For whether a given ritual has value seems now to depend on whether the mental states that are properly projected on to it have themselves a value. If they have a value, it does: and it doesn't if they haven't a value.

This objection does not have the force it seems to have—for three reaons. Two of these we are already in a position to appreciate. For the third we shall have to return to the parallel between ritual and art.

In the first place, ritual gains value—gains *some* value, that is—from the mere fact that it can reflect complex conditions of the mind, utterly irrespective of any value we set upon these conditions. The capacity to bear multiple projections, expressiveness, fit—that is the most general way I can put it—mere fit, then, between the inner and the outer is something to which in itself we are inclined to assign value: value, moreover, which we think of as related to significance or meaning. The inclination rests, I take it, upon the thought that fit humanizes nature, or that through fit we make ourselves at home within the world.

But, secondly, and far more to the point, is this: Suppose we try to evaluate ritual by evaluating the mental constellations that we project upon it—how do we set value upon mental states themselves? And there is one criterion which recommends itself, though just why is a difficult matter, which concentrates upon the outer manifestation of the mental state, and rules that inner states are of value just in case their outward manifestation is something that lends itself to calm and steady contemplation. If the outward manifestation repels contemplation—and not just superficially, of course, but on the part of someone who offers it full and informed attention—then the inner state stands criticized. An analogy, which might soften the strangeness of the criterion, suggests itself: Ritual on this view subjects a particular kind of life to much the same sort of ordeal as autobiography subjects a particular life. In each case what the ordeal amounts to is exposure to the light of day, and it is no small matter, no mere coincidence, whether what is exposed can stand up to the test.

In ethics I am a naturalist, but there is naturalism and naturalism, and in the university of Cambridge I do not have to make the point how few forms of the doctrine have any chance of survival.[5] I have nothing to say for forms of naturalism which try to define moral terms in non-moral terms, or to identify moral phenomena with non-moral phenomena. The naturalism I favour is not a linguistic or an ontological doctrine. Naturalism for me consists in the claim that morality originates in certain natural movements of the psyche, which do not themselves require reference to morality either to describe or to explain them. More specifically, it originates in our primitive capacity to tolerate certain conditions of ourselves and our primitive incapacity to tolerate other conditions of ourselves. Now, it is intuitive to think that, as internal conditions get externalized, or in the wake of projection, so our capacity or our incapacity to tolerate them will be put most sharply to the test. And the criterion for judging internal states, by reference to their outward manifestation, which I have said recommends itself, does so just because it exploits this thought.

In this lecture I have no chance to argue for or defend the underlying thought. Let me hasten to show that one absurd consequence does not follow from it. It does not lead to the optimistic conclusion—or to what my predecessor in these lectures to whom I have already made reference called, on rather different grounds, the pessimistic conclusion—that every ritual, or every social phenomenon, that has stood up to the test of time is all right, and we have no reason to look for improvement. To show that this is so I shall have to return to the parallel to ritual, art, and in the course of doing so I shall have a chance to present the further, the third, reason why the value of any ritual does not simply derive from the value of the mental states that may be projected on to it.

5. Thus far in considering art—the expressiveness of art, that is—I have considered it in a single perspective, which might be thought of as as the perspective common to artist and spectator. I have talked of the expressiveness of a work of art as though it depended solely upon the fact that the work has a surface, the surface has a certain character, and the character of the surface permits, facilitates, encourages the projection on to the work of a certain constellation of mental states. This is to view expressiveness in the perspective common to artist and spectator, just because what it brings into sight—fit, the match between outer and inner—is something equally accessible to artist and spectator. Neither is privileged over the other in his grasp of it, and it explains the characteristic interest that each develops in the work. Fit explains at the same time why the artist makes the work and what the spectator makes of it. All that has to be added—so long as we continue to occupy this point of view—is how each, in taking his own interest in the work, is reinforced by knowing that the work may hold the very same interest for the other.

But this is not the only perspective in which the expresiveness of art may be viewed. Shifting our position, we may see it in another perspective, open in the first instance only to the artist, and so only secondly to the spectator. In this perspective quite another aspect of expressiveness is brought into sight. This aspect relates to the artist's activity, and it is for this reason that the perspective is primarily the artist's. For if a work of art derives its expressiveness in part from its surface, or from how it appears, expressiveness also accrues to the work through the artist's activity of giving it this surface or bringing it about that it appears as it does. If we want to understand what a work of art expresses, we must take stock not just of the product but also of the process that culminates in the product: for the process too has a contribution to make to the overall significance of the work.

The contribution can be of two kinds. It can be positive, or it can be negative. The creative process can enrich or enhance the work's expressive meaning; it can depreciate, it can impoverish it. Once we grasp this, once we see how this comes about—and then additionally we see how just the same thing holds for ritual and the observance of ritual—we shall have before us the third reason I promised why the value of a given ritual isn't simply derivative from the value of the mental states with which it fits.

Now, it is no small mark of the austerity, of the high seriousness, of art that, while there are several ways in which the activity of making the work can detract from its significance, there is only one way in which it can add to it. It can add to it only when that activity constitutes a process of self-knowledge—with all that that implies: for self-knowledge invariably brings in train self-change, self-reparation. And the creative activity can become a process of self-knowledge when the work of art reflects with sufficient precision some complex constellation of inner states which the artist seeks to externalize. In such cases the artist's activity assumes the character of a benign odyssey, from which the work of art in turn draws benefit.

Contrast this with ways in which the significance of the work is diminished by the nature of the artist's activity. I shall indicate two ways in which this may come about. First of all, the work of art may insufficiently, too imprecisely, fit the internal states that it is supposed to reflect, and, if this happens, not just any old how, but along a particular dimension, in that something felt to be shameful or degrading or frightening, something (to go back to an earlier thought) whose outward manifestation could not be steadily contemplated, fails to get externalized, then the artist, in making the work of art, not only fails to acquire self-knowledge, he strenuously attains to self-error. The surface with which he endows the work of art presents an idealized version of the psyche, and in apprenticing himself to that surface he struggles to acquire a picture of himself which by many indications he has already shown himself not to believe true.

I have used the word 'projection' to pick out the activity by which a work of art, endowed with a particular surface, acquires an expressive value. The word 'projection' is part of the vernacular. "The youth," Emerson writes, "intoxicated with his admiration of a hero, fails to see that it is only a projection of his own soul which he admires." The word is also part of a theoretical language: the language of psychoanalysis. From this theoretical language I take another word to characterize this first way in which the creative process can contribute negatively to the expressive value of the work of art: 'denial'. The artist is engaged in denial when he constructs a work that idealizes its expressive content.

The second way in which the creative process can contribute negatively to the expressive value of the work is this: The fit between outer and inner need leave nothing to be desired (though it probably will). Nevertheless the increment in self-knowledge that might reasonably be expected of the creative process does not occur, and the reason why is to do with the spirit in which the process was undertaken. The work may now bear upon its surface whole truths, not half-truths, but just the motive with which the artist inscribed them upon the surface interferes to prevent his reading them. There are a number of more specific thoughts that may serve to define the exact motive: the artist may wish to triumph over what the work could show him; he may want to disown it, or treat it as the belonging of another; he may make it serve his designs upon the spectator, to lure him or to scandalize him. But, whatever the fine detail of the motive, the upshot is the same. The artist has externalized some mental constellation so as to rid himself of it, or of its consequences, and this way in which the creative process can contribute negatively to the expressive value of the work I call, once again taking a term from the language of psychoanalysis, 'projective identification'. In denial the artist immures himself in self-ignorance: in projective identification he repeats the losing of a piece of self-knowledge.

But to think that the artist's activity could contribute, either positively or negatively, to the expressive meaning of the work of art seems exposed to a powerful objection. At its simplest the objection is this: Isn't any such view committed to supposing that there could be two works of art, indistinguishable in themselves, identical, that is, as to their surfaces, which nevertheless differ in expressive meaning, and do so solely in virtue of their history? The difference is to be ascribed not to anything in either work but to how they became what they are. And this is surely counterintuitive.

But before I try to meet this objection, I have an admission to make. It will not have escaped your attention—and you may wonder whether it has, whether it possibly could have, escaped mine—that in considering expressiveness I have presented the whole phenomenon back to front. For what I have done amounts to treating art as though it were a kind of mail-order business in which the artist orders the work from himself.

Having chosen a surface from some mental catalogue, he commissions himself to produce a work that would bear just this surface. Stripped of metaphor, what I have done is allowed myself to talk of creativity as though a work of art could be fully specified antecedently to its being created. Of course, this is an absurd assumption, and I have put the matter as I have only for ease of exposition, reasonably confident that up till now this put me at no great risk. Up till now, but no longer. For the present objection trades on this very assumption: since, in supposing that there could be two works of art, indistinguishable in their surface but distinguishable in their history, does it not assume that the surface of a work of art can be adequately described without reference to the process of which it is the product? Elsewhere, in arguing otherwise or that the work of art and the artistic activity are interdependent, I have put it by saying that a work of art is essentially a *work* of art.

However, it may seem that the objection has not yet been fully met. For, even if the surface of a work of art may be variously described depending upon how it came about, and the correct description is that which chimes with how it actually came about, the question remains whether these differences in description correspond to sensible differences in the surface, to different ways in which the work might be perceived. Do they identify real differences in the product or merely differences in the process? An analogy suggests itself: The surface of a work of art may be variously described depending upon who brought it about, and the correct description—"it is an autograph Rembrandt, not a studio picture"—is that which chimes with who actually brought it about. But the question arises here, Do these differences in description, or (as we would say) in attribution, correspond to sensible differences in the surface, to different ways in which the work may be perceived—or only to historical differences?

The only succinct argument that I can think of in either case resembles an evolutionary argument. One reason, and an exceptionally important reason, why certain processes have come to be recognized, and, having been recognized, have survived, as the processes of art, is just that different ways in which they are employed, different hands which use them, more generally differences in attitude or character or mood or motive, show up unmistakably, not obviously but ultimately unmistakably, in differences of product. Question this if you wish; question it if it seems to you a facile or too easy an argument; but in questioning it, take very good stock indeed of just how much of the traditional value set upon art you thereby put seriously in doubt.

6. If we now think of the performance of a ritual as the counterpart to the creative process from which a work of art emerges, then we may understand how the meaning that a ritual possesses inherently may on a given occasion be enhanced by the way in which it is performed—and this enhanced meaning may then be transferred to the life of the person who performs it. Alternatively, we may perceive how the inherent meaning of the ritual may be depreciated by the way in which it is performed: for the pathology of ritual imitates the pathology of art. For this reason ritual must have one of the characteristics I ascribed to it: that it can be variably done.

Readers of Proust will recall how the gilded youths he portrays manage to capture for their lives some meaning—perhaps only a very little meaning—from the code of behaviour in which these lives were circumscribed. The manners of the Faubourg were undoubtedly trivial, anachronistic, verging upon the absurd, but just because they could be variably performed, they enhance to some small degree the lives of those who perform them: the bow, the placing of the silk hat upon the floor, the raising of the voice, the *petits soins,* assume the character of musical scales expressively practised. By contrast, those of us old enough to have been brought up in a certain way, with a great preaching of manners, were told—in so far as we were told anything—that the advantage of manners was that they covered up. Our natural feelings might fluctuate, but good manners could be relied upon to give an even, inexpressive surface to life.

An example of a ritual of our own secular age would be truth-telling, by which I do not mean that truth to self, that inner veracity, which I have suggested is an aim of all ritual, but the practice of telling truths that is often held to be the supreme virtue between close friends or lovers. That this practice can contribute to inner veracity is beyond doubt, but it also exemplifies with remarkable lucidity the pathology I have tried to outline for ritual. A truth may be told incompletely, and the part that is told may be told just so that the rest may be left untold. What is confided may be not undamaging to the teller—a risk is run, for which full credit is due—but the credit due obscures the crucial silence. Or the confidence may be total. Everything is said, but it is said so as to be forgotten: forgotten rather than forgiven. Ibsen and Henry James understood these duplicities of communication.

7. I have come a long way from the incident from which the title of this lecture has been derived, and I return to it none too soon, you may feel. For, by generalizing the incident, by making it serve for a whole range of actions which have in common that they give a life, or deprive it of, meaning, have I not lost sight of something important, of what lends eeriness to the incident, or allows it to haunt the mind? The ancient ceremony whose decay Confucius laments has this character: it prescribes the killing of a sentient animal. The Chinese gentleman leads a richer life, the sheep bleeds to death. Is this an acceptable exchange?

Now, the very assumption that the sacrifice of a sheep at the new moon could ever—could, that is, even within the context of a certain form of life—give meaning to a human life might be challenged. There are a number of ancient rites, as also a number of modern sports, that require a death—generally the death of an animal, though sometimes the death or the simulated death of a human being—and I would think it persuasive to maintain that such activities invariably belong to the pathology of ritual: they are invariably exercises in denial. The ritual in itself denies, and then, derivatively, those who perform it deny, the fact of human aggression: the fact, that is, of aggression as a human motive. The denial is effected in much the following way: First, the end to which this motive inherently moves—that is, the taking of a life—is isolated; it is bracketed; then it is ordained that this end should be enacted, should be repeated, over and over again, but always, on each enactment, at each repetition, the life is to be taken out of a motive as far removed from aggression as possible—in the case of the ancient rites, from piety, or decency, or reverence for higher authority, and in the case of blood sports, out of high spirits or in a mood of stern endurance. Opponents of these practices often ascribe them to sadism. I am sure that this is wrong, and that what they are designed to achieve is, rather, the belittlement or making light of sadism—as well as, perhaps, the belittlement of death itself. At the kill the ideal huntsman dismounts, like the high-souled Arjuna descending from the chariot of Sri Krishna, penitent that he should ever have been taken in by the delusion of suffering, slaughter, death.[6]

Nevertheless, it is clear that this is not at all how Confucius saw the matter, nor did he sense any pathology in the ritual whose full rigour he demanded, and so, looking at the matter for the moment in his perspective, let us return to the question, If the sacrifice of the sheep gives a human life significance, can the gift be justified?

I said at the beginning of this lecture that it would not be, at any rate directly, against Utilitarianism, and you may feel that now is the moment when my good faith is put to the test. For if, strictly speaking, Utilitarianism doesn't give a clear answer to this question, it gives a clear method for arriving at an answer once we have the facts of the case, and the facts of the case may themselves seem clear enough for the Utilitarian answer to be in little doubt. Unless one is prepared to think that the sheep doesn't suffer, or that the sheep's suffering is of no moment, or that the gentleman's prosperity of mind quantitatively outweighs the agony of the sheep, Utilitarian condemnation of the sacrifice is a certainty. Or so it seems.

Or so it seems. For I want to argue that eligible Utilitarianism as I call it, or Utilitarianism that has a chance of commanding our acceptance, is not so evidently required to give this answer, to deliver itself of this condemnation. But, first, an observation—the briefest: that Utilitarianism too serves the denial of human aggression. It achieves denial in stages. First (once again) it severs the end to which the motive moves from the motive itself: it then assimilates the end to what are in fact the ends of very different motives by placing them all on a common scale, a scale of painfulness, and saying of them that they differ only quantitatively or in degrees of unpleasure: then it rates human actions by how their ends figure on this scale. This reorganization of human action effected, cruelty inflicted is domesticated by reappearing in our moral thinking as simply a special case of pain caused.

In talking of eligible Utilitarianism I am not proposing a brand new moral theory and annexing to it a familiar name. The theory is to be found in the writings, in the distinctive writings, of John Stuart Mill, and it begins by taking seriously the idea that, if Utilitarianism is to be a compelling moral theory, then the pursuit of utility—crucially the pursuit by others of their utility—must itself independently seem a worthwhile aim.[7] However, so long as utility is identified with a sensation, or an adjunct of sensation, called 'pleasure', the pursuit of utility will not necessarily seem a worthwhile end, and Utilitarianism will not be a compelling moral theory, at any rate for a community of evolved human beings—even though there is no moral theory that will seem more compelling. The problem, then, which eligible Utilitarianism confronts, is to redefine utility in such a way as to preserve its contact with pleasure but also so as to make its pursuit, or conformity to it as a primary principle, worthwhile, and the crucial step is to hold that, for each individual, utility is always mediated by certain secondary principles to which he subscribes. Instead of the individual seeking utility in an unmediated way, the lessons of which he abridges into a conception of his utility, he now has a prior conception of his utility, spelt out in terms of these secondary principles, and utility accrues to him as he succeeds in realizing it. However, this conception, if it is to do justice to its name, if, that is, it is to be a conception of utility, must satisfy certain constraints. Supremely it must reach back to the individual's original experiences of pleasure, reproducing those experiences in a way which fits in with psychological development. But other things will also be true of it. It will owe a great deal to the norms and expectations of the environment. It will encompass whatever the individual has come to believe about what will give meaning or significance to his life. And it is something that has to be formed. The individual must form it for himself, and inevitably he must form it by a process of trial and error, or through what Mill called, boldly, 'experiments of living'.

Eligible Utilitarianism, having thus reinterpreted the pursuit of utility as a pursuit occurring under the conception of one's own utility, must now bring its normative requirements into line. What it does essentially is to propose a bifurcation within the individual's ethical system. He incurs a dual loyalty. There is still Utilitarianism proper, which enjoins the maximization of utility, and which always holds, but which is compelling only when individuals have formed conceptions of their utility and seek utility under them. But there is also, underlying Utilitarianism proper, what I call preliminary Utilitarianism and, whereas Utilitarianism proper is concerned with utility, preliminary Utilitarianism is concerned with individual conceptions of utility, and it enjoins whatever is necessary for individuals first to form, then to maintain, their conceptions of their own utility—and, for that matter, to have respect for those of other individuals. Now, not only does preliminary Utilitarianism, like Utilitarianism proper, always hold, but, unlike Utilitarianism proper, it is invariably compelling; furthermore, when the injunctions of the two ethics conflict, then, unless the cost in utility is outrageously high, the injunctions of preliminary Utilitarianism take priority. I have said that eligible Utilitarianism is not an invention of my own, for which I have purloined a distinguished name. Any reader of John Stuart Mill's essay *On Liberty* will recognize both in the arguments concerning the proper limits of state action and in those concerning liberty of opinion not merely the appeal to preliminary Utilitarianism but also the priority assigned to it.

The relevance of this to the debated question, What verdict would Utilitarianism pass upon the sacrifice of sheep?, should be evident. For the sacrifice of the sheep, and indeed ritual generally, must belong to the sphere of preliminary Utilitarianism, and within this sphere no mechanical method for arriving at clear answers exists. If we had well-confirmed laws governing the development of human character, or what Mill called a science of 'ethology', answers might be readily forthcoming.[8] In their absence such issues must be settled by trial and error, where the criteria of error are essentially contestable and the trial involves evidence far more ramified than straightforward or ineligible Utilitarianism would consider admissible.

8. Traditionally thinkers upon human nature have regarded the body as the chief impediment to that calm, reflective conduct of life, regulated by the individual's conception of his own happiness, punctuated by ritual, which is calculated to invest life with significance. Urges arising from the interior of the body demand satisfaction, will tolerate no deferral, and are deaf to reason. Imperious bodily desires confront ethical ideals. The wiser amongst the ethical teachers of humanity have tried to anticipate this confrontation, and their ideals have adopted some of the body's demands, if in a carefully edited version. But the accommodation once effected, conflict breaks out again, now between the compromise ideals and residual desire. St. Paul edged himself towards the wisdom of compromise when he asked whether it was not better to marry than to burn: but, monogamy once established as an ethical ideal, it has then had to withstand the bitter onslaught of unaccommodated human sexuality. The struggle that rages between these two is characteristic of the conflict at the core of human society: between instinct and the ordering of life, between nature and culture.

Such is the traditional view. But it may need to be revised. A thinker to whom this lecture already owes a heavy debt, Sigmund Freud, has offered us a new view of the conflict in which the forces appear to be drawn up more ambiguously. The ideals of humanity, the ethical, attempt to silence the demands of the body, but, like the firing-squad in Manet's great *Execution of Maximilian*, they do so using the weapons, wearing the uniform, of their enemy.[9] "They use the weapons of the enemy": For in the economic theory of the mind Freud has maintained that the only energy available to the ego with which to fend off instinctual attacks upon itself is energy derived from the instincts. The mechanisms of defence upon which the ego relies for its security have to be fuelled by neutralized energy, or energy stripped of sexual or aggressive tone. And "they wear the enemy's uniform": In a number of writings Freud has allowed us to see how from the very beginnings, from earliest infancy, the ego in conceptualizing its own activities—where these, of course, include the mechanisms of defence—employs internal representations that are modelled upon the body and its activities. Freud talked of the ego as "first and foremost a bodily ego," and one of the things he had in mind was the way in which the most basic mental acts in the infant's repertoire—acceptance, denial, interrogation, or their primitive precursors— are entertained under crude corporeal phantasies of ingestion, expulsion, penetration. Milk flooding the infant's mouth, teeth upon the nipple, vision clouded by tears, retention of the faeces, screaming, urinating, vomiting—all these offer prototypes of action and passion to which elementary, and then less elementary, processes of the mind are assimilated, and the interest that the mind pays on these generous loans is that, as the relevant part of the body—mouth, anus, urethra, eye—becomes eroticized or is experienced as an instrument of aggression, so the mental process itself incurs the same hostility as the instinctual impulses against which it was initially recruited.[10]

The peculiar inescapability of the human body, or the way in which in any deep conflict, such as that which necessarily surrounds the submission to the ethical, the body, particularly in its more primitive functioning, is likely to make an appearance on both sides—on one side as fact, or in its own reality, on the other side as idea, or through lending content to certain crucial internal representations—this sets new and altogether dramatic limitations upon human aspiration. It gives if not a new, then certainly the most general, application to the Patristic saying for which Freud felt great affection, citing it on a number of occasions, always in connection with the vainglory of culture: *Inter urinas et faeces nascimur.* And this ubiquity of the body, and above all the presence of its elementary processes and their products in mental representation, underlie what I have already identified as the pathology of art and the pathology of ritual. We must suspect the intervention of crude corporeal phantasy whenever an activity, consecrated by social convention or individual commitment, which might have been expected to lead to self-knowledge, does not do so. It becomes pathological: it leads away from self-knowledge.

I have talked of truth-telling as a ritual of the modern age, and in one of the earliest works of literature touched by modernity we find a singularly poignant account of how the telling of a highly charged truth can, for the teller, assume the character, both in itself and in its consequences, of a piece of physical expulsion. The young Mademoiselle de Chartres, beautiful, virtuous, a great heiress, arrives at Court. At marriage is arranged with the Prince de Clèves, brave, honourable, prudent. He is passionately in love with her: she respects him profoundly. They marry. Then to her horror she falls in love with the incomparable Duc de Nemours: her love is returned. She flees his company. Deeply troubled, she confesses her love to her husband. He is distraught, he suspects her, he falls ill and dies. After a period of mourning the Princesse de Clèves and the Duc de Nemours can at last meet and admit their love for each other. She tells him how he inspired sentiments in her which she had never known before, and then she adds, "Cet aveu n'aura point de suite." Nothing follows, nothing is permitted to follow: she abandons him, and life, and is dead within a few years. That the Princesse de Clèves should feel guilt for the Prince's death, that she should decide to remain faithful to his memory, might seem things that are fully explained by the morals of the age. But just the way she connects these two feelings, as well as her consciousness that it is an imaginary duty that she obeys, compel us to look elsewhere for a full understanding. The looming presence of the dead husband, ghostly even while alive: the nature of the princess's mourning, and her sudden access of omnipotence: her attachment to illness and to the deliverances of illness: the significance she assigns to *repos,* to peace of mind—all suggest that, in confessing her passion to the prince, she had also conceived herself as placing some bad bit of herself inside him, now buried with him, and which she can reincorporate only in death. For this most virtuous of women, the telling of a truth is projective identification.

9. There is a well-worn phrase, "You must take him as you find him." I would adapt the phrase and say to moral philosophy, "You should take morality as you find it."

In this lecture I have tried to suggest that morality, narrowly conceived, is naturally and inextricably entwined with another process, not part of morality thus conceived, just because too indifferent to consequences, and this is the cultivation, the self-cultivation, of the individual. And this process is itself so susceptible to distortion or error that in turn it is inextricably bound up with its companion process, which contributes to the impoverishment, to the enfeeblement, to the destruction, of individuality. And then moral philosophers come along and suggest that we must make cuts, that we must observe distinctions, and that the proper sphere of moral philosophy is confined to what I have called 'morality narrowly conceived'. We do nothing similar—observe—with art. We do not—I believe, though I speak without authority—do this with religion. The philosophy of art and the philosophy of religion are not confined by these purist ambitions. And the irony is that, if we accede to them in the matter of morality, not only do we have on our hands a phenomenon that may excite our reverence but certainly eludes our understanding, we also succumb to one of the crudest phantasies that moral pathology throws up: the phantasy that morality marks the spot where human beings discard human nature. In one of his finest essays Sir Leslie Stephen devised a name for the home of such beliefs. He called it 'the world of dreams', 'dreamland'.[11] Dreamland is crowded with moral philosophers.

II The Ends of Life and the Preliminaries of Morality: John Stuart Mill and Isaiah Berlin

1. In the introductory chapter of *On Liberty* John Stuart Mill claimed that for him utility was the ultimate appeal on all ethical questions, and that he renounced any advantage that might accrue to his argument from considerations of abstract right.[1] In "John Stuart Mill and the Ends of Life" Isaiah Berlin challenges Mill's claim.[2] He puts it forward as his view that, though Mill avowed a commitment to utility, the commitment is not real. In support of the avowed commitment Mill was compelled to stretch the notions of happiness and pleasure to the point of vacuity. Meanwhile his real commitment was to various distinct values such as individual liberty, variety, and justice. These values may at a number of places make demands that coincide with those of utility—in so far, that is, as these themselves are coherent—but Mill's demands cannot be given a consistently utilitarian interpretation.

In many writings Berlin has urged upon us a single message of great power and moment. It is that human values are necessarily many, not one, and that of the many values there is not one to which the others are properly subordinate. Values come in systems, and systems of value possess the kind of complex structure that allows the different constituent values to interact. What morality rejects is monism, and the pluralism within which it can find accommodation is a pluralism of a loose kind or pluralism without hierarchy.

It is worth pointing out that this message, which has profound and subversive implications for both practical and theoretical thinking yet to be absorbed, relates exclusively to the internal nature of an individual's morality. It says nothing about the relations between the moralities of different individuals, and specifically it does not say that there must or even can be a multiplicity of such moralities. Berlin himself, who has always held to a version of voluntaristic meta-ethics, possibly believes in this kind of pluralism too. But the pluralism here under discussion is perfectly compatible with the belief in a single system of values, to which the different systems of value held by different individuals ought to conform and upon which they may be expected to converge. The message that I have attributed to Berlin is consistent, as far as I can see, with ethical convergence, with ethical objectivism, and even with ethical realism.

Now, once Berlin's message is clearly before us, it is plausible to think that his reading, or re-reading, of Mill derives from it. The derivation would take roughly the following course: Berlin finds Mill a sympathetic thinker with many of whose views on moral and social topics he finds himself in deep agreement; he finds it impossible to believe that these views could be arrived at on the basis of the monistic morality that Utilitarianism must insist on; therefore, whatever he may profess, Mill is not really committed to Utilitarianism; rather he is committed to a pluralistic morality, moreover to a loosely pluralistic morality, and it is from this that his best thinking depends.

In this essay I want to tread a narrow path. I accept wholeheartedly Berlin's strictures upon moral monism and indeed upon anything other than a loose form of pluralism in morality. I share his high opinion of Mill, who for me also is a sympathetic thinker on moral and social topics. However I reject Berlin's reading of Mill and I accept Mill's claim about himself. In other words, I believe that Mill did remain a utilitarian and I think that he certainly continued to think of utility as he said he did: that is, as the ultimate appeal on all ethical questions. But the crucial qualification here is, to my mind, provided by Mill himself when he goes on to say that he intends utility "in the largest sense" or utility "grounded in the permanent interests of man as a progressive being."[3] For it is central to my way of thinking about Mill that this significantly extends the notion of utility, that it is vital to the understanding of Mill's revision of Utilitarianism, and that it does not, as Berlin thinks, stretch the notion of utility to the point of vacuity. For me it is just this qualification, properly understood, which explains simultaneously how Mill remained a utilitarian and how he emerges as an interesting and sympathetic thinker. And, by qualifying the notion of utility as he does, Mill, to my mind, produces not only a more plausible morality, but a morality that can be more plausibly regarded as utilitarian, than that constructed upon the cruder notion or notions of utility held alike by his immediate predecessors and many of his numerous successors.

A residual question remains: Berlin insists upon the diversity of human values. Mill ascribes complexity to the single value to which he subscribes. Given that Mill in talking of complexity succeeds in doing justice to everything that Berlin has in mind by diversity, given that Mill shows that utility, properly understood, can lay claim to the appropriate complexity, is Mill still right to think of utility as the complex value appropriate to occupy the central place in morality? I shall not attempt an answer to this residual question.

2. In 1826 John Stuart Mill underwent a severe mental crisis, to which so much of his earlier life contributed, and from which so much of his later life was to draw benefit. Mill himself wrote of the crisis as an event in his intellectual development. It was clearly more than this, but it was also this, and it is solely as an event in his development as a moral philosopher that I wish to consider it.

One day Mill found himself putting to himself the following question:

Suppose that all your objects in life were realized; that all the changes in institutions and opinions which you are looking forward to, could be completely effected at this very instant: would this be a great joy and happiness to you?[4]

He did not have to wait long for an answer. The question was posed, and

an irrepressible self-consciousness directly answered, 'No!' At this my heart sank within me: the whole foundation on which my life was constructed fell down. All my happiness was to have been found in the continual pursuit of this end. The end had ceased to charm, and how could there ever again be any interest in the means? I seemed to have nothing left to live for.

One striking detail about the incident, or about Mill's telling of it, is the way in which Mill frames the original question. For he does not ask, as one might expect, Do I still find the utilitarian ideal a good ideal? Am I in accord with it as a moral or political objective? Instead he asks whether the realization of utilitarian objectives will give him pleasure, whether the satisfaction of the utilitarian ideal will in turn satisfy him, and at first this might strike the reader as a peculiarly personal or poignant touch, showing how deeply this crisis of belief affected his whole being and how it had shaken the more drily abstract way of looking at things which had been natural to him. The briefest reflection will show that this is a misinterpretation of Mill. In framing the question as he did, just what Mill shows is how firmly he still stood within the utilitarian framework. For, according to Utilitarianism, it is a constraint upon morality that, for any given moral judgment, general or particular, there should be a precise match between the content of the judgment, or what it obliges an agent to do, and its motivational force, or its capacity to incite the agent—the agent, that is, who has fully understood it—to act in conformity with it. Further, Utilitarianism prided itself on being a morality—indeed the only morality—which could meet this constraint. By assigning content to the moral judgment in the way in which it did—that is, as what would result in the greatest net balance of pleasure over pain for its recipients—it claimed to provide the agent with a uniquely good motive for putting it into practice—that is, the prospect of the greatest net balance of pleasure over pain for him too. Accordingly Mill was accepting one cardinal tenet of Utilitarianism and using it to challenge another when he began to suspect that the fulfilment of the utilitarian ideal would not bring him happiness. As this suspicion hardened into certainty, his mental crisis peaked.

Mill's recovery from depression coincided with the attempt he made over the subsequent years to bring the content and the motivational force of Utilitarianism back into line. Or—as it might more realisitically be put, for Mill never really took altogether seriously the idea that there could be a morality which, once properly grasped, would prove irresistible—with the attempt he made to recapture motivational appeal for Utilitarianism. Reflection must have shown that there were in principle two ways of doing this. Starting from the simple Benthamism with which he had become so thoroughly disillusioned, either he could rethink the content of utilitarian morality, so as to enhance its appeal, or he could put forward a revised account of human motivation with the aim of showing that utilitarian morality, content unchanged, had after all the capacity to move to action.

There was an evident difficulty for Mill in pursuing the second course: It would have required him to deny the most crucial experience of his life. In rewriting human motivation he would have had to rewrite his own motivation, and he would have had to say that, at the very moment when he was utterly convinced that the ideals in which he had been brought up no longer moved him, he did in fact have a motive, however best described, for acting on them, the deliverances of self-consciousness notwithstanding. In other words, Mill would have extricated himself from his mental crisis only at the expense of unlearning the lesson it seemingly had taught him, and it is no surprise that, in his attempt to recapture motivational appeal for Utilitarianism, he chose the first course.

Mill's revision of the content of utilitarian morality can most conveniently be considered if it is looked upon as falling into two stages. The two stages are not chronological stages, and there are good reasons for thinking that Mill's thought is ill-suited to strictly chronological study—which, it is no accident, his detractors greatly favour.[5] Mill was a very perceptive thinker, and he often ran ahead of himself in grasping the conclusions to which his current thinking would lead him. At the same time he was very preoccupied with the impression that his words might make on a reader, and sometimes, in order to dispel the suspicion that he had abandoned the leading ideas of his earlier years, he would use phraseology which no longer consorted well with his deeper thinking. To consider then, as I propose to do, the shift that Mill effects in utilitarian morality as falling into two stages—one of which is the shift from a morality that employs a monistic conception of utility to one that employs a conception of utility that is pluralistic but with hierarchy, while the other is the shift from a morality that employs a conception of utility that is pluralistic but with hierarchy to one that employs a conception of utility that is pluralistic and without hierarchy—is not to advance a rigidly historical thesis. Evidences of the second stage are already to be found in the essay on Bentham (1838), while the first stage still leaves its mark on *Utilitarianism* (1861).

In explicating the revision that Mill effects upon the content of utilitarian morality, I shall do so with an eye to the two questions that may be raised about it. The first is: Does this shift in content succeed in restoring appeal to Utilitarianism? The second is: Is this shift really a shift within Utilitarianism, or isn't it, rather, a shift out of Utilitarianism?

Finally, with Mill's revision of Utilitarianism fully before us I shall draw attention to a corollary that Mill appended to Utilitarianism. Its effect is to show that utilitarian morality may be set within a larger framework of ordinances. This larger framework I shall call an ethic, and that Mill proposed a three-tiered ethic is, I shall suggest, one of the most interesting, as well as one of the more neglected, aspects of his work as a moral philosopher.

3. In our consideration of Mill's revision of Utilitarianism, there is one problem, which might be expected to have priority for someone out to revise Utilitarianism, which we do not have to trouble ourselves with. For reasons whose adequacy need not detain us, Mill took the problem as solved. The problem is that of the transition from a purely egotistic morality, which is the form in which, according to a well-established tradition, Utilitarianism initially proposes itself, to a non-egotistic morality: that is, to a morality which enjoins the maximization of pleasure but is indifferent to who it is to whom the pleasure accrues, and, specifically, is blind to the distinction between agent's pleasure and the pleasure of others.[6] For the purposes of this essay this transition is assumed.

The first stage in the shift that Mill effects in the content of utilitarian morality consists in the move from a monistic conception of utility to a conception of utility that is pluralistic but with hierarchy. Alongside the primary principle of hedonism, or the maximization of pleasure, secondary principles make their appearance. Examples of such secondary principles would be the education of the mind, the cultivation of sexual love and family affection, patriotism, the maintenance of personal dignity, or the attachment to beauty, and, of course, it must be appreciated that these secondary principles, like the primary principle, may be non-egotistic. Secondary principles fix the agent's ends—their ends are his ends—but there is no reason why his ends should be self-interested or exclusively for him. However, what is characteristic of this stage of Mill's thinking, and what defines it, is that secondary principles are strictly subordinate to the primary principle, and it is because of this subordination that the pluralism brought about by the introduction of secondary principles is hierarchical.

In order to see how hierarchy manifests itself, let us take as the central case—for it is the clearest case—that in which a moral agent invokes utilitarian morality in order to decide how he ought to act.[7] Once we have grasped how hierarchy manifests itself here, we can use this understanding in order to grasp the effects of hierarchy in what may be regarded as derivative cases: for instance, where a moral agent decides whether he has acted as he ought to have, or where a moral critic decides how others ought to act or whether they have acted as they ought to have.

Now in the central case, the moral agent in reaching a decision may consult the primary principle; alternatively he may consult one or another of his secondary principles. Let us suppose that he consults secondary principles. He does so, and he arrives at a decision. Then it is open to him to consult the primary principle and arrive at a decision on the basis of it. It is not required of him to do so, but, other things being equal—that is, the costs not being prohibitive—it is a rational course of action. It is so just because, should the two decisions diverge, then what he ought to do is given by the decision arrived at on the basis of the primary principle. The original decision must be abandoned. Of course, if the secondary principles have been at all carefully thought out, such divergences will be a rare thing. Nevertheless, should they occur, the primary principle operates in the agent's reasoning as though it were the only principle in the field, and this is one way in which secondary principles show themselves to be subordinate to the primary principle, or in which hierarchy manifests itself.

This way is the straightforward way in which hierarchy manifests itself, and to see the oblique way let us now suppose that the agent, in reaching a decision how he ought to act, consults the primary principle. In such a case what he will do is that he will survey the various actions that are practicable for him, he will assign to each the consequences that it is most likely to have for himself and for others, and he will calculate for each of these consequences the net balance of pleasure and pain that it is likely to produce, and then arrival at a decision will be a matter of selecting that action whose consequences maximize pleasure or produce the greatest net balance of pleasure over pain. Non-egotism is preserved by indifference to who it is to whom the pleasure accrues. Now, in computing the pleasure and pain for each action, the agent will have to consider how his action interacts with the actions of others, and therefore he will need to know the courses of action on which those others who are affected by the action are embarked. However, these courses of action will themselves have been decided upon in one or the other of two ways: either on the basis of the primary principle or on the basis of some one or more of the secondary principles of the person embarked on it. Let us now suppose that all the courses of action on which those others affected by the agent's action are embarked have been decided upon on the basis of secondary principles, and that this is known to the agent. All persons affected by his action are acting on secondary principles. In that case, in computing the pleasure and pain that action is likely to produce, the agent will surely find it natural to equate, for each person, pleasure with the achievement of the end or ends fixed by the secondary principle or principles on which that person is acting. This determines the way in which, at any rate in the first instance, the agent will consider the interaction of his action with the actions of others. But, once again, this calculation having been made, then, though it is not required, it is, other things being equal, rational for the agent to make a complementary calculation. This time, in computing the pleasure and pain that his action is likely to produce, the agent, one allowance apart, ignores the fact that those others whom his action affects have decided upon the courses of action on which they are embarked on the basis of secondary principles. He assumes all persons affected by his action are acting on the primary principle, and in consequence, for each person, he equates pleasure, not with the achievement of the end or ends fixed by the secondary principle or principles on which that person is in point of fact acting, but just with whatever the primary principle enjoins for him—the one allowance that the agent makes being that he still has to count as pain for each person any disappointment that person might experience from frustration of the secondary principle or principles on which he is actually, if misguidedly, acting. On this new assumption the agent will arrive at a fresh decision concerning how he ought to act, and should the two decisions diverge, it is the second decision that he should prefer. He should, in other words, act as though the primary principle operates, this time not in the agent's reasoning, but in the reasoning of others, as the only principle in the field. Here we have the oblique way in which secondary principles show themselves to be subordinate to the primary principle, or in which hierarchy manifests itself.

The subordination of the secondary principles to the primary principle at this stage in Mill's thinking has, as a consequence, that the ends fixed by the various secondary principles stand to the end fixed by the primary principle in a special relationship: they stand as means to end. The agent's ends are, and are to be assessed as, means to pleasure. This means–end relationship totally coheres with the motivation that prompts this first shift in the content of utilitarian morality. What motivates this shift is something essentially practical, and is best expressed by Mill when he talks of utility as "too complex and indefinite an end"[8] for a moral agent always to have to take stock of in calculating what he ought to do or what would be best for himself and others. Such a calculation remains a calculation about utility, but it might be more practical to arrive at an answer by working it out in terms both simpler and more definite than utility. These terms are just what secondary principles provide through fixing subsidiary aims.

If Mill's first revision of utilitarian morality makes it easier for the agent to operate, it also does more than this, and it is this additional thing it does that enhances the appeal of utilitarian morality. For the revision brings it about that an agent, in deciding what he ought to do, has no longer to regard as irrelevant a whole body of thoughts, and also the attitudes and feelings connected with these thoughts, had by him or had by others, and which must be reckoned by any sensitive person as amongst the most interesting that either he or they are likely to entertain. I refer, of course, to those thoughts which define either his ends or the ends of others, for these thoughts must now enter into his calculations in so far as he thinks of pleasure accruing to himself or to them through the satisfaction of secondary principles upon which they act. So far, but no further. This body of thoughts acquires relevance for his calculations, but the relevance is merely provisional. Once it seems to the agent that pleasure is less likely to accrue this way, once the ends of the secondary principles no longer convince him as the best means to the end of the primary principle, then these thoughts cease to have a claim upon his attention. He may, indeed he must, put them out of his mind.

The purely provisional way in which these thoughts enter into the agent's calculations, and, correspondingly, the way in which they can be appropriately displaced by the direct thought of pleasure or utility, attest, of course, to the hierarchy that at this stage constrains the new-found pluralism of utilitarian morality. But they attest to something else as well. They attest to the degree to which the concept of pleasure, or happiness, or utility—and so far I have not found it necessary to distinguish between them—is itself found quite unproblematic. More specifically, the concept is not felt to require any of the interesting thoughts I have just referred to, or the ends fixed by secondary principles, for its elucidation. All this however is to change as utilitarian morality undergoes its second revision, to which we now turn.

4. The second stage in the shift that Mill effects in the content of utilitarian morality consists in the move from a conception of utility that is pluralistic but with hierarchy to one that is pluralistic and without hierarchy. Not merely do secondary principles appear alongside the primary principle, but now they are not subordinate to it. The ends fixed by the

secondary principles no longer stand to the end fixed by the primary principle in the means–end relationship. Or at least they no longer stand to it exclusively in this relationship. They also serve to elucidate it.

That the ends fixed by the secondary principle now serve to elucidate the end fixed by the primary principle has the implication that by now this latter end, or utility, has ceased to be unproblematic. And this is so. It is characteristic of Utilitarianism under its second revision that utility is found problematic, but it is important to grasp how. The point is not that—or is not merely that—Mill, the moral philosopher, finds utility problematic. Rather, in his moral philosophy Mill reconstructs the fact that the moral agent finds, indeed must find, utility problematic. Mill's philosophy then goes on to represent how the moral agent tries to resolve the problem for himself. He is represented as trying to make utility un-problematic by subscribing to secondary principles.

Why the moral agent finds utility problematic has to do with the highly abstract nature of the concept. Grasping this highly abstract concept, the agent finds that it doesn't contribute, in the way that Utilitarianism leads him to believe that it should, to a decision concerning how he ought to act. Even with all requisite information at his disposal, he will still have an inadequate grasp of what he should do to maximize utility. The ab-stract concept *utility* needs to be filled out, and this filling out can be thought of in two parts. In the first instance, the moral agent is required to have what might be called a conception of his own utility. Only then can he consider how his utility is to be advanced. This conception is however not something that can be given to him or that he can learn. It is something that has to be formed, and it is formed through the process of trial and error. He tries out various secondary principles and finishes by subscribing to those whose ends give him or teach him what he wants. But, in the second instance, the moral agent requires that others have a conception of their own utility, for only then can he consider how he is to advance their utility. And, once again, this conception is one that they have to form, they form it through trial and error, and it is codified in their secondary principles.

But it is one thing to believe that utilitarian morality cannot be suc-cessfully pursued unless each forms a conception of his own utility and that such a conception is formed through subscribing to secondary prin-ciples, and another thing, and evidently unjustified, to equate the agent's subscription to just any set of secondary principles with the formation of a conception of his own utility. Surely there must be some constraint upon the secondary principles subscribed to, or upon the ends that these principles fix. To put the point another way: it may very well be that the pursuit of morality requires the subscription to secondary principles; but what has to be true of the secondary principles for the morality that they permit to be truly thought of as a utilitarian morality?

Actually it is an exaggeration to say, as I have said, that at this stage of Mill's revision of utilitarian morality utility is found problematic, if this is taken to mean that utility is found altogether problematic. There remains an unproblematic aspect of utility, and to mark the distinction that is at stake here it would be useful to employ the traditional distinction between pleasure and happiness. Unproblematically utility connotes pleasure, where pleasure is thought of as a kind of sensation or adjunct of sensation, and, so long as utility is given this highly restricted interpretation, the moral agent may arrive at utilitarian decisions about how he ought to act without either his forming for himself or others' forming for themselves conceptions of their own utility. Such decisions are decisions about the maximization of the privileged sensation or adjunct of sensation. It is only when the moral agent appreciates that utilitarian decisions cannot be circumscribed in this way that utility becomes problematic for him. Any issue from this problematic situation is possible only if two conditions are met. In the first place, utility must be recognized to connote more than just pleasure. It also connotes, and it must be perceived to connote, happiness. Secondly, for the concept of utility in its broader connotation to gain application, it is required that the agent and others form conceptions of their own utility. This they do, as we have seen, through subscribing to secondary principles. If however we now ask what these secondary principles must be like, or what is the constraint laid upon the ends fixed by secondary principles if the conception to which these principles contribute is to be regarded as a conception of the person's utility or if the morality that they help to constitute is to be regarded as a utilitarian morality, the answer is easier to find. The constraint appears to be this: the ends fixed by the various secondary principles must be systematically related to pleasure.

But to say that the ends of the secondary principles must be systematically related to pleasure if Utilitarianism is to be safeguarded does not say enough. There are various ways in which the ends of secondary principles may be systematically related to pleasure. For instance, some moral philosophers would argue that the systematic relationship is to be of a conceptual kind. The ends must derive from the concept of pleasure. I wish to suggest that the systematic relationship must be of a genetic kind. And I also wish to suggest that this is how Mill thought of the matter. In other words, Utilitarianism as revised by him requires that it is possible to arrange pleasure and the ends fixed by the secondary principles of a moral agent on one and the same dendrogram, where the ends lie on the branches, pleasure is at the base of the tree, and the diagram as a whole represents the emergence of the moral agent according to the best theory of human nature.[9]

From this last point an important consequence follows. To be able to say what it is for a morality that consists in a primary principle enjoining the maximization of utility and various secondary principles that are not subordinate to the primary principle to be overall a utilitarian morality presupposes that we have in our possession a developmental psychology of a certain richness. It is only through such a psychology that we can decide whether the secondary principles appropriately relate to the primary principle. It is unnecessary to observe that Mill did not have such a psychology. He conceded the point—notably in the essay "The Subjection of Women"—and in at least one place he gave it as his opinion that this lack constituted the biggest single gap in contemporary knowledge.[10] However, there is a passage where he clearly recognizes just what has to be the internal structure of a morality that is pluralistic and without hierarchy and also utilitarian, and how this structure presupposes a theory of human nature. I refer to the passage in *Utilitarianism,* widely ridiculed, in which Mill talks of higher and lower pleasures.[11] To see how this passage bears upon the present issue, we need to orientate ourselves appropriately. For generally this passage is read for what Mill has to say about the difference between higher and lower pleasures, or how it is that one pleasure can vary qualitatively from another. But the passage can also be read for what Mill has to say about what higher and lower pleasures have in common, or why it is that both are kinds of pleasure. Roughly, Mill's view is that higher and lower pleasures are both kinds of pleasure because they are functionally equivalent at different levels of a person's psychological development—which, of course, is also, to the same degree of roughness, just the reason why one kind of pleasure is qualitatively superior to the other. Thereby Mill throws everything on to the question of psychological development and how its levels are to be identified and what lies on each level. Given his lack of a psychological theory, Mill is naturally unable to answer these questions, but what is crucial for the proper interpretation of Mill is that he saw just what it is that was necessary if such answers were to be produced or just where they were to come from.

I shall call Utilitarianism under its second revision, or where its content is given by the primary principle of hedonism and various secondary principles not subordinate to but elucidatory of it, 'complex Utilitarianism,' and I turn to the question how, or how far, complex Utilitarianism restores appeal to Utilitarianism.

The crucial way in which complex Utilitarianism restores appeal to Utilitarianism is that it compels—it doesn't just permit, it compels—the moral agent, in deciding what he ought to do (or in coming to any related decision), to take account of what I have already referred to as thoughts that are amongst the most interesting that human beings entertain: that is, thoughts definitive of the ends fixed by secondary principles, whether the agent's own or those of others. And, in taking account of these thoughts, the agent is also required to take account of the feelings and attitudes that group themselves around these thoughts. And the account that he is required to take of these mental constellations is something that is by now ineliminable. It is not merely provisional, and it is not to be set aside in deference to some consideration which overrides secondary principles and their aims. Utilitarianism at last pays attention to man in his full complexity as a developed human being, and it would have to be a very gloomy or very desiccated self-consciousness that returned the answer "No" to the question whether the pursuit of man's happiness, when man is thus envisaged, was an end that held the promise of satisfaction.

5. However, it might now seem that Utilitarianism under its second revision, or complex Utilitarianism, gains, or regains, appeal, but only at the cost of scope. Let me explain.

A moral agent, we are now told, has to take ineliminable account of both his and others' secondary principles. But this is impossible unless both he and others have secondary principles, and furthermore—for otherwise the account he takes of them would be eliminable—hold them not subordinately to the primary principle. He and others must have formed conceptions of their own happiness, and they must moreover have knowledge of each other's conceptions. But this is not a universally satisfied condition: it represents an achievement, first of all, in the life of the species, and then, secondly, in the life of the individual. Complex Utilitarianism gains its appeal from the way in which it pays respect to the full faculties of man: but, by the same token, it appears to lose its hold when man has not entered into possession of his full faculties. In its attempt to do justice to the developmental nature of man, complex Utilitarianism takes on or acquires a developmental nature. Or so it might seem. Is this so, and is this how Mill saw it?

Mill, we know, like his father and like Bentham, professed to think that any non-utilitarian morality was ultimately untenable. But did he think that utilitarian morality was binding in those circumstances—whether of general history or of personal biography—in which it did not hold appeal?

Explicitly Mill never raised the quesiton. But implicitly—or so I be-lieve—he must have, just because he supplied the question with an an-swer, and an answer which, as I have already said, constitutes one of the most interesting and also most neglected aspects of his work as a moral philosopher. For what Mill did was to set complex Utilitarianism within a larger structure, appropriately thought of as a three-tiered ethic, to each tier of which he then assigned distinct conditions under which such an ethic was binding or in which it obliged the agent to act in conformity with it.

On one tier of this ethic, the uppermost tier, there is Utilitarianism proper, by now glossed as complex Utilitarianism. Complex Utilitarian-ism enjoins the maximization of utility, as utility is elucidated in the moral agent's conception of happiness and in the conceptions of happi-ness entertained by the various recipients of his action. Complex Utili-tarianism is binding when, or in so far as, people have indeed formed their own conceptions of happiness, know of the conceptions of others, and pursue utility accordingly. It binds just when men have entered into possession of their full faculties. On the tier below this, or the middle tier, there is simple Utilitarianism, where this includes both Utilitarianism em-ploying a monistic conception of utility and Utilitarianism employing a conception of utility that is pluralistic but with hierarchy. Simple Utili-tarianism binds when, or in so far as, men have not formed conceptions of their own happiness, and pleasure rather than happiness is what they pursue for themselves and others. It is the ethic of men whose faculties are still undeveloped. Then, on the third tier, the lowermost, there is what I shall call 'preliminary Utilitarianism', and I claim that it is one of the most innovative aspects of Mill's ethical thought that he identified and found a place for preliminary Utilitarianism. What preliminary Utilitarianism enjoins is whatever is necessary for people either to form, or, having formed, to maintain, conceptions of their own happiness—or, for that matter (though I shall not pursue this aspect), envisagements of other people's conceptions of their own happiness. The conditions under which preliminary Utilitarianism is binding are disjunctive: that part which is concerned with the formation of people's conceptions of their own happiness holds when such conceptions are not fully formed, and that part which is concerned with the maintenance of such conceptions holds just when they are formed. Preliminary Utilitarianism invariably binds. And, finally, when the injunctions of preliminary Utilitarianism conflict with the injunctions of either simple or complex Utilitarianism—whichever is relevant—then, unless the cost in utility is too severe, the injunctions of preliminary Utilitarianism take priority. Education up to the point where happiness can be attained is more important than the attainment either of pleasure of or happiness.

I shall end by drawing attention to the three separate places where Mill argues for policies or practices on the basis of preliminary Utilitarianism. Two occur in the essay *On Liberty*.

The first passage is in chapter 4, where Mill, having divided the actions of the agent into the 'self-regarding' (his phrase) and the 'other-regarding' (not his phrase), exempts the former altogether from the sphere of State intervention. For this exemption might not be the verdict reached by appeal either to simple or to complex Utilitarianism, and for two distinct reasons. In the first place, though it is a matter of dispute just how Mill effected the division, it seems as though self-regarding actions are not to be equated with those which in no way impinge upon others. They must be those actions which affect others, if they do, only in some discountable fashion.[12] Accordingly there is always the possibility that a self-regarding action is in its net effect more adverse than some other action practicable for the agent. Why should not such a self-regarding action, on grounds of Utilitarianism, either simple or complex, be the object of State intervention? Secondly, self-regarding actions, however defined, have an effect upon the agent. Why should not Utilitarianism decide that those with a benign effect upon him ought to be enforced by the State and those with a malign effect upon him be prohibited? Against both these considerations Mill's counter-argument, his support for the self-regarding action despite its adverse consequences, seems to be that self-regarding actions are crucial to those 'experiments of living' without which individual conceptions of happiness would either not be formed or, having been formed, wither away.[13] Here we witness in effect preliminary Utilitarianism overruling either simple or complex Utilitarianism.

The second passage is to be found in chapter 2, where Mill discusses liberty of opinion, which once again is treated as total. Mill's argument in favour of total liberty of opinion appeals to two considerations: truth and rationality. In both cases the content of the appeal is subtle, but the question arises: Why should a utilitarian, even a complex utilitarian, set such supreme value on truth and rationality? These may, of course, and almost certainly will be, amongst the ends fixed by the secondary principles of the various citizens. But does this fully explain the absoluteness of Mill's commitment? It seems that, once again, preliminary Utilitarianism must make its contribution to the argument, in that, if, in this case, it does not overrule Utilitarianism proper, it certainly supplements it.

The third passage is in *Considerations on Representative Government*. Mill says that representative government is the ideally best form of government in that it is "the one which in the circumstances in which it is practicable and eligible is attended with the greatest amount of beneficial consequences, immediate and prospective."[14] Here, it might seem, speaks Utilitarianism proper. But not so. For, as Mill develops the argument, he brings forward two criteria by which the merit of political institutions is to be judged. One concerns the way in which they "organize the moral, intellectual, and active worth already existing, so as to operate with the greatest effect in public affairs." The other concerns the way in which political institutions "promote the general mental advancement of the community." If these criteria can in part be ascribed to Utilitarianism proper—and this I do not deny—they largely attest to the influence of preliminary Utilitarianism.

It is not surprising that critics are to be found who will see in these passages evidence of Mill's backslidings from Utilitarianism. Given their failure to perceive the complex character of Mill's commitment to Utilitarianism—more complex, it now turns out, than a mere commitment to complex Utilitarianism—their criticisms are altogether understandable. However, concern for the proper interpretation of Mill requires us to reject them. Properly interpreted, Mill can be shown to concur not only with Berlin's concern for a loose pluralism in morality but also with his other, no less urgent, no less generous, and certainly related, concern for the all-important value of liberty. But that is another though not all that different a story.

III The Good Self and the Bad Self: The Moral Psychology of British Idealism and the English School of Psychoanalysis Compared

1. Some may think that in my choice of topic for this lecture I owe my distinguished predecessor in the chair of philosophy at University College London an apology. For the Dawes Hicks Lecture is a lecture in the history of philosophy, and the thought would be that in taking philosophy to include moral psychology I am obviously at fault, for I have violated well-established frontiers. If I choose not to answer such a charge directly, one reason is this: that, rigidly delineated though such frontiers may be, the arguments in support of their being drawn as they are vary considerably. Another reason is that perhaps the best answer to the charge is the indirect answer: so that, instead of disputing where the frontiers should run, one is more profitably engaged in showing how the existing lines may be safely transgressed, or, indeed, how in some historical phase progress was made in spite of them, progress which could not have been achieved if they had been held in respect. But, if there is to be even the hope that the history of philosophy can in this way give anything to philosophy, it follows that it must not begin by borrowing from philosophy too rigid or exclusive a conception of what philosophy is. So I remain unapologetic in my choice of topic.

Idealism and psychoanalysis may seem an incongruous pair. The history of their transplantation to Britain is, it is true, in many ways a history of common experience. Originating in the German-speaking world, both encountered fierce opposition on arrival in this country. In the course of time both gained exponents, adherents, disciples, some of great distinction, but in neither case more than (comparatively) a few. And yet both have been held responsible for a wide range of nefarious consequences: intellectual, ethical, social, and practical. But here I want to call attention to another feature that transplanted idealism and transplanted psycho-analysis have in common. For, if we look at the work of their most eminent representatives—and I shall confine myself to the ideas of F. H. Bradley and Melanie Klein—we can, I suggest, discern a joint contribution that they make to the understanding of moral phenomena: a contribution which at once belongs to moral psychology and justifies the claim of moral psychology to be a philosophical discipline.

2. Bradley's *Ethical Studies* is divided into seven essays. Too many readers of the book—not a class with a superfluity of members—hasten to identify Bradley's own ethical views with the heavily collectivist theory which he expounds in Essay V under the Hegelian heading, "My Station and its Duties." They do this, despite the fact that in the very first sentence of the next essay Bradley says of this theory that "however true"—which is his way of saying "however many truths it may contain"—it provides "no sufficient answer to the question What is Morality?"[1] This remark however is lost on them, for by this time they have brought their reading of Bradley to a close and have shut the book.

Such precipitance on the reader's part is unfortunate, and unfortunate for two reasons, which are connected. Already in Essay II Bradley had introduced his own ethical theory. "The final end," he had written there, "with which morality is identified, or under which it is included, can be expressed not otherwise than by self-realization."[2] But it is not until Essay VII that a full-scale account of the theory of self-realization is given, and by stopping short where he does the precipitate reader deprives himself of this. But he also deprives himself of a proper understanding of Bradley's criticisms of alternative ethical theories, given in Essays III and IV, which he will have already read, and is certain to have admired. And the connection is this: that, in criticizing Hedonistic theory and Deonto-logical theory, Bradley concentrates on the account that each theory provides of moral action; and why moral action, and therefore an adequate account of it, are of supreme importance to ethical theory becomes fully clear only once we entertain, if not assertorically at least hypothetically, the theory of self-realization.

Indeed this last point, as an observation on Bradley's procedure, could be expressed more forcefully. For it would be little exaggeration to say that in criticizing the theory of Pleasure for Pleasure's Sake or the theory of Duty for Duty's Sake—as he calls them—Bradley in effect criticizes each not so much as an ethical theory in its own right but rather as an interpretation of the theory of self-realization. Now, if this is so, it follows that the crucial question that Bradley has to ask of each theory is, Does it properly exhibit moral action as self-realization?

Should we now wonder why Bradley proceeds in this way, the answer seems to lie in something that he says in the course of introducing his own theory. He was, he conceded, in no position, metaphysically that is, to prove the theory. And he went on, "All that we can do is partially to explain it, and try to render it plausible."[3] The partial explanation unfolds in two stages. The first stage consists in looking at what can be gathered from alternative ethical theories—or, more strictly, from the accounts of moral action that they provide—about self-realization, and thus seeing what there is that remains to be said. And the second stage consists in the appeal to moral psychology. And as for rendering his theory plausible, Bradley's hope is that plausibility will attach to the theory as the explanation unfolds.

If we start with Bradley's criticisms of alternative theory, a preliminary is to recognize the requirement that he places upon an account of moral action: a requirement which derives from the view that he takes of action in general. For Bradley all action is intentional in a fairly strong sense in that we cannot be said to *do* anything that we did not intend to do: though, of course, our actions may fall short of our intentions—we may not do the whole of what we intended to do. So, if moral action is, as Bradley maintains, self-realization, what it is not is, amongst other things, action in which the self is realized fortuitously or coincidentally. There must be some corresponding idea or set of ideas under which the action was done. It follows from this that, if an ethical theory is to attain to adequacy, it must provide an account of moral action that assigns to it the appropriate intentionality: or, to use language that is peculiarly appropriate to Bradley's thinking, the theory must capture the volitional structure of moral action.

So the first question to be asked is, Does Hedonism do this? Now, according to Bradley it is characteristic of authentic Hedonistic theory— that is, theory at once consistent and consistently Hedonistic, of which he thought that, avowals to the contrary, there was precious little around— that it presents the moral agent thus: that on each and every occasion that he acts morally, he wills some particular pleasure. He wills, in other words (the gloss is Bradley's, and we shall see its significance), "a state of the feeling self."[4] If such an agent's will is invariably actualized, it follows that his existence will unfold as a succession of pleasurable states. Now, if we ask whether such a succession amounts to self-realization, the answer must depend on the relations between the various pleasurable states—whether, that is, they fit together into, or form, a pattern or whole: and, since there is nothing in the Hedonistic account of what the man wills that corresponds to such an outcome, that account as an account of moral action must be defective. For it to be adequate to the intentionality of moral action, it must ascribe to the moral agent not only the idea of this or that particular end but also some general standing idea under which he wills the end he does.

If Hedonistic theory is thus deficient, the second question to be asked is, Does Deontological theory show us how to repair this deficiency? According to Bradley it is characteristic of this theory that it presents the moral agent thus: that on each and every occasion that he acts morally, he wills to act under one and the same idea, which is also of the greatest generality. The idea under which he wills may be called—"indifferently" Bradley says[5]—Freedom, Universality, Autonomy, or the Formal Will. But the trouble with this idea, it would seem, is that, in any of its guises, it goes too far—it goes all the way, we might say—in the direction of generality. Bradley characterizes it as "mere universal," and what he means by this might be put by saying that the agent may quite properly be said to be able to will anything under it, alternatively to will nothing under it. Anything: in that any particular end is compatible with it. Nothing: in that no particular end is indicated by it. If what is wrong with Hedonism is that, if the moral agent wills as the account it provides specifies, and his will is actualized, he will not necessarily achieve self-realization, what is wrong with Deontological theory is that, if the agent wills as the account it provides specifics, there is no clear sense that can be given to supposing that his will is or indeed could be actualized. Of no one particular action rather than another can it be said, as needs to be said, that *it* matches his intention.

However, to put the matter so might suggest that, at any rate on the present showing, Hedonistic theory has for Bradley a start over Deontological theory as an interpretation of the theory of self-realization. For, whatever else self-realization may be, it is surely action—it is, in Bradley's words, a "doing,"[6] a "putting forth"[7]—and, this being so, must it not be for him a relative merit of Hedonistic theory that it assigns to the moral agent a volitional structure from which some kind of action could follow, and, equally, a relative demerit of Deontological theory that from the volitional structure it assigns him no action could conceivably follow?

But Bradley does not think like this. He does not allow Hedonistic theory even a temporary advantage over Deontological theory, and we must try to see why. It is certainly true that Hedonistic theory assigns to the moral agent an intentionality from which action could ensue, but Bradley's point is that the action that ensues or would ensue is quite improperly related—improperly, that is, from the point of view of a theory of moral action—to that intentionality. It is related as means to end, so that, for instance, if a better means were found to the same end, that should be preferred as a way of realizing that intention. But it is a requirement on moral action not only (as we have seen) that the action should not be fortuitous, that is that there should be an intention, but also that the action should not be merely instrumentally related to the intention: the end should be realized not merely through the action but in the action. But, if the end is, as Hedonistic theory would have it, a particular state of the feeling self—just that—then this requirement cannot, in the nature of that end, be satisfied. So, to adapt a distinction of Bradley's: at best Hedonistic theory could offer an ethic of self-realizedness, not—which is what we are after—an ethic of self-realization.

A good and natural way of expressing Bradley's criticisms of these alternative theories would be to say that each theory is one-sided. And this is just what Bradley says.[8] But when he says it, he wants the phrase to be taken—well, if not literally, then at any rate as a living, rather than as a dead, metaphor. For it is for Bradley a truth, a theoretical truth, about volition that it has two 'sides', a universal side and a particular side,[9] a truth which he thinks is displayed in, or which we can grasp through, the very form of the assertion "I will this or that," for in saying this we mean (and I quote) "to distinguish the self, as will in general, from this or that object of desire."[10] Accordingly, a theory which is to go beyond Hedonistic theory and Deontological theory must afford full recognition to both sides of moral volition, and in doing so it must, of course, repair those injustices which each side has suffered from the theory that recognizes it exclusively. And then it must do something which in the nature of the case neither of the theories so far considered could even attempt: it must exhibit how in moral action the two sides are brought into relation. It is just this additional task that I had in mind when I talked of the appositeness of the phrase 'volitional structure' to Bradley's form of ethical inquiry.

What Bradley has then to do for his ethical theory is to show what the particular end is in moral volition, what the self is in moral volition, and how it is that the two are brought into conjunction so that the latter realizes itself in willing the former. It is in pursuit of such an account that Bradley turns away from existing ethical theory to psychology, and we thus enter upon the second stage in his partial explanation of what he regards as true ethical theory. The two stages are related thus: that, having gained from alternative philosophical theory the general form of moral volition, Bradley looks to psychology to inform him about its content, and when he has, as it were, placed one inside the other, he will then be able to say what the volitional structure of moral action is. He will still not have proved his ethical theory, but he may have made it seem more plausible against our moral intuitions, and, in doing so, he will, with luck, have sharpened them.

3. Bradley's appeal to psychology starts not with the complex phenomenon of moral action but with about the simplest type of action that can be said to have a volitional structure. Its simplicity Bradley takes as showing that it possesses not only logical priority, but also temporal priority in the history of the individual. His name for it is 'appetite', and his account, which is to be found in Essay VII of *Ethical Studies,* "Selfishness and Self-Sacrifice," runs as follows:

An agent perceives a sensuous thing, which he subsumes under one idea or more. His condition is such that the idea of this thing, or perhaps better, the idea of having the thing, arouses in him a complex of feelings. On the one hand, he experiences a painful feeling, connected with the fact that he does not have, or that he lacks, the thing—a feeling which may, or may not, be a continuation of existent want. On the other hand, he experiences a pleasurable feeling, because the having of the thing is somehow connected for him with satisfaction. The two feelings, pain and pleasure, set up a tension, and the felt tension, otherwise called desire, moves the agent to have the thing.[11] An example: A small child sees and recognizes a lump of sugar. His condition is such that the thought of not having the sugar excites in him feelings of hunger. And it is also such that the thought of having the sugar excites in him feelings that would accompany his eating sugar. The first experience is painful, the second pleasurable, and the conjunction leads him to reach out a hand for the sugar or to cry for it.

If we now ask what the content of the volitional structure is in this case, we get this answer: The particular side, or end, is represented by the idea of the sensuous thing. The universal side or self is represented by the pleasure that is excited by the idea of the thing and that moves the agent towards the thing itself. And the two sides are related through physical want.

An instant way of bringing this account into focus, or of holding it steady, is to concentrate on the role it assigns to pleasure, and then to contrast this with the role that is assigned to pleasure in a typically He-donistic account of action. What does this allow us to see? In the first place, on the present account pleasure does not appear at all on the par-ticular side, which in the Hedonistic account it monopolizes: what is willed is now willed under the idea of a particular thing, not of a particu-lar pleasure. And, secondly, where pleasure does appear on this ac-count—that is, on the universal side—it is pleasure itself that appears there, not the idea of pleasure, which is all that the Hedonistic account lets in: this, according to Bradley, must be right, for, at any rate in the ordinary kind of case, it is only feeling, of which pleasure, as we have seen, is an instance, that can move to action.

From this last point it would seem to follow that in any account of action—even the most complex type of action—the self, or universal side to volition, will in part at least be represented by pleasure. And this is indeed Bradley's position. What is distinctive about the account of appe-tite is that the pleasure to which it makes reference is of so peculiarly primitive a kind. But that only records—though it does not exhaust—the fact that the type of self that appetite presupposes is itself a primitive type of self: a fact that Bradley brings out when he says, as he does repeatedly, that in appetite the self 'affirms' itself—affirms, that is, not 'realizes', itself.

Now, I would contend that it is prima facie a strength of Bradley's account of action and its volitional structure that, even on its lowest level, it accommodates some form of self: just as I would also add, parentheti-cally this time, that it is prima facie an advantage for any developmental psychology, like, say, psychoanalytic theory, if it can postulate, from even the earliest stages of mental life, an ego however rudimentary.[12] But I say prima facie in both cases: for this lead can be maintained only if a fur-

ther, genetic thesis is provided, itself involving only perspicuous transitions, showing how what is presumed present from the beginning evolves
into its final, complex form. And it would be my claim that, out of what
Bradley has to say in the original text of *Ethical Studies* and in the additional material appended nearly fifty years later in 1924, there can be
reconstructed just such a genetic thesis, taking the reader from the primitive self that affirms itself in appetite to the good self that realizes itself in
moral action.

Ostensibly what Bradley does it to provide a systematic account of
different types of action, in which each type is more complex than its
predecessor, and where difference in type of action is paired off with
difference in type of object of volition. He produces what may be thought
of as a hierarchy at once of action and of object of volition. However, in
doing this Bradley also provides, I claim, a genetic thesis about the self,
because at each new level in the hierarchy, it becomes apparent that a
new and more evolved type of self is required into being if the particular
and the universal sides of volition are to engage with one another. And
this genetic thesis reveals its adequacy for his moral theory in that the
most evolved type of self it posits, or the self at the very top of the hierarchy, can reasonably be thought of as realizing itself in willing the most
complex object of volition.

But to understand this account we must first grasp what is meant by a
type, or, more significantly, by different types, of object of volition.
Clearly this is not the same as different objects of volition—presumably
the object is of the same type when now I will a plate of smoked salmon
as when in childhood I willed a lump of sugar. A reasonable suggestion,
seemingly in line with Bradley's thinking, is that we can talk of not just
different objects of volition, but different types of object, when and only
when there are different objects, and, furthermore, when in having—
equally in lacking—one of these objects, the agent would stand in a quite
different relationship to it from what he would stand in to the other, if
he had or lacked that: where the terms 'object of volition', 'have', and
'lack' are all used quite schematically and as mutual correlatives.

So: In the case of appetite to have the object of volition is—at any rate
approximately—to gain physical mastery over it or to consume it: to lack
the object is for it to be beyond one's reach. That exemplifies one relationship to the object of volition. But now consider the following sequence of possible ends that an agent might adopt as the object of his

volition: one, the presence, or proximity of a loved figure in the environment; two, the state of satisfaction or happiness of such a figure; three, conforming to, or ultimately, four, the adoption of, that figure's will and character. If we consider this sequence, it should be apparent that, as an agent progressed through it, acquiring new ends, then at each point in the sequence the relationship in which he stood to the object of his volition—stood to it, that is, either in having it or in lacking it—would radically alter. And, in describing the agent's movement through this sequence as a 'progression', I have in mind the further fact that the relationship of agent to object, as it altered, would also become increasingly more abstractly identified. The pattern that realizes this relationship must be characterized on ever higher levels of generality. And it is this that warranted my saying of Bradley that he produces, not merely a list of different types of object of volition or a list of different types of action, but a hierarchy. For, of course, readers of Bradley will have recognized, and others may have suspected, that the sequence of ends I enumerated just now—the presence of another, the welfare of another, obedience to another, the adoption of the will of another—was not selected by me at random but corresponds to what Bradley thinks is willed by the agent as he engages in increasingly complex types of action. They are the objects of volition that the once merely appetitive child progressively makes his own.

This being so, we can already see one line of determination along which more complex types of action might be thought to require into being more evolved types of self. For each new type of action requires a self that can form—form and maintain—a more and more abstract view of what counts as the success, alternatively as the failure, of his will. On the universal side of volition there must be, we might think, some representation of mounting complexity that attaches to the realization of the particular side.

But, if this were so, everything would lie in the cognitive domain, and the genetic thesis would be about a self that emerges or develops largely intellectually. And the cognitive plays no part, or next to none, in Bradley's moral psychology, at least at this stage. The development of the self in which Bradley is specifically interested falls within the emotional domain, and it derives from the way in which, according to him, different types of object of volition, and therefore different types of action, make from the beginning demands upon the feelings and desires of the child:

more precisely, from the way in which they enlarge his capacity to experience pleasure and pain. And in this connection we may note two distinct, though clearly interrelated, lines of determination.

It would be true to say of appetite that the child experiences pleasure in having the lump of sugar only when he wants the sugar and then only because he wants the sugar. Let us now look at these two conditions in perhaps artificial separation. So: "Only *when* he wants the sugar"—that is, the child takes no pleasure in the object as such: it is for him neither permanently nor independently pleasant.[13] "And then only *because* he wants the sugar"—that is, the pleasure that the child experiences when he gets pleasure is always in contrast to some pain that he simultaneously or, more likely, antecedently, experiences. The pleasure—and it is a favoured phrase of Bradley's—the pleasure is "felt against"[14] the felt absence of the object of appetitte. It is then in both these respects that, as the child comes to engage in new types of action, his capacity to experience pleasure (and pain) in relation to the object of volition develops: and this development is in turn crucial for—indeed one might say partly constitutive of—the emergence of the self.

First, then, the child extends the range of objects in which he may take pleasure. And, if I have already indicated how this goes, I should now fill in the detail. It goes, then, from the transient thing that will satisfy appetite, to the same thing conceived of as an enduring object, to a loved person who is always with the child, to the well-being or happiness of such a person, to that person's will or set of precepts, and finally to persons and causes with which the child is not personally involved. At each stage—Bradley is at pains to point out—the extension of what is found pleasant is based firmly on the previous stage. So consider the all-important extension from an object that habitually satisfies appetite to the satisfaction or happiness of a person in the environment. What ensures this transition, according to Bradley, is that there are persons in the environment who are already linked with the habitual satisfaction of the child's appetites. It is, he says, "a fact which deserves more attention than it receives"[15] that the first figures to whom the child is permanently attached are those who have satisfied his first recurring wants and are a fixed aspect of the environment. And he specifies mother and nurse.

Bradley is anxious that the growth of 'interest'—as he calls it, following Hegel—should be safe against two fairly ready misinterpretations. It is not the case, he insists, that this process depends—as some eighteenth-century moralists would have us think—on the workings of sympathy: so that the child's pleasure is caused by another's pleasure through the intervention of associated ideas, first of the other's pleasure, then of the child's. For apart from the question whether such a mechanism could indeed account for the result required of it, appeal to it denies the basic fact that the child's pleasure in new objects is as direct as any it received from satisfied appetite. But nor is it the case, Bradley also insists, that the child simply remains confined to the pleasure of satisfied appetite, and that its interest in other people, their happiness, their injunctions, their aims, is no more than a cultivation of these various things as means to its own pleasure which remains distinct from them.

Bradley's own account of the extension of interest is in terms of objectified feeling. So an object excites pleasure in a child, and he then comes to invest this object with that feeling, so that from then onwards he experiences the object in much the same way as up till then he had experienced his sensations of satisfied appetite. He feels it "as part of himself": [16] or again, without it he "does not 'feel his self' at all." [17] And the point is illustrated, in a way that may remind us of later theory, thus: "The breast of his mother, and the soft warmth and touches and tones of his nurse, are made one with the feeling of his own pleasure and pain." [18] If, Bradley maintains, an explanation of this process is still demanded which is cast in terms of ideas and their vicissitudes, then we should think, not that the ideas of the object and my pleasant feelings are associated, but that the two ideas are integrated or become one: though Bradley might have been wise to point out that this is not so much an explanation, as a consequence or register, of the objectification of feeling.

So much for the first way in which, as the child comes to engage in new types of action, his capacity to experience pleasure and pain in relation to the object of volition develops. Interest enlarges, or the range of objects in relation to which he experiences pleasure extends beyond that which satisfies transient appetite.

Secondly, as this occurs, the pleasure that the child experiences in the object is no longer felt against, or is no longer felt exclusively against, pain. There are three considerations relevant here, for two of which we have already been prepared. The first is that, as we move up the scale of action, the requirement to find a place for pain in the account of volition weakens. When to have the object of volition means, as in appetite, to possess it physically, then the equation of lacking the object with being deprived of it or the sense of privation, which is painful, is plausible. But, as having the object is increasingly a matter first of doing something or other, and then of being something or other, the equation loses plausibility. The initial condition ceases to seem one of privation. And at the same time—and this is the second consideration—the child is increasingly drawn to the object for its own sake, so that he takes pleasure in it because of what it is, and permanently is, rather than, as in appetite, because of how he is and transiently is. But the third consideration is the most important. And that is that, as the scope of interest enlarges, as feeling comes to be widely objectified, as the significance of the object becomes increasingly independent of the child's immediate state, so the relevant background to any single action of his lengthens, so that it now takes in not just the fact that here and now he lacks the object of volition but also the fact that on repeated occasions in the past he has had the object. Past satisfactions are now stored: for it is no longer the case that satisfaction endures only until want returns, but it is somehow laid down in external achievement or internally in the form of character and habits, and, thus laid down, is perpetually pleasant. "The child," Bradley says, "has done something; and what he has done he still in some shape or other has, if it be only in credit; he possesses an objective issue of his will, and in that not only did realize himself, but does perpetually have himself realized." [19]

4. This last quotation might suggest that, in Bradley's eyes, we have now reached a self of the relevant complexity that, insert it on to the universal side of a volitional structure, see that an appropriate end occupies the particular side, and we can think of the ensuing action as self-realization. However, it is his view that, before this can be correct, we must add to the account of the self—to the account of the self, I say, rather than to the self, for it may be that a self that will satisfy the account thus far given will satisfy the rest—two further stipulations. The first is that there should be knowledge of good and evil and the corresponding capacity to will each as such. And the second is the division of the self into the good self and the bad self. The two conditions, or the processes that lead up to them, for each is the product of slow growth, are intimately connected.

"The existence of two selves in a man," Bradley writes, "is a fact which is too plain to be denied." [20] Two selves, note, aiming respectively at the good and the bad, and not just two collections of desires, some of which we happen to think good and the others bad. In the beginning however these two selves are represented in the young child by something like two centres of pleasure, of which one is under the influence of the extension of interest, while the other is not. Given the role of pleasure in volition—and we have seen something of this—the consequences of there being two such centres within the child should be discernible. Not only will he act upon different desires at different times, not only will action upon these different desires establish within him different habits, but at these different times the world will seem to him so different that it will not occur to him to will otherwise than as he does. And at times the two centres can be so brought into conjunction that the world will seem to him these two different ways at one and the same time.

A crucial stage however in the development of the two selves out of the two centres of pleasure is reached when interest has grown to the point when the precepts and prohibitions—the will, in other words—of a loved figure become the object of the child's volition. This stage is crucial for two reasons.

In the first place, the conflict between the two sets of desires, issuing from the two centres, always active, now becomes sharpened: and that is because one set is now experienced as conforming to, whereas the other set is recognized as contravening, this will. And the conflict is then further sharpened as the will, originally, of course, encountered as external, or as "the will of the superior," in Bradley's words "ceases to be external and becomes autonomy."[21] And, secondly, it is at this stage, and not coincidentally, that the child acquires knowledge of good and evil, and, once the knowledge has been acquired, good and evil are then appropriated by the centres, so that each centre has now a distinctive and unified way of expressing its aim. So, to put the two reasons together, not only is the conflict between the two sets of desire accentuated, it now gains a new self-consciousness.

I said that it was not coincidental that it was at this stage, as internal conflict grows, that Bradley thought that the child acquired knowledge of good and evil. What I had in mind was Bradley's insistence that good and bad can never be known, nor ideas of them acquired, from something purely external. The modern absurdity of 'moral education', which occupies some contemporary philosophers of morals and of education, finds no place in his thinking. "Knowledge of morality," Bradley insists, is knowledge of specific forms of the will, and, just as will can be known only because we know our will, so these forms of will demand personal and immediate knowledge. Hatred of evil means feeling of evil, and you can not be brought to feel what is not inside you, or has nothing analogous within you. Moral perception must rest on moral experience.[22]

The relevance of this important idea in the present context is this: that, if, initially, the division of the self into a good self and a bad self is facilitated by the child's learning of good and evil, under which ideas the two selves can then organize themselves, nevertheless, once this knowledge has been acquired, facilitation will occur in the other direction. The child's knowledge of good and evil will be further deepened by the felt division of the self into good and bad, and by the recurrent experience of internal conflict:

> It will not do for the subject merely to be identified with good on the one side, bad on the other, to perceive their incompatibility and feel their discrepancy. He cannot know them unless he knows them against each other.[23]

5. There are two distinct parts of Melanie Klein's theory that contribute to our understanding of morality, and these also, I wish to suggest, by conforming with Bradley's moral psychology, go some way to underpinning it. These are the account of internal objects, and the account of the depressive position. In arguing for their relevance to Bradleian theory, I shall consider the two accounts in turn.

In discussing Bradley's ideas, I made no attempt to relate British Idealism to the philosophy of Hegel. Similarly in discussing Klein's ideas, I shall not attempt the hotly debated question precisely how the English school of Psychoanalysis relates to Freud's own theory—though it is my own conviction, which I shall therefore state baldly, that one is the proper continuation of the other.

But, however this question is to be decided in general, it is clear that the Kleinian account of internal objects takes off from certain hypotheses of Freud's about the development of the ego, initially put forward in two of his greatest papers, "On Narcissism"[24] and "Mourning and Melancholia,"[25] and then more systematically presented in *Group Psychology and the Ego*.[26] So: In order to explain internal objects and their formation, Klein invoked just what Freud had invoked to explain the watching, measuring, criticizing agency that occupied him in the Narcissism paper and also the lost love-object incorporated in the ego which he thought to be at the base of melancholia. In both cases appeal is made, on the one hand, to the appropriate developmental state of the instincts, including anxiety, and, on the other hand, to a few psychic mechanisms, of which clearly the most relevant is introjection. And, as these example suggest, the strength of the explanation must lie, in part, in the wide range of phenomena it can account for, from the case where a bad object is taken in defensively, so as to ward off anxiety, to that where a good object is taken in constructively, so as to strengthen or extend mental structure.

One significant respect in which Klein goes beyond what Freud explicitly asserts, though not beyond what he suggests, is in what she has to say about how the various psychic mechanisms operate, or in what mental activity their functioning consists, and her view is that in each case their functioning consists in phantasy.[27] More precisely it consists in phantasy twice over. For—suppose we concentrate on introjection—then the initial incorporative process can be identified with a phantasy of ingesting the object through the contemporaneously dominant bodily zone or channel: say the mouth, or possibly the anus. And, then, as a consequence of this initial phantasy there is set up in the mind of the person who has entertained it a disposition to entertain further phantasies in which a counterpart object to the object internalized—an internal object—is represented as being—that is, as living or dying—inside the person.

If it is now asked how this mental activity, phantasy, is to be understood, the suggestion most in keeping with Kleinian theory is that it should be understood as a piece, occurrent or dispositional, of imaginative activity, normally unconscious, and engaged in (and this we shall see is important) under a belief in the omnipotence of thoughts. Elsewhere I have argued for this interpretation,[28] but here I wish only to indicate a particular advantage that it has for us. And that is that it can account for a distinction, of general importance for psychoanalytic theory, but peculiarly relevant for our concerns, between two types of introjection.[29] One, which is identification, concludes with the internal object represented as within, or part of, the self: the other, which might be called mere internalization, concludes with the internal object represented as over and against the self. And my suggestion about the nature of phantasy would then explain this distinction by reference to a difference, phenomenologically accessible, between two kinds of imaginative activity—that is, between the case where the person imagines someone else 'from the inside' or centrally, and the case where the person imagines himself centrally and someone else from the outside or peripherally. For, within the dispositional piece of phantasy, which is relevant here, we can then pair off identification with imagining someone else centrally, and mere internalization with imagining someone else peripherally.[30]

But let me explain what I meant by saying that the distinction within introjection is peculiarly relevant for our concerns. I meant that the Bradleian account of the development of the moral self out of a more primitive self seems to presuppose something very like identification, and, once we have the structure of this mechanism reasonably straight, then we can, by appending it to that account, make that account at once clearer and stronger.

The first and most obvious place where identification fits on to the Bradleian account is in connection with the growth of 'interest'. (And it is noteworthy, though no more than that, that Bradley himself makes much use of the term 'identification' in connection with the extension of interest.) For recall that Bradley rules out two possible interpretations of this process: one is that the child engages in some complex piece of ratiocination in which he puts himself in another's place so that then pleasure will accrue to him, the other that he remains incorrigibly selfish and attends to another's pleasure but only to ensure, consequentially, his own. And perhaps we can see how identification, interpreted as I have suggested, is well calculated both to bring about the requisite result and to do so without mediation. For it will ordinarily be the case—that is, outside phantasy—that the child, by centrally imagining someone else, will, if he feels anything, feel what the person whom he imagines would, or would be believed to, feel. If the child felt otherwise, this would destroy the centrality of that person in his imagination. And what phantasy adds to this ordinary linkage is that, by requiring that the imaginative activity is engaged in under the belief in the omnipotence of thoughts, it ensures that the child feels something. He will feel something, that is, unless he is too psychically damaged to feel at all: and then we would think of him as also too damaged to phantasize. And if he does feel what the person whom he centrally imagines would feel, his emotional range will enlarge.

My suggestion then is that one part of Kleinian theory—the theory of internal objects—allows us a better insight into a phenomenon vital to the development of the self—the extension of interest—which Bradleian moral psychology merely asserts.[31] But probably other psychological theories or fragments of such theories could do this, and therefore how strong a claim to relevance Kleianian theory can make must depend on the extent to which, in explaining one aspect of Bradleian moral psychology, it can also explain others.

Now, if within Bradleian moral psychology the emergent self characteristically comes to seek pleasure in new ends, or rather new types of end, it is no less characteristic of it that, as it finds the pleasure that it seeks, it ceases to feel this exclusively or even predominantly 'against' pain. And this occurs, as we have seen, for three reasons: the pain of privation becomes less in evidence; the pleasure in the object gains in intrinsicality; and past pleasures are now somehow stored in the self and perpetually available to it. And my next suggestion is that this aspect too of the development of the self finds an explanation in the Kleinian account of internal objects, though the explanation it offers requires us to adjust somewhat our overall view of the matter.

For, let us first note that the new relations between pain and pleasure that Bradley writes of seem to correspond very closely to a certain constellation of emotional attitudes and capacities that Klein identifies as the diminution of frustration, the increasing capacity for good experiences, and—most significant in her view—the growing security that the child derives from its knowledge of past satisfactions. And this constellation she not only associates with, but also hopes to explain by reference to, the stable establishment within the ego of a good internal object. And, if we wonder why this should be so, why lasting identification should bring in train these benign consequences, the answer in part rests with what it is that on Kleinian theory is introjected. For the object in the external world that is taken in in phantasy is not simply that which transiently gratifies the infant's appetite: it is, rather, the permanent source of that which gratifies appetite. In the most archaic (and therefore the most significant) case, it is not milk that the infant introjects: it is the breast.

But, if it is true that the account of internal objects can be used to explain both the growth in interest and the new relations between pleasure and pain, what is also true—and this is what I meant by an adjustment to our overall view of the matter—is that, in explaining both phenomena, the account establishes what had so far been lacking: this is, a priority between them. For the new relations between pleasure and pain now take precedence, structurally and hence temporally, over the growth in interest. And this is so because, whereas the new relations between pleasure and pain derive from the mere establishment of an internal object, or from the initiating part of the phantasy, the growth of interest derives from the ongoing part of the phantasy, or from the relations with—that is, the relations in phantasy with—the internal object.

But it is now time for us to take a closer look at the initiating phantasy itself: the phantasy of incorporation. For that phantasy reflects or represents what in my reconstruction of Bradley I called a particular kind of object of volition: and the point I want to make now is that the phantasy of incorporation represents a fairly primitive kind of action in that the whole associated pattern of what it is to have, and what it is not to have, the object of volition is rudimentarily conceived. It is not the most primitive kind of action, such that having the related object is equated with consuming it: for some objectification of feeling would appear to have occurred. (What is introjected is not milk, but the breast.) Nevertheless it falls within the stage of appetite, and this allows me to make my next point: and that is that the Kleinian account of internal objects provides us with a smooth, uninterrupted sequence of events, which starts in a primitive type of action, goes through the incorporative phantasy modelled on this type of action, through the constellation of feelings that this phantasy sets up, through the dispositional or ongoing phantasy in which the introjected object makes its appearance, through the growth of interest that this ongoing phantasy then permits, and closes on new and more evolved types of action in which the child transcends appetite. In other words, by making just one assumption Kleinian theory strings together into a single perspicuous story events that Bradlein moral psychology also insists, though without indicating how, must be connected by only easy or natural transitions. And the one assumption that Kleinian theory makes, which is, of course, totally unrealistic in the short run, but reasonable on a longer term, is that regression does not occur, and it is certainly worth any curious reader's while to observe how close in spirit are what the two theories have to say about how such disturbance or inhibition might occur. What Bradley refers to as Lust—an "unfortunate" term, he later admitted,[32] meaning, I suppose, totally misleading—and what Klein refers to as Envy, are both essentially rooted in insatiability, and their phenomenology is described in surprisingly similar terms.

And now in relating Kleinian theory to Bradlein moral psychology, I have allowed the account of internal objects to overrun that of the depressive position, to which I now turn.[33] In broad outline the depressive position arises when the infant comes to perceive that the good and bad objects with which it has felt itself to be surrounded are really only part-objects or aspects of one and the same thing which therefore has at different times been loved or hated. In venting its rage upon the hated mother the child has in reality or (worse) in omnipotent phantasy damaged the mother it loves. Two broad possibilities are open to it. On the one hand, the infant may be unable to tolerate the perception, and then resorts to such crude mechanisms as splitting or denial, or alternatively to the manic defence. On the other hand, it may be able to accept the perception, and then, under the influence of guilt or depressive (as opposed to persecutory) anxiety, it will struggle to repair, preserve, or revive, the loved injured object. And 'loved injured object' here covers both external and internal objects: for as the child's perception of the external world is corrected to take in whole objects, the inner world is correspondingly modified in its population. Now, in claiming that the growth of interest, and in consequence the capacity to engage in new types of action, can be explained in terms of the infant's relations with its internal objects, I refer to those relations only in so far as they are motivated by the emotions and anxieties characteristic of the depressive position. And in order to grasp the full contribution of the depressive position to the growth of the moral life, we must further appreciate that some of the reparative activity in which the infant engages will be of a symbolical character: that is to say, the infant will express itself in external creativity and achievement, and, internally, in trying to reclaim lost or split-off parts of the self, in trying to harmonize the desire with which it can readily feel simply assailed. The ego, no longer preoccupied with preserving itself, can attempt to integrate itself.

6. Certainly the most striking feature in common between the moral psychology of Bradley and that of Klein is their connection of the good, or the idea of the good, with harmony or unity, and when I wrote a book on the philosophy of Bradley, this was the only point of comparison that I made.[34] In favour of this connection, and of the associated claims that the bad is primarily directed against the good, and that the bad is deficient in harmony or unity, all of which might conveniently, though perhaps not all that precisely, be summarized as the thesis of the dependence

of the bad upon the good, our two thinkers have, of course, very different arguments: very different considerations weigh with them: and instead of enumerating and correlating these arguments—which would require another lecture to itself—I shall just make rather general observations about the thesis that they are designed to support.

First, let me make clear, in case it is not so already, that the thesis is not necessarily a bland or optimistic thesis. Klein, for instance, combined a belief in the dependence of the bad upon the good with the attribution to the child of phantasies quite incompatible with the sweet, amnesiac myth of early innocence. Writing of the first few months of life, she describes the situation thus:

> In its oral-sadistic phantasies the child attacks its mother's breast, and the means it employs are its teeth and jaws. In its urethral and anal phantasies it seeks to destroy the inside of the mother's body, and uses its urine and faeces for this purpose. In this second group of phantasies the excrements are regarded as burning and corroding substances, wild animals, weapons of all kinds, etc.; and the child enters a phase in which it directs every instrument of its sadism to the one purpose of destroying its mother's body and what is contained in it.[35]

But that this is compatible with what I have called the thesis of the dependence of the bad upon the good emerges when we consider what the theory tells us are the objects of the child's sadism or that which it is directed upon. Originally turned against the ego, in which form it is properly identified as the death-instinct, when deflected outwards infantile aggression, or envy as it came to be thought of, flows along one or other of two reasonably distinct channels, both of which can be said to be, in the first instance, laid down by the good or the libidinal. So, if aggression or envy is directed against the breast, a typical infantile target, then it is so either because, though the breast once had the power to satisfy the infant's desires, it seemingly no longer can, or because the breast still possesses an unlimited flow of riches but wishes to keep this for its own, or another's (say, the father's), gratification. "Envy spoils the primal good object" is the relevant formula.[36]

But, mere misunderstandings to one side, I want to say something very general about the place of the thesis of the dependence of the bad upon the good in our moral thinking, and, in doing so, I shall concentrate for the moment on its most significant constituent—the ultimate unity of the good—and then say this: that, whatever initial implausibility it may possess, some such belief as this, taken very roughly and therefore in need of much refinement, is a prerequisite of a certain form of naturalism to which both our thinkers subscribe and which, I am inclined to think, is, not only the one form in which naturalism is acceptable, but the form in which it is correct. Indeed, I would think that one might profitably use the tenability or otherwise of this form of naturalism as a sort of test for naturalism. If naturalism is not acceptable in this form, then it is not acceptable.

The form of naturalism to which I refer has nothing to do with the analysis of the moral judgment, which in this century is the locus where naturalism has characteristically set itself up. The naturalism I have in mind concerns the origins of morals, and its claim is that, in so far as the distinction that we ordinarily draw between what is good and what is bad is licit—and already we can see that this kind of naturalism leads to a critical or revisionary ethical theory—this distinction derives from the way in which our earliest feelings, desires, and wishes represent themselves to us. For they represent themselves to us from the beginning as—and here, of course, our vocabulary will be necessarily inadequate—either favourable, comforting, benign, or as unfavourable, harsh, divisive. Take our desires, for instance: these do not present themselves to us, their owners, as simply being what they are for, and all—innocently, one might say—begging for satisfaction as vociferously as their strength determines. On the contrary, some are acceptable, familiar to us, whereas others stand apart from us, for all their force and fury. Now it seems to me that, if morality does presuppose some primitive way in which our endowed propensities are experienced favourably or unfavourably, then it is likely that those of our propensities which we do experience in a favourable light should be on the whole those which are, and are held to be, reconcilable. In this connection, however, it is surely a genuine gain in realism that, in the elaboration of such a naturalism, Kleinian theory adds to the materials with which Bradley's moral psychology makes do both the experience of depressive anxiety or guilt and the desire to restore, or create anew, an internal harmony.

It is only in the context of this naturalism that I can explain an omission in this lecture, which is deliberate. For I have ignored a topic on which Bradley has little to say but Klein has a very great deal to say. And the topic is heteronomy, or the mental phenomenon whereby precepts are given to the agent internally but as if from another, where, in other words, the commander from whose mouth they issue is phantasized peripherally, and the reason for the omission is that it seems totally in keeping with the thought of Bradley, and the view is quite explicit in Klein, that such forms of internal regulation, extremely effective though they may be, do not necessarily contribute to our undisturbed sense of the distinction between good and bad, in so far as this is licit. It is largely due to the misunderstanding of certain remarks of Freud's that it has come to be thought that the conception of the super-ego—a term not so far heard in this lecture—has a systematic connection with the development of morality in its benign form. The term 'super-ego' has a not uncomplicated history in Klein's theory, as her editors have recently made clear, but it was a constant theme in her thinking that the injunctions or fulminations of internal figures not lying at the core of the ego play at the best an unreliable, at the worst a deleterious, role in the moral life.

7. This is all that can be said in this lecture about the moral psychology of British Idealism and the English School of Psychoanalysis. I conclude with some observations about the worth of saying it.

My proximate motive in setting what Kleinian theory has to say about the development of the self by the side of the Bradleian account was to make the point that, in doing all that he thought he could do for his ethical theory, Bradley was appealing to what must be regarded as psychology. The case that he presents for the theory of self-realization rests heavily on substantive issues concerning the mind. But, of course, I would not have thought to subject the reader to these ideas unless I had felt that the Bradleian-Kleinian form of inquiry is somehow on the right lines, nor would I have been quite unapologetic in imposing it under the heading of a lecture in the history of philosophy, had I not also felt that the example of moral philosophy pursued as a branch of psychology is one to be taken very seriously indeed. But why do I feel this?

Suppose we start, as (and I use both senses of the phrase) the better part of twentieth-century moral philosophy has done, from the other end of the line: with the view that moral philosophy has nothing to do with substantive issues and is essentially involved with the analysis of the moral judgment. Sooner or later such a view encounters this difficulty: that it is possible to devise a judgment that satisfies the analysis, and yet is clearly unacceptable as a moral judgment because, say, its content is too trivial; the only reasons that anyone could have for holding it true would be arbitrary, perverse, inhuman, or some such. And so the original view of moral philosophy must give way to another, broader view on which its subject-matter is not just the analysis, but, more comprehensively, the nature, of the moral judgment: where the nature of a judgment comprehends the general implicatures of the judgment, and also, perhaps, the characteristic speech-acts directed upon it. But difficulties are not at an end: for, however deep an understanding moral philosophy might gain of the nature of the moral judgment, the question of its peculiar authority, of what it can stir up in us, cannot be fully answered within the limits that the present view of the subject imposes. Even if we know everything about what constrains the moral judgment, we shall still not know what about it constrains us. Another way of putting the point would be that the so-called autonomy of the moral judgment, which an 'internalist' account of morality is supposed to grasp, can be grasped only if the account assumes an agent to whom it has first attributed, under the guise of rationality, all the requisite moral attitudes, sentiments, and anxieties.

Now this last consideration suggests a fairly considerable shift in our view of moral philosophy, and in the direction of psychology: so that on the revised view its task is, amongst other things no doubt, to exhibit those beliefs, desires, and related attitudes, which would indeed make moral action—from the agent's point of view, that is—rational. But this view too runs into several difficulties. In the first place, a great deal about morality will remain unsaid if we fix our attention entirely on what moves the agent to moral action: we surely need to attend to what he experiences if he desists from moral action, and also to what there is to morality that also moves him to resist moral action. Secondly, if we concentrate on what moves the agent to moral action, a great deal about morality will have been presupposed: for many of the beliefs, desires, and other attitudes invoked to rationalize moral action will be themselves, in some broad or even narrow sense, the products of morality. Thirdly, and more obscurely, the rationalization of moral action must involve reference—as, indeed, must the rationalization of all action to some degree or other—not only to the beliefs, desires, and attitudes of the agent, but also to how the agent stands to them, and in particular to the desires: to whether (to recycle that phrase) he does or does not identify with them.

And this third difficulty specifically suggests yet another view of moral philosophy, which would permit it not only to take account of the first two difficulties but also to evade a further objection that might have occurred to the reader: the objection that this last view robs moral philosophy of the universality and conceptual character that we look for in philosophical inquiry. And the new view would be that the central task of moral philosophy—for, again, there will be other tasks—is to explore the nature or structure of that process whereby our propensities or dispositions, supremely our desires, are modified or selected, our attitudes to them are developed, so that we are then capable of being appropriately moved to moral action.

Such a view of moral philosophy is, of course, precisely designed to meet the third objection against the last view: the objection, that is, that the view does not take account of how we stand to what rationalizes our actions, and specifically of how we stand to our desires. But in meeting this objection the new view also goes some way towards meeting the first two objections. Unlike its predecessor the new view can take full account of the ambiguities and ramifications of moral action, and it does not have to presuppose morality in the account it gives. It can do all this just because it brings into the centre of attention not a synchronic slice of the agent's mind but a diachronic process in which his mind evolves. Thus it retains moral philosophy within psychology, but relocates it. However, if it retains moral philosophy within psychology, it also reinstates it as a conceptual inquiry. For one way of viewing the psychological process under inquiry is as that process which provides the appropriate conditions for the application of the concept or concepts of morality, and indeed moral philosophy is concerned with the process only in so far as it does lead to this outcome. In this respect it seems to me that moral philosophy is in a very similar position to that occupied by the philosophy of the self, whose topic of inquiry is also a process. It may indeed be that it is with one and the same process that the two branches of philosophy are concerned, the difference being that this single process is viewed in the two cases with different interests in mind. Such a conclusion is fairly close to the approach of the two thinkers I have discussed here. But, however that may be, in the case both of moral philosophy and of the philosophy of the self, the precise depth to which philosophical inquiry must cut into the process itself, or exactly how far it should engage with substantive issues, will depend on the estimate one makes of how implicated the sense of the relevant concepts is in the empirical theory under which the process falls.

I end on a question: Is it ironical, or is it by some happier coincidence, that, if one takes the most austerely anti-psychological ethical theory of our day, the imperativist theory, the point at which it seems to come closest to our moral intuitions—that is, where it makes reference to the self-addressed command—is precisely where it conforms to an important truth of moral psychology and one which has been considerably exposed in this lecture:[37] that morality begins only where the interior dialogue breaks out, a dialogue which on the Bradleian account engages just the good self and the bad self, and which in Kleinian theory pulls in the more numerous and ethically more ambiguous figures of the inner world?

IV The Bodily Ego

1. "The ego," Freud writes in *The Ego and the Id,* "is first and foremost a bodily ego."[1] "The bodily ego," a striking phrase, does not recur in Freud's writings. Nevertheless I believe there to be a thesis of the bodily ego which plays an important part, certainly in Freud's later, but probably also in his earlier, thinking. In this essay I want to consider the nature of this thesis, and to say something about its place within Freudian theory.

2. The thesis of the bodily ego contributes to the question how mind and body are related, or the mind-body problem. Currently, it is true, this problem is interpreted very narrowly: only one relation—that of identity—is taken into account, and only the question whether mind is identical with body is raised. To this question the thesis of the bodily ego has nothing to say, and the contribution that the thesis does make to the mind-body problem becomes apparent only when the full range of theoretically interesting relations between mind and body is taken account of. Let us see how those relations arise.

To the question whether mind is identical with body or whether for every mental particular—a thought, a feeling, an access of desire—there is some physical particular with which it is identical, the answer may be Yes or No. Those who answer Yes subscribe to the identity thesis and are, on ordinary metaphysical assumptions, materialists. Those who answer No are generally dualists or epiphenomenalists, unless their No is so hesitant and guarded as to reflect a doubt whether mental and physical particulars are sufficiently well-regimented for identity either to be asserted or to be denied between them. Freud answered Yes to this question: he was a materialist, but there are shades and shades of materialism.

Someone who subscribes to the identity thesis might do so for one or other of two different reasons. He might believe that the identities in question are analytic, so that for every mental description of a particular there is some physical description with which it is synonymous. Such a person would accept the identity thesis because he accepts some metalinguistic thesis which at once entails and trivializes it. But he might not believe in any such synonymy, and for him the identities obtain solely because of what mental particulars are. The identities are metaphysically rather than analytically true. All who hold the identity thesis for the first of these reasons, and some of those who hold it for the second, are not only materialists but also reductionists: they believe that the mental language is at least in principle eliminable. When the identity thesis is held for metalinguistic reasons reductionism is an obvious consequence, but the connection is less clear in the case of someone who holds it for metaphysical reasons: probably what is at stake is whether mental properties are or are not identical with physical properties. Freud's materialism was not based on linguistic considerations, and he rejected reductionism. His theory requires the mental language.

Anyone who is not a reductionist about the mind must ask himself the question, What is so special about mental descriptions? If he rejects the identity thesis, this question asks nothing less than, What is special about mental particulars? If however he accepts the identity thesis, his question may be reformulated as, What is special about a certain subset of bodily particulars? or What special aspect or aspects of this subset of bodily particulars is it to which we attempt to do justice when we apply mental descriptions to them? It would be in this way that the question presented itself to Freud, and there are two familiar answers, each of which provides a condition for the mental. Each aims at necessity, their disjunction at sufficiency, and, in most cases, if either is met, so is the other. The two conditions, constitute a common ground between the dualist, the epiphenomenalist, and the non-reductive materialist.

According to one answer, when we apply mental descriptions to bodily particulars, we do so because the particulars are associated with a phenomenology. The point has been put recently[2] by saying that there is something that it *is like for* the subject that houses the particular to be in the state corresponding to the existence of the particular. According to the other answer, the application of mental descriptions to bodily particulars records the fact that such particulars are associated with an internal representation: in other words, the existence of the particular corresponds to a state of the subject which allows him to be related cognitively, conatively, or affectively, to things in the external world (where this includes things in the internal worlds of others) and also to things in his own internal world. (I prefer to say of the particulars to which we apply mental descriptions that they are 'associated' with a phenomenology or with an internal representation rather than that they have a phenomenology or include an internal representation because these latter ways of putting it involve mental predications, and it seems right to make such predications of a bodily particular only when it has been picked out by means of a description in the mental language.)

If either of these answers is correct, or both, the next question to ask is whether they give rise to a further relation between mind and body. If mental particulars, which either are or aren't bodily particulars, have a phenomenology or include an internal representation, does either of these facts relate the mind to body in a way over and above identity or diversity? Spinoza and William James addressed themselves to just this question. So does the thesis of the bodily ego.

3. Primarily the thesis of the bodily ego says something about the way in which mental states are related to the body through their representational aspect: however this link, as we shall see, is sometimes reinforced by another link, which passes through the phenomenology of mental states.

Let us introduce the thesis of the bodily ego through a theory of Spinoza's, which also claims that mind and body are related representationally. The theory is very bold, and its claim is that every mental state is representational of a bodily state and specifically of that bodily state with which it is identical. Freud's theory, or the thesis of the bodily ego, diverges from Spinoza's at three crucial points. First, Freud's theory is not a theory about every mental state. It ranges over primitive states of mind, or states of mind that have succumbed to some fairly primitive form of mental functioning. Secondly, Freud's theory concentrates not upon the outward-looking representations that mental states include—that is, those which permit the subject to relate to the world—but upon the inward-looking representations or those by means of which a mental state represents itself to itself. And thirdly—and now we come to the central claim of Freud's theory—it is asserted that those mental states over which the theory ranges represent themselves to themselves as, at least in part, bodily states, though by no means those bodily states with which they are identical. Just which bodily states occur in these self-representations is certainly no arbitrary matter. It has, as we shall see, two determinants. First, there is the overall psychic organization of the subject, and, secondly, there is the precise role or function that the mental state discharges for the subject who has it.

But, first, what is this talk of self-representation of mental states? Why should we be expected to believe in such things? More specifically, if mental states are internally represented, isn't it enough to think that one mental state will be represented by another mental state? Why should we have to believe the surely more cumbrous thesis that (at any rate some) mental states are *self*-representing?

I suggest that whether a certain mental state is self-representing or not is just the issue whether its efficacy requires that it should be represented in the mind. Once its essential function or role within the psychology of the person is found to involve a representation of itself, the conclusion seems inescapable that this representation is part of it, that is, is a self-representation. Of course what such an argument requires is that we should be able to assign to mental states something that may be regarded as their function, but that this is so is a thesis about the mind which must remain an assumption for the length of this essay. Some difficulties with the thesis may be removed when it is recognized that the function may be, and often will be, a matter of bringing about further mental states.

Above, in summarizing the thesis of bodily ego, I began with the claim that certain mental states are self-representing and I then went on to indicate the content that the theory ascribes to those self-representations and then to link this ascription with, in part at any rate, the efficacy of the mental state. This is obviously the correct expository order, but it is important to recognize that it reverses the evidential order. For the best reason that there could be for postulating self-representations of mental states relates to what such representations can do for the mental states they are of—or, ultimately, for the subject who has such states. In illustrating this point, which is a general point, I shall not confine myself to those mental states to which the thesis of the bodily ego applies, but I shall also take states which are self-representing but where the self-representations are veridical and not distorted.

I start with belief and a recent argument[3] designed to show that we cannot legitimately assign beliefs to creatures who lack the concept of belief. The argument—if I follow it—does not rest upon the presumably incontrovertible fact that anyone who can be said to hold a belief must be capable of reflecting upon the belief that he holds and for this reason will certainly need to have the concept of belief. To argue in this way would be to make the necessity of having the concept of belief something that is consequential upon holding beliefs, whereas what the present argument wishes to establish is that having the concept of belief is part of, or essential to, holding beliefs. For it the central consideration would seem to be this: We form beliefs, we revise them; these are the vicissitudes of belief, and we have to allow both if belief is going to enter appropriately into the explanation of behaviour. Now, if we consider the formation of beliefs it is evident that the subject, in order to form a belief, must have the concept of truth: for truth is what belief aims at, and so without the concept he would have no reason to choose this rather than that as what he believes. However, if we now turn to the revision of beliefs, we can see that the concept of truth is not enough. To make intelligible to himself the switch from one belief to another, the subject must also have some such concept as that of holding true, where what is held true may or may not actually be true. And further reflection shows, first, that this concept has a real part to play in the formation of belief too, and, secondly, that this concept is just the concept of belief.

If this argument works, it does so by showing that beliefs could not achieve what they do for the subject—that is, explain his behaviour and his changes of behaviour—unless the subject had the concept of belief. In this way the argument is of the pattern I suggested. It is, it is true, not made explicit in the argument that the concept of belief should actually be *used* in the formation or revision of beliefs—that is, that it should figure representationally rather than be kept in reserve, as, say, an idle part of the subject's recognitional capacity—but the argument seems not to carry the reader along without such an assumption. And so, if I am right about this, the proper conclusion to the present argument is that beliefs are necessarily self-representing.

Belief is a disposition, and it is natural to think that the case for the self-representation of mental phenomena gets stronger as we turn our attention from dispositions to occurrent states. The occurrent mental states whose specific efficacy seems most readily explicable by reference to the way in which they are represented, or represent themselves, are memory and imagination (or at any rate one form of imagination, which I shall call make-believe). Memory does what it does for the subject in part because memory states are labelled as states whose content relates to the past. Make-believe does what it does for the subject in part because states of make-believe are labelled as states whose content is not to be assessed against considerations of truth. I have argued[4] for both these propositions and hence for (on my view) the conclusions that derive from them—namely, that memory states and states of make-believe are self-representing—and now I want simply to add one point which will turn out to be germane to the topic of this essay. In the case of memory, though not as far as I can see in the case of make-believe, there seems to be a connection, not lost on philosophers, between the self-representation of memory (whether this is how they saw it or not) and the phenomenology, or, more specifically, a crucial part of the phenomenology, of memory—I mean the sense of pastness or of familiarity that permeates at least one kind of memory. It is in part because memory feels as it does that it labels itself as such—just as it is in part because it labels itself as such that it is enabled to do what it does. It is a fine point whether phenomenology and self-representation are fundamentally distinct aspects of a mental state like memory or whether one isn't ultimately derivative from the other. But they certainly collude in a variety of ways, and this collusion will recur within the scope of the thesis of the bodily ego, to which I now turn.

4. In the essay "Negation"[5] Freud considers the origins of intellectual life, and in particular he concentrates upon a phenomenon which anticipates the formation of belief. Let us call this the formation of proto-belief. Belief and proto-belief differ in this respect: that, whereas belief is, as we have seen, a truth-directed phenomenon, proto-belief is pleasure-directed. The formation of belief issues in holding something true or false: the formation of proto-belief issues in finding something good for us or bad for us. Holding something true or false conditions our expectations of the world. By contrast, though finding something good for us incites us to maintain it before the mind, and finding something bad for us incites us to expunge it from the mind, in neither case is the question of any match or mismatch between the thing found good or bad and the world paid heed to. With proto-belief there is, as Freud puts it, no 'reality testing'.

In the preceding summary 'something' is clearly to be glossed as 'a thought' or 'a judgment'. But then it might be asked, How could a thought ever be retained or dismissed for reasons that were altogether independent of truth? Of course, we may—as in make-believe—suspend considerations of truth, but then equally we don't accept or reject what we make-believe. So how could we accept or reject a thought, as we are alleged to do in the case of proto-belief, and yet take no interest in its truth-value? It is of this that Freud offers an explanation, and he does so by reference to the way in which the thought represents itself. It represents itself as something corporeal: or, more specifically, either as something that can be brought into the body and made part of it, or as something that starts off as a part of the body and can then be pushed out of it. Freud characterizes the formation of proto-belief in the following way:

> Expressed in the language of the oldest—the oral—instinctual impulses, the judgment is 'I should like to eat this', or 'I should like to spit it out'; and, put more generally: 'I should like to take this into myself and to keep that out'. That is to say: 'It shall be inside me' or 'it shall be outside me'. As I have shown elsewhere, the original pleasure-ego wants to introject into itself everything that is good and to eject from itself everything that is bad.[6]

A thought makes itself suitable for this kind of treatment by the way in which it represents itself: it represents itself as a piece of food, or as a piece of vomit, or (since proto-belief not merely persists into, but flourishes during, the anal phase) as a piece of shit.

A feature of the discussion in "Negation" is that the thoughts Freud has in mind are not singled out by reference to their content. They are, by and large, thoughts which arise from perception or from sensation: and the fact that they misrepresent themselves in this special way is just a reflection of the mode of mental functioning that currently prevails within the subject. It is the stage of development the subject is at, or the fact that he is still in the grip of the primary process, that accounts for the occurrence of his mental states under these confused images, and what is of psychoanalytic interest here is the fragment of psychological development to which it introduces us.

However, the thesis of the bodily ego also ranges over certain mental states in virtue of their content rather than of the stage of development to which they attest, and in the case of such states, barely surprisingly, their content is of inherent psychoanalytic interest. Such states occur originally during the ascendancy of the primary process and therefore their later occurrence is, strictly speaking, regressive, but they nevertheless play a crucial role not only in the evolved life of the individual but also in the evolution of his life. I am thinking particularly of the mental states that make up the two psychic mechanisms of introjection and projection. These mental states are phantasies, and to see just how these phantasies add up to a psychic mechanism, the thesis of the bodily ego is of real importance. I shall here discuss only introjection, since the structural similarities between introjection and projection suffice for the case to carry over.

In the best account of introjection, which can partly be derived from the interpretation of Freud's writings[7] but which needs to be supplemented by later writers,[8] phantasy appears twice over. In the first of its two appearances phantasy manifests itself in an occurrent form. A figure in the environment is perceived by the subject either as particularly loving and benign or as especially frightening and malign. This perception is itself most likely due to phantasy, but this preliminary phantasy would manifest projection. Whichever way round the figure is perceived, but in either case because it is perceived the way it is, the subject thereupon engages in a phantasy in which the figure before its mind is depicted as being brought into the subject's body. Typically entry is effected through the mouth, but sometimes through the anus. This first appearance of phantasy I call 'the incorporative phantasy'. In its second appearance phantasy manifests itself in a dispositional form. As a result of the incorporative phantasy the subject acquires a disposition to phantasize in a certain way. The figure whom in the incorporative phantasy he took into his body is now phantasized as engaging in a variety of activities, all of which take place within the confines of the subject. Just how the location of these activities is represented in the phantasies will, as we shall see, vary. This second appearance of phantasy within introjection I call internalization—though this is a comparatively idiosyncratic use of the term—and the connection between the occurrent phantasy and the dispositional phantasy is at once causal and intentional: internalization is the effect of the incorporation, and there is seemingly—an appearance we shall later need to correct—an identity of figure between the two.

However, to achieve cogency the account needs supplementation, and this is what the thesis of the bodily ego can provide. The thesis adds that the two phantasies essential to introjection represent themselves corporeally or that their self-representations assimilate them to bodily activities. There are two claims here. The first is that these phantasies are self-representing: which, as we have seen, means that a representation of them within the subject is essential to their efficacy. The second claim is that these self-representations are a specific kind of self-*mis*representation, and once again the justification of the claim depends—though this time not wholly—upon an appeal to efficacy. Otherwise the claim reflects the libidinal stage or organization that exerts hegemony over the subject.

In what way does the thesis of the bodily ego fill a lacuna in the account of introjection? The account begins with a perception, in which a figure in the environment is perceived by a subject as either very benign or very malign, and this figure the subject then phantasizes taking into himself. It is reasonable to suppose that what the subject wishes to achieve is, in the case of the benign perception, to protect the figure from harm, and, in the case of the malign perception, to protect himself from harm the figure might do him. But why should he think that either aim could be achieved by phantasizing that the figure enters his body? The subject may phantasize anything he wishes, but surely the figure, still out there in the environment, will remain either just as vulnerable or just as dangerous as he was initially perceived to be. Is there any source from which the subject can acquire confidence that, if he phantasizes in a certain way, a certain effect in the world will be assured? Or is there any belief that the subject could have which would justify him in his own eyes in resorting to incorporative phantasy as an appropriate response to a situation of danger?

An answer suggests itself. The subject's resort to incorporative phantasy would be explicable if it could be shown that the subject believes that in phantasizing the incorporation of the figure he thereby alters the situation of the figure: he is removing him from a position in which he can suffer, alternatively in which he can inflict, harm to a position where he is safe, alternatively where the subject is safe from him. The simplest belief of this kind would be that in phantasizing the incorporation of the figure the subject thereby incorporates him, and this in turn could be accounted for if, not merely did the subject's phantasies include a representation of themselves, but these representations represented them as the very bodily activities that they are of. It is essential to the incorporative phantasy that it represents itself as an actual incorporative process, and this bridges the gap, which otherwise would open up, between resort to phantasy and the lowering of anxiety. This, it hardly needs to be pointed out, is an appeal to efficacy in that what the subject needs from introjection is relief from anxiety.

However, this is not the only respect in which the initial account of introjection needs to be supplemented by the thesis of the bodily ego. Corporeal self-representation cannot stop short at the incorporative phantasy: it must extend to internalization for two distinct reasons. In the first place, unless this is so, the efficacy of the incorporative phantasy, which was the reason for introducing corporeal self-representation initially, would be in jeopardy. For once the external figure has been (as the subject experiences it) brought inside him, the subject needs to be reassured that such security as has already been achieved will not be at risk: in other words, he must believe that the incorporated figure will remain inside him. And a way of doing this that suggests itself is that the subject should experience the dispositional phantasy as a corporeal process of containing the figure in the very place where he is phantasized as being: that is, inside the subject's body. But, secondly, how mental states are represented or self-represented is not a piecemeal issue but is determined on the level of overall psychic organization. Corporeality of representation reflects the prevailing mode of psychic organization so that, given two closely associated phantasies, if one is represented corporeally, the other will be too: if the incorporative phantasy is represented corporeally, so also must be the dispositional phantasy to which it gives rise.

The plausibility that attaches to this account of introjection is still not completely before us until we see how phenomenology enters the picture and makes its distinctive contribution to efficacy. It is a long-standing thought of Freud's that an experience that has a powerful visual or kinaesthetic content can readily be taken by the subject for the very thing that it is of—with, at any rate in the case of waking experiences, the immediate discharge of energy. Under the impact of the wish, a 'false identity' is established between an image—or a memory, as Freud is inclined to call any image that owes its content to previous perception—and a phenomenologically similar percept, and in consequence the subject undergoes a hallucination. Such thinking is already much to the fore in those parts of the *Scientific Project*[9] where Freud discusses early mental functioning: so much so that two recent commentators on the *Project* have summarized his position by saying that "hallucination is in a sense *the* mechanism of the primary process."[10] Hallucination in this sense is of crucial importance in *The Interpretation of Dreams,* and it appears as a premiss in an empirical argument that Freud adduces to substantiate a central tenet of his dream-theory. Freudian dream-theory maintains not just that dreams express wishes but that they provide wish-fulfillment, and in direct support of the theory he cites the 'infantile' or 'intelligible' dreams of children,[11] in which manifest and latent content coincide and where, say, a child wanting strawberries dreams of having strawberries. But this would be no evidence unless we believed that in the subject's perspective the representation of a wish as fulfilled appears to fulfil that wish. Dreams can constitute wish-fulfilment only if, in being dreams of gratification—and the advantage of infantile dreams is that this is an evident fact about them—they are thereby believed to gratify.[12]

Freud cites the phenomenon of hallucination to show how a mental state of one kind can come to serve the same causal or functional role as a mental state of another kind and can do so in virtue of a phenomenological link: so, for instance, memory, which resembles or seems like perception, comes to function as perception, that is, it regulates discharge of energy. Now, as far as Freud's explicit account is concerned, there is no suggestion that this false identity operates through the self-representation of mental states, so that, for instance, when a memory state acts for the subject like a percept, it includes a self-representation that represents it as a percept. Nevertheless this could be the right way of reconstructing Freud's account of hallucination. (Similarly an appeal to self-misrepresentation of mental states might be the right way to explain Freud's account of what he variously calls 'the omnipotence of thoughts' or 'the over-valuation of psychic phenomena'.[13] Indeed the right way to explain this latter phenomenon might even be by an appeal to a corporeal self-misrepresentation of mental states.)[14]

However, in this essay I do not intend to pursue these questions, closely related though they evidently are to its topic. For, if I am right, there is already reason to suppose that some mental states do misrepresent themselves and do so by representing themselves corporeally. This supposition in part derives, as we have seen, from considerations of efficacy, and in part it gains credibility from its link with the theory of psycho-sexual development: for the precise corporeal form that mental self-misrepresentation takes depends upon the stage of development that the subject is at. Now my present suggestion is that, given that there are such errors of self-representation amongst certain mental states, might it not be that the phenomenology of those mental states contributes to that outcome? Certainly, on the face of it, it is not implausible that, say, the phantasy of devouring an external figure should, on the basis of how it seems or feels, help to lure the subject into thinking that he was actually devouring the figure or that the experience in itself should strengthen the illusion that Freud called 'psychic cannibalism'. But at this point I leave the suggestion.

5. I have said that in introjection the link between the two constituent phantasies—the incorporative phantasy and internalization—is twofold: It is causal and it is intentional. It is causal in that the earlier phantasy is productive of the later phantasy, and it is intentional in that the earlier and later phantasy are about the same thing or there is an identity of figure between the two. The second point, as I have already hinted, is not quite right. The incorporative phantasy is a phantasy about an external figure and taking it into oneself: the phantasies of internalization are about a figure taken into oneself, and they concern his doings inside the body. Strict identity does not hold between the external figure and the internal figure that results from its incorporation. The best way of mirroring the relationship between the two seems to be as that between a real-life person and a fictional character modelled upon that person.

In those passages in which Freud talked of introjection, he would seem, with varying degrees of explicitness, to think of the product, or output, of the incorporative phantasy as an internal figure. The boldest claim of this kind evidently concerns the super-ego, which is the internal version of the father in the Oedipal drama. But, as he came to recognize the frequency of introjection in an individual life—which in turn must mean that introjection transcends a purely defensive role[15]—Freud was led to believe in a wide variety of internal figures, and in the late *Outline of Psychoanalysis* he posits an 'internal world'[16] which is populated by such figures. Freud's insight was, of course, intensively exploited by Melanie Klein and her followers. In reaction against what are held to be the excesses of Kleinian theory and in defence of a greater parsimony, defenders of psychoanalytic orthodoxy have come to obscure Freud's point.[17] By proposing the terms 'mental representation' and 'representational world' instead of 'internal object' and 'internal world', they have misrepresented the point as though it were, in the first place, a point about what phantasies *are* rather than about what phantasies *are of,* and, secondly, a point about *all* phantasies rather than about *certain* phantasies. It did not require the genius of Freud to discern that phantasies as such are internal events. What Freud did discern was that there are certain phantasies such that the only adequate way of describing their content is to say that they are of an object that is located inside and persists within the subject's body. There are, in other words, phantasies of external objects and phantasies of internal objects, and phantasies of internal objects derive by an appropriate causal route from incorporative phantasies. It is significant that in Kleinian theory where internal objects are made so much of, the distinction between the two kinds of phantasy and the specific causal origins of each kind are insisted on.[18]

That introjection should in this way bring into being an internal object at once clarifies, and may be clarified by reference to, what emerge as two discrete applications of the thesis of the bodily ego to mental phenomena. In "Negation" Freud was talking about how a thought or judgment, where this may be equated with the content of a mental act, may come to represent itself as a bodily phenomenon—in this case, a bodily part. By contrast, in the discussion of introjection (and projection) Freud was talking about how a mental act itself might come to represent itself as a bodily phenomenon—in this case, a bodily process. Continuous with this second line of thinking is the corporealization of what the mental act is directed upon: and that is not a thought or judgment but that which the thought or judgment is of. Bodily representation extends from phantasy to the figure in the environment who occurs in the phantasy: and, given that the phantasy is represented as a bodily process, the figure is represented as the kind of thing that the bodily process would be directed upon. Psychic cannibalism, in other words, consumes a person.

However, it is one thing to see why psychoanalytic theory, when it is conceptualized in such a way as to preserve the subject's perspective, needs to introduce internal objects, but it is another thing to resolve the difficulties that attach to such a notion. I shall consider two obvious difficulties.

In the first place, in what sense are internal objects *internal?* I have already said that the marks of internality are varied, and it might be useful to bring them under two broad headings. On the one hand, there are what I call the substantive marks of internality, by which I mean a subset of those properties which the object is phantasized as having. Amongst such properties would be ambivalence, the pursuit of archaic sexual aims, implacability or an exaggerated radiance of character, and an immediacy of access to the subject's mental processes. On the other hand, there are what I call the formal marks of internality, where these derive not from the content of the phantasy but from the structural properties of phantasy as such. Such marks would include radical incompleteness of character, deathlessness, a mutability of goodness or badness in accordance with the psychic ups and downs of the subject, and an imperviousness to reality-testing or to any matching against the external prototype.

Secondly, in what sense are internal objects *objects*? The seriousness of the difficulty comes from the combination of three factors. Internal objects are non-actual: the explanatory role for which they are cast requires them to be the subjects of *de re* truths: and they give the appearance of not having well-defined identity conditions. I have already given a hint of where to my mind the likeliest analogy for internal objects is to be found: in fictional characters—though the third factor is present only in some fiction. I do not know of an altogether satisfactory theory of fictional characters, but the most adequate accounts,[19] by rooting fictional characters in the imaginative experiences or the make-believe activity of their authors, prepare us for the way in which internal objects derive their existence from the incorporative phantasies of the subject they inhabit.

6. Thus far, in talking of the thesis of the bodily ego, I have talked of the bodily ego itself solely in so far as it makes a benign contribution to individual development. This however is not the whole story, and that it isn't enhances the value of the thesis, for it enlarges its explanatory scope. Corporeal representation is, we have seen, obedient to the phase-specific intimations of psycho-sexual development, and in consequence, if and when this development meets with setbacks, there will be corresponding disturbances and inhibitions amongst those mental phenomena which are represented in a way that makes reference to some phase in this developmental story. Even within normal development, Freud, following Abraham, pointed out that any internal object that owes its existence to a phantasy of oral incorporation is susceptible to a defect characteristic of the oral phase: ambivalence.[20] But in "The Psycho-analytic View of Psychogenic Disturbance of Vision,"[21] an essay which for some reason he seems to have held in low esteem, Freud went well beyond this and produced a general account of how a bodily organ that "enters into close relations" with the sexual instinct exposes itself to just those risks of

functional disturbance to which sexual development itself is prone, and an account of this sort is presupposed in much of the work of Melanie Klein and W. R. Bion.[22]

The philosophical interest of the thesis of the bodily ego is that it ties not just the mind to the body but the development of the mind to the development of the body. This tie turns out in life itself to be a mixed blessing. If Freud is right and his thesis true, it leads us to an important though well-kept secret of human psychology.[23]

V Psychology, Materialism, and the Special Case of Sexuality

1. One way, a good way, of thinking of psychoanalytic theory is that it provides us with what used to be called an anthropology. There is still no better word for it. By an 'anthropology', I mean an account of human nature that is explanatorily rich. It posits an internal structure, of the appropriate complexity, which, operating in accordance with one or more functioning principles, accounts for a wide variety of output. The output may be external, it may be internal: behavioural, or purely mental. The structure itself is modified over time as the result of pressures from without and from within.

Regarded as an anthropology, psychoanalytic theory offers us three kinds of thing. They are not always distinguished. So, in the first place, it offers us new phenomena, or phenomena that it claims to have discovered. An example would be infantile sexuality. Secondly, it offers us new concepts, or concepts in terms of which either new or old phenomena might be explained. An example would be fixation point, which can be used to organize a great deal of developmental material. And, finally, there are phenomena that psychoanalytic theory has discovered and that require for their conceptualization not just new concepts, but new kinds of concept. The reason for this lies, of course, in the discovered phenomenon itself: the phenomenon functions with a distinctive kind of causality, and what is therefore required is a concept with a corresponding kind of explanatoriness. Prime examples of this third kind of thing that psychoanalytic theory has to offer us are the phenomena, hence the concepts, of the so-called mechanisms of defence: projection, introjection, and projective identification.

Let me now give it as my conviction that the primary task of philosophy vis-à-vis psychoanalytic theory is to articulate the kind of understanding—the diversity of understanding, we might say—that psychoanalytic theory promises of human nature. This essay is an attempt, a somewhat sporadic attempt, at the articulation, the philosophical articulation, of psychoanalytic theory. It puts to one side the epistemic issue, or the issue how to test psychoanalytic theory. It does so in the belief that, as Adolf Grünbaum has put it,[1] it takes real ingenuity, not just semantic analysis, to devise effective ways of testing theories: the more so in the case of interesting or innovative theories. Any such ingenuity would be misplaced if the theory itself had been imperfectly grasped.

2. There are two facts about Freud which we need to hold on to if we are to appreciate his theory. They are facts about his intellectual orientation. He was committed to psychology in science, and to materialism in philosophy. He was a psychologist, and a materialist.

That Freud was *a psychologist* involved a commitment on his part both as to the *explicanda* and as to the *explicans* of the science he set out to construct. It was a science that would explain psychological phenomena by reference to psychological phenomena. This is not quite precise: More precisely, what it set out to explain was either psychological phenomena or phenomena that were directly caused by psychological phenomena and could be identified only in terms of those causes; notably actions. And it set out to explain them by reference to psychological phenomena and phenomena that directly caused psychological phenomena, notably bodily stimuli and events in the perceived environment. And 'psychological phenomena' may be thought of as phenomena that bear at least one or other of the following two properties: intentionality, or thought-content, and subjectivity, or what philosophers used to call 'feel' and what is now often referred to by the phrase 'what it is like for a subject to be in that condition'.[2] When these two properties both hold of a given psychological phenomenon, they characteristically fuse, and for this amalgam I use the term 'phenomenology'. Psychological phenomena may be conveniently classified into (one) mental states, which are transient, like moments of panic, passing thoughts, pains, dreams, perceptions: (two) mental dispositions, which underlie mental states, like desires, beliefs, skills, habits: and (three) mental activities, which are things that we do internally, like forming intentions, inferring conclusions, repressing desires, and introjecting figures in the environment.[3]

That Freud was *a materialist* committed him to denying the existence of entities other than those which physical science studies and which obey its laws. Whether Freud believed that there were properties that could not ultimately be identified with physical properties or that there were laws that could not ultimately be correlated with physical laws is probably not worth pursuing. There is no reason to think that Freud's views on these issues were determinate, or even that he recognized these issues as such.

There is no incompatibility between the two commitments to which Freud was obliged. Nor did Freud, except perhaps intermittently, think that there was. Indeed Freud thought of them as connected commitments. He believed that materialism should exercise an influence over any well-thought-out psychology. He wavered over what form this should take.

The Three Essays in the Theory of Sexuality is a good place to find illustrated the different ways in which Freud thought that materialism could or should influence psychology. And, since some of those ways are, to my thinking, benign and others malign, a consideration of them is not mere archaeology. Or so I hope.

However a note of reserve. It is not necessary to be a materialist to recognize that sexuality is in some intimate way tied up with the body. Sexuality is bodily in a way that transcends the broad fact that our psychology, the whole of it, is essentially embodied. It is bodily in a way that prudential calculation is not, nor even is anger. Freud was aware of this fact, and he attempted to do justice to it, and my reservation is that it is not easy to keep apart the overall influence that materialism had upon Freud's theory of sexuality, and the specific way the theory attempted to do justice to the nature, to the singularly corporeal nature, of sexuality.

3. I start with the most audacious theme in the *Three Essays:* the discovery of infantile sexuality. And the question I ask is, Why did Freud think that this is what he had discovered? Why, for instance, did he think that the infant who tries to recreate through thumb-sucking the pleasure he had passively experienced while satisfying a vital need was initiating himself into sexuality?[4] The *Three Essays* contain, in fact, a range of answers to this question. They propose several criteria of the sexual as these apply to—which is what is here at issue—a mental state. I shall look at these criteria with an eye to the broader issue, or to what they show us about how Freud conceived of psychology under the shadow of materialism.

The *first proposal* is that a mental state is sexual if it is the correlate of specific chemical changes occurring in the body.[5] Here the deference to materialism is evident, but it is important to be clear just why this proposal is inadequate from the point of view of psychology. Certainly the concept 'correlate of certain chemical changes' can be used to pick out psychological phenomena. Just because 'chemical change' is a concept of chemistry, it does not follow that 'correlate of certain chemical changes' is a concept of chemistry. A psychological phenomenon can be identified by referring to its physical correlate. But the inadequacy is this: that, if this is done and the concept 'correlate of certain chemical changes' is used to pick out a psychological phenomenon, it will not pick it out by reference to its psychological properties. We shall be left totally in the dark about both the intentionality and the subjectivity of the mental state. For a reason to which I shall return, this constitutes a real impairment in a concept intended to play a crucial role in a psychological theory.

However, within the *Three Essays,* we find a supplementary view, seemingly endorsed by Freud, which enriches such concepts as 'correlate of certain chemical changes' in such a way as to make them phenomenologically informative. Enriched in this way, these concepts make reference to a chemical state or a chemical transformation twice over. For they invoke certain chemical changes in that the psychological phenomena to which they apply must be correlated with these changes: then they invoke them a second time in that the psychological phenomena must also be perceptual of these changes. What underwrites this conceptual enrichment is the theory, the philosophical theory, that some psychological phenomena—and, though the scope of the theory is not clear, this includes states of sexual excitation or pleasure—are, amongst other things, perceptions of the physiological states with which they are correlated.[6] Now, if we accept this view, then it follows that, once we know what chemical changes these psychological phenomena are correlated with, we also know, at least in principle, or but for a lack of imagination on our part, what these states are like phenomenologically. The theory that affords us this increment of information is in effect a version of the famous James-Lange theory of the emotions.[7]

Introduced into the present context, this theory of the emotions has the effect of psychologizing the first proposal about the nature of sexual states, in that the proposal now not merely allows these states a psychological content, it goes some way towards saying what this is. But this, it might be felt, is purchased at a heavy price in plausibility. Why should we think that some mental states are perceptions of chemical changes? And if some are, why sexual states?

A *second proposal* that Freud considers about what makes a mental state sexual also identifies the sexual through its causation, but not solely: for it adds to the causal criterion an explicit psychological specification. According to this proposal, a sexual experience is one that has been caused by stimulation of one of several especially sensitive areas of the body, and the experience consists in feeling pleasure at that area.[8]

This proposal defines sexuality in terms of the erotogenic zones, and Freud would appear to have backed away from it for two reasons which are seemingly unrelated. One is that Freud came to the view that any zone of the body might become erotogenic.[9] The other is that pleasure at an erotogenic zone did not seem to him to be, at least for men, an accurate characterization of what *genital* sexuality seeks: it did not seem to him to do justice to orgasm, or what he called the "discharge of the sexual products."[10] I have called these two reasons seemingly unrelated, but perhaps they come together in this way: that the nature of an erotogenic zone cannot be captured simply by enumerating an open-ended list of parts of the body: we must also specify the common interest taken in them. But there is no one single form of interest that they hold for us. (It is significant that, whatever reasoning it was that turned Freud against defining sexuality in terms of specific zones of the body, he thought that these zones could still be used for characterizing the successive organizations of the libido. For, even if there is no common interest that we take in all excitable zones of the body, there is a characteristic interest that we take in each, and there is a common way in which this interest is then extended to other parts of the body. So, for instance, in the oral phase we seek a particular kind of pleasure primarily in the mouth, and then derivatively we find it in what we, but not anatomy, think of as a mouth. This patterning of pleasure over the body gives a thematic unity to the actions and passions of each libidinal phase.)

A *third proposal* that Freud considers can be seen as leading on beyond the second: it is purely phenomenological. It identifies the sexual in terms of the pleasure it involves: the pleasure, note, not the source of pleasure. In point of fact, this proposal is a cluster of proposals, the members of which correspond to different ways in which Freud conceived of the phenomenology of sexual pleasure. For some of the time he seems to have hoped, but without much conviction, that sexual pleasure could be reduced to a single or 'specific' quality.[11] But basically Freud renounced any such easy solution to the problem, and he looked for a phenomenological criterion of a more structural kind. In this connection, he tried to understand sexuality in terms of a distinctive intertwining of pleasure and unpleasure or pain.[12]

That such an account is wanted is for Freud implicit in a fact of usage: that, as he puts it, "the concepts of 'sexual excitation' and 'satisfaction' can to a great extent be used without distinction."[13] Now Freud sees in this usage a paradox, which he expresses by saying that under the aegis of sexuality we equate pleasure with unpleasure. It might be thought that what Freud was doing, in proposing this paradox, was to pin down, perhaps in an exaggerated fashion, some surface feature of our sexual lives: that he was referring, say, to the ambivalence, to the element of sado-masochism, which none of us can escape. But this is not the case. The paradox that Freud proposed was conceptual, and of a kind that needed, not just acceptance, but resolution, and, if his attempt to resolve it in the third of his *Three Essays*[14] is not altogether persuasive, what is of real interest is how the problem arose for him. For here again we find the intersection of materialism and psychology in his thinking.

The starting-point for Freud was an old idea about the way the mind lies under the sway of a recurrent physiological cycle. The cycle begins with the accumulation of tension in the body, through either an external or an internal stimulus. The cycle ends with the discharge of this tension, brought about through activity that, in terms of energy expended, is commensurate with the stimulus.[15] This cycle underlies sexuality. Add now to the cycle the James-Lange theory to take us from the physiology of this sequence to psychology, and pain or unpleasure is equated with the perception of tension and thus takes its place at the beginning of the cycle, and pleasure is equated with the perception of discharge and occupies the end of the cycle. And now the stage is set for thinking that a distinctive mark of sexual pleasure is that it is inconceivable without a certain kind of unpleasure, which Freud finds it natural to call 'excitement'. It might even be held that all that sexual pleasure is the dramatic cessation of unpleasure.

However a fundamental question which might be asked, and one which goes deep into the sources of Freud's paradox, is, Why should Freud have thought of pleasure and unpleasure in what is such a relentlessly atomistic way? Does not sexual intercourse itself suggest a more global conception of pleasure? On such a conception, when pleasure accrues to a cycle of behavior which begins in excitement, ends in orgasm, and is held together by anticipation and recollection, no one segment of this cycle monopolizes pleasure. There is, in the current gallicism, no 'site' of pleasure.

There is, as far as I can see, no direct reason why materialism should favour an atomistic over a global view of pleasure and unpleasure. But there is an indirect reason. For there is a tendency implicit in materialism to posit, in the first instance, as simple a psychology as possible, and then to treat more complex psychological formations as learned or acquired variants upon this base. As an illustration of such a simple psychology, we might imagine the following account of how a particular desire arises: A creature experiences a certain pleasure, at, say, a certain part of its body, in the course of satisfying a vital need. Then it seeks to recreate for itself this pleasure: it now pursues the pleasure actively, instead of under-going it passively. Quite possibly, in the course of doing so, the creature finds that some object—its own body or the body of another—reveals itself to be indispensable to the regular re-creation of this pleasure, and to the extent, but only to the extent, that this is so, this object gets incor-porated into the orbit of the creature's quest. Desire for this object is established in the creature's psychology.[16] Now two things are to be ob-served about this account. It employs, indeed it depends upon, the at-omistic account of pleasure that figures in Freud's paradox. And it is structurally identical with a whole strand of Freud's thinking about sexu-ality: that is to say, the strand that thinks of aim as fundamental to sexu-ality, and of object as something that is, in Freud's phrase, only 'soldered' on to it.[17]

My suggestion is not that materialism requires this kind of stratifica-tion of psychology. It is only that it encourages it. And my suggestion is that, for all the elegance implicit in this strand of Freud's thinking about sexuality, it is the other strand, or that which takes a more global view of pleasure and which assumes an object for sexuality right from the beginning, that is more realistic. Such a view is emphasized in Kleinian theory, to which I shall return.

Two further proposals that Freud considers about the nature of a sexual experience, and which bear specifically on the question why an early and seemingly innocent experience like thumb-sucking should be considered sexual, have a feature in common: They both propose rela-tional accounts. They both hold that the sexual nature of thumb-sucking depends, or partially depends, upon its relations with something else, and the two accounts diverge in what they think this something else is. One account takes a synchronic view, and it holds that an early sexual experience is essentially related to, in that it draws upon, the component instincts: that is, the instinct to look and the instinct to be looked at, the instinct to inflict cruelty and the instinct to undergo it.[18] The other account takes a diachronic view, and it holds that what makes an early experience sexual is that it is related to, in that it lays the foundations for, the later and indubitably sexual life of the individual.[19]

I am confident that it is this second kind of relational account that weighed most with Freud in his assertion of infantile sexuality. But, once again, such an account will not do by itself. It must be supplemented by a phenomenological characterization of the experience that it pronounces sexual. And now we must ask, Why is this so?

There are two reasons why this supplementation is necessary. The first is comparatively shallow, and it is the implausibility of thinking of an experience as sexual solely in virtue of its consequences. What the experience is like must come into it. The second goes deeper, and it is that without a phenomenological characterization of the experiences that are said to affect later sexual development, the claim that they do is ungrounded. This is a point I shall take up later.

What I hope is now apparent is that this identification of experience, particularly of seemingly innocent experiences, as sexual and the construction of a theory of psycho-sexual development go hand-in-hand. Each of these two constituents is complex, and the theory of psycho-sexual development is very complex. It is overall an audacious theory, though this should not obscure the fact that some of its parts are ineliminable parts of commonsense psychology.

4. In considering the different ways in which Freud proposed to identify the sexual nature of an experience, I have contended that some betray, whereas others do not, the influence of materialism upon the construction of a theory that was psychological in its ambitions. Now I turn to two further ways in which materialism obtruded into Freud's anthropology, affecting far more than his theory of sexuality.

The first is the economic aspect of psychoanalytic theory, or the way in which Freud correlated transformations of belief and, above all, of desire within a subject with shifts of psychic energy. Energy cathects now this idea, now that, and sometimes circulates in the system free or unbound. The hypothesis of psychic energy, or what is called the economic model, one of Freud's oldest ideas, plays a role within his theory that is extremely difficult to circumscribe. Historically it certainly suggested to Freud a number of theses that are indisputably psychological in character. In this connection we can think of the postulation of reaction-formation, the general account of obsessional neurosis, and, above all, the first account of anxiety according to which anxiety is transformed libido. However it is arguable that the hypothesis of psychic energy suggested these things to Freud only in so far as the concept itself is taken metaphorically, or as a vivid way of talking, in a vocabulary borrowed from materialism, about certain very familiar facts of psychology: such as that desire will out. For the truth is that the distinctive aspect of psychic energy—namely, that it is a quantitative phenomenon—goes uninterpreted, and therefore it is arguable that the concept as used by Freud does not have, taken literally, any explanatory or even any descriptive power. It provides a vocabulary without, or at least in advance of, a theory.

The second general way in which materialism manifests itself within Freudian theory has gone largely ignored. It inspired a characterization of our earliest way of thinking and feeling, which at once underwrites and supplements what Freud has to say about the omnipotent mode of thought. For this characterization I have purloined a term of Freud's, and I call it 'the thesis of the "bodily ego."'[20] What this thesis asserts is that in the beginning our psychology is such that we conceive of mental states on the model of corporeal entities, and of mental processes on the model of corporeal processes. We conceive, say, of a thought as a piece of food in the mouth, or as faeces, and we then conceive of accepting the thought as swallowing the piece of food, or of rejecting the thought as excreting faeces. In later life this mode of consciousness, as we might call it—using consciousness in the broad or determinable sense, for the mode occurs, of course, on the conscious, preconscious, and unconscious levels, though mostly on the unconscious level—is largely transcended, but never totally. Furthermore it is a mode to which we may, and in certain circumstances do, regress.[21]

5. We can, I have said, distinguish between the benign and the malign influence that Freud's materialism had over the construction of his theory. Very roughly, the influence was benign when it led the theory to identify,

and it was malign when it led it to efface, the phenomenology of the experiences the theory ranges over. This is a more fundamental issue than whether the account the theory gives of this phenomenology is correct or incorrect.

We are back to the question, Why is it important for psychoanalytic theory to fill in phenomenology? I hinted at the answer when I questioned the acceptability of identifying a sexual experience solely through its causal influence upon later sexual development. The answer is this: In so far as a mental state has *as such,* or because of the mental state that it is, an effect upon the subject's psychology, including his behaviour, it is likely to have this effect in virtue of its phenomenology: likely, though not necessary. In certain cases, broadly thought of as computational, the effect of the mental state will be brought about solely through its intentionality or its thought-content. This corresponds to the narrow domain to which cognitive psychology, or functionalist theories of the mind, have in effect confined themselves. But generally it is the total content, or the phenomenology, of the state that is causally active. This is borne out by the fact that, for many types of psychological state, someone who had never experienced a state of that type would not be able to understand how the state could have the efficacy that it has. Someone who had never experienced terror could not understand how terror could make the most resolute of people turn and run. Someone who had never experienced the pangs of love could not understand how they might drive someone to ecstasy or suicide.[22]

These two examples are cases where a mental state causes another mental state or causes certain behaviour, and it does so in virtue of its phenomenology. It is important to realize that the same holds for the causal influence of a mental state upon a mental disposition. In so far as a mental state establishes a new disposition or modifies an existing disposition, it is likely to do so in virtue of its phenomenology. A fixation-point, for instance, is best thought of as a disposition, activated by frustration, to seek pleasure in specific kinds of activity. And my claim is that, not only is a fixation-point established through mental states, early in date, in which such pleasures were freely enjoyed, but it is the pleasurable character of those states that is causally responsible for the content of the disposition, or the fact that it is a disposition to pursue just those activities.

The point that I am insisting upon about the importance of phenomenology within psychology can be forcefully made by using the well-entrenched distinction between the two relations, 'cause' and 'causally explain'.[23] 'Cause' is a fully extensional relation, 'causally explain' is not. If physics or physiology discovers that one event causes another, then we can assert this connection under any description of the two events. We can assert it, for instance, under physiological or under psychological descriptions of those events, given that such descriptions are available. The same does not hold for 'causally explains'. To say that one event causally explains another is true only for those descriptions of the two events which pick out whatever feature of them it is in virtue of which one causes the other. So, when psychology discovers that one mental event causes another, though this assertion remains true under all descriptions of those events, including whatever physical or physiological descriptions are available, in the vast majority of cases one of these events can be said to causally explain the other only under descriptions of them that are psychological or that quote their phenomenology. And the same holds *mutatis mutandis* when the mental event causes the establishment of, or an alteration in, a mental disposition. For this reason, since psychological, specifically psychoanalytical, theory aims to be explanatory, it must resist the pressure, whether it comes from materialism or elsewhere, to pass over or omit phenomenology.

It is to my mind apparent that amongst followers of Freud it is Melanie Klein and her co-workers who have best appreciated this point, and we find in their work, theoretical and clinical, many arresting applications of it. The emphasis upon phantasy facilitates this kind of theorizing, and in illustration of my claim I might cite the Kleinian elucidation of the so-called defence mechanisms.[24] For what Kleinian theory has done is, developing certain suggestions of Freud and Ferenczi, to append to projection, introjection, and projective identification phantasies with a highly specific phenomenology which serve as the vehicles or media of those mechanisms. The content of these phantasies is replete with references to expelling something out of, or putting something into, one's own body, or to forcefully breaking into the body of another, and it is of a piece with ordinary views about psychological causation to think of these phantasies, given their phenomenology, as adequate for bringing about the consequences that psychoanalytic theory attributes to the defence mechanisms they mediate. These consequences amount, in the case of each mechanism, to the establishment of a disposition to engage in further phantasies, which mould the subject's thoughts, feelings, and perceptions. As an application of this last point it seems that, in the current state of the theory, which assigns no suitably charged phantasies to the mechanism of repression, we should perhaps think that repression merely *causes* its specific consequences, whereas projection, introjection, and projective identification *causally explain* what they induce. This fits in well with the historical fact that repression was a first thought of Freud's about what was to prove the rich field of defence. In due course repression may need to be reformulated, and in the process it may turn out to be the disjunction of several distinct mechanisms.

VI Desire, Belief, and Professor Grünbaum's Freud

1. Virtually all those who are not either ignorant of Freud or totally sceptical of his findings believe that he altered, radically altered, our conception of the mind. He effected a change in what we think we are like, and it was a big change. Astonishingly enough, it is philosophers who have been of all people the slowest to recognize this fact. They have been slowest to recognize that this fact has anything to do with them.

2. Of course there are philosophers who have discovered that Freud's new conception of the mind has consequences for the philosophy of mind. And what these philosophers show is that there are two very different ways of understanding the alterations that Freud made to our conception of the mind, and they have split on which view they have taken of what he did. They have divided themselves, implicitly for the most part, between a more extreme and a far less extreme understanding of how he altered our thinking about the mind.

On the more extreme view, what Freud did was that he reconceptualized the mind from scratch. He rejected the traditional concepts used to grasp mental phenomena, and he asked us to substitute for them other concepts that he devised for this purpose. Wittgenstein, who held some such view,[1] suggested that one fact that might blind us to this crucial feature of Freud's work is that he (and his translators) went on employing the traditional vocabulary of the mind. Freud continued to talk of 'desire', 'belief', 'thought', merely prefixing these words with the qualifier 'unconscious'. But 'unconscious' is (on this view) no ordinary qualifier. It subverts the word it qualifies. It does so by snipping the word off from its standard evidential links with the world. There is, for example—and the example is Wittgenstein's own—no coherent way of understanding 'unconscious thought' as though it picked out a psychological entity that is just like a thought except that it happens to be unconscious. To understand 'unconscious thought' we must start with the phrase as a whole, not with its familiar-seeming constituents.

On the less extreme view, Freud certainly arrived at a new conception of the mind, but he did so by taking over more or less intact the ordinary, the commonsense, conception of the mind, and then adding to it. It was because he preserved the core of the traditional conception that he preserved the traditional vocabulary in its traditional meaning. In so far as he added to the commonsense conception, this was to accommodate new mental phenomena that he discovered and, if his additions to the commonsense conception, if the outer layers of conceptualization that he wrapped around it, have attracted so much attention, the reason is that these newly discovered phenomena turn out to play such a large role in what we do, as well as in what happens to us. They are crucial to the way we lead our lives.

And now are we prepared for the following paradox: that the more extreme view of how Freud altered the conception of the mind—that is, by reconceptualizing the mind from the beginning—has a tendency to trivialize his achievement, whereas the far less extreme view of the matter—that is, that he added on to the traditional conception—readily allows us to see how he deepened our view of ourselves?

3. What lies behind this paradox is that, if the extreme view were in fact true, if Freud's concepts were concocted totally *de novo,* if the traditional schemata for the mind had been totally abandoned, it would not be easy to see how psychoanalytic theory offered us any form of explanation. This is certainly how Wittgenstein thought, and Richard Rorty, a contemporary upholder of the same view, is like-minded.[2] For Wittgenstein the non-explanatory nature of psychoanalytic theory, which is just a special case of the non-explanatory nature of all psychology, is the premise from which he derives the conclusion that psychoanalysis is just a new 'notation' or 'convention'. Rorty, by contrast, starts from Wittgenstein's conclusion—Freud's theory, he writes, is just "one more redescription of things to be filed alongside all the others, one more vocabulary, one more set of metaphors"[3]—and from this he derives as his conclusion something like Wittgenstein's premiss. The weaknesses inherent in both arguments need not detain us, and all I wish to point out is the intimate connection between thinking of Freud as a total conceptual revisionist and denying his theory genuine explanatory value.

I turn then to the less extreme view, which presents Freud as someone who extended the pre-existent conception of the mind, and what I shall do, by way of vindicating this view, is to take Freud's conception not statically or in itself, but in action, in explanation, and to show how the kind of psychological explanation that Freud made possible is an expansion, effected step by step, of that provided by the commonsense conception of the mind.

Now I assume that what is distinctive of ordinary psychological explanation is that, when it explains an *action,* which is what it characteristically does, it does so by appeal to a desire and a belief on the part of the agent, where the desire and the belief are appropriately related to one another and also to the action itself.[4]

Let us look at these two relationships in turn:

First, the desire and the belief are appropriately related to one another just in case, given what the desire is for, the belief asserts what, in the circumstances in which the agent finds himself, is the best way open to him of satisfying such a desire. The belief may be thought of as, relative to the desire, an instrumental belief, though it is important not to misunderstand this phrase. For what the belief indicates is not necessarily something that is a mere stage on the way to satisfying the desire: it may indicate something that in the circumstances is, or is equivalent to, satisfying the desire. The belief is instrumental in a broad sense, which covers informing us not only how to achieve our end but what achieving that end amounts to. Secondly, the desire and the belief are appropriately related to the action that is to be explained just in case two further conditions are satisfied. The first is that the belief indicates that very action, or asserts that in the circumstances *it* is the best way of satisfying the desire: in which case the agent has a reason for doing the action. The second condition is that the desire and the belief should jointly have caused the action.

Since this form of explanation is so widespread, it is appropriate to illustrate it with examples of suitable banality. A woman wishes to see a certain play. She believes that the best way to do so is to go to the booking-office and buy some tickets without delay. So under the influence of this desire and this belief, she goes to the booking-office straight away and buys the tickets. A man wishes to quench his thirst. He believes that the best way of doing so is to pick up the glass of water before him and drain it. So under the influence of this desire and this belief, he drinks the glass of water.

For these explanations to work, first, the person must actually have the desire and the belief. Secondly, the desire and the belief must make the action rational for the agent to do: they must "rationalize" it for him. Thirdly, it must be the desire and the belief that caused the agent to carry out the action. It is important to appreciate—and the significance of this now obvious-seeming point is due to the work of Donald Davidson—that rationalization by itself does not explain an action: additionally, causation is required. So long as an agent has a desire and a belief that rationalize an action, he has a reason for doing it. He may have a reason for doing it long before he does it, but from that it doesn't follow that, when he actually does it, this is the reason why he does it. He might do it for some other reason. To close this gap, or to convert a reason that the agent had for doing an action into the reason why he did it, this reason must be causally efficacious. In other words, it is only in the light of its causal history that we can explain an action.

Something further to be noted about ordinary psychological explanation is that, not only does the appeal to a desire and a belief suitably related to one another and to a certain action explain that action, but it also establishes it as an action. An action, it has been said, is something that an agent does and about which it is appropriate to ask, in some relevant sense, *why* the agent did it. The desire/belief schema of explanation glosses this 'why'. It reveals the relevant why to be that which the practical syllogism interprets.

Freud, then, inherited this explanatory schema, and he made ample use of it in, for instance, the narratives of his case-histories, or the descriptions of the waking hours from which the dream gains its material, or the stories that unfold in the manifest content of dreams. However he revealed his own conception of the mind in three things, three distinct things, which he did to this explanatory schema. He *deepened* the schema: he *elaborated*, or *produced variations upon*, it: and he *contextualized* it. Let us look at these three developments in turn.

(a) In *deepening* commonsense explanation, Freud preserved the proforma or schema that common sense employs, and introduced into it as terms or explanatory factors non-conscious desires and beliefs—factors which common sense either completely overlooks or invokes with less than total conviction.

So, an agent does something, and this is explained by appeal to a non-conscious desire and belief on the agent's part which at once rationalized the action and conjointly caused it. The non-conscious desire and belief are related to each other and to the action in virtually the same way as their conscious counterparts are in everyday explanation. An example, which Freud gave out of his own experience, is this: On his way to visit his elder brother, who was staying in England, Freud failed to make the right connection in Cologne, although the train he needed was standing in the station with its destination clearly marked: in consequence of this slip Freud had to stay the night in Holland. This lapse is explained by Freud's unconscious (or perhaps preconscious) desire to see the great Rembrandts at the Hague and in Amsterdam plus his belief that, if he missed his train, he would have to spend extra time in Holland and could see them readily.[5]

Notoriously Freud greatly enlarged the number of things we do that should be regarded as actions in virtue of the fact that, contrary to appearances, they admit of desire/belief explanation. It is one of the themes running through *The Psychopathology of Everyday Life* that some of the slips and errors of ordinary occurrence are properly thought of as intentional actions.[6] *Some,* I say: for some other slips and errors are, as we shall see, to be diagnosed as having different kinds of causal history, and hence are amenable to different forms of explanation, and hence are not actions at all.

What can be appropriately regarded as an addendum to deepened desire/belief explanation, with the normal explanatory schema still holding, are cases where the place normally occupied by belief in this schema is taken over by phantasy, which is cousin to belief. So, for instance, when Freud's famous patient the Rat Man found himself settling down to work between midnight and one o'clock, this piece of behaviour is explained by the desire to earn his father's love in conjunction with the phantasy that his father, in fact long dead, would return as a ghost at the bewitching hour and would be delighted to find his son hard at work.[7]

However, as Freud came to appreciate, phantasies, being exclusively unconscious factors, tend not to operate in the same orderly way as instrumental beliefs: they cannot be recruited as minor premises in some practical syllogism that the agent can be credited with running through unconsciously before he acts. The upshot is that, when phantasies are causally operative in behaviour, the behaviour tends to call for one or another of the new forms of explanation to which I now turn.

For Freud's conception of the mind, as I have already indicated, made itself felt not just in introducing non-conscious factors into the existing form of explanation—though this is how philosophers have generally seen the matter—but in innovating new forms of explanation, which may be regarded as variations upon the original form. Each of these new forms is a response to the discovery of some further aspect of the mind which has a causal influence upon human behaviour: more specifically, the form of explanation is designed to capture the nature of the causal influence that this new factor exerts. Each form has its prototype in ordinary or non-psychoanalytic habits of explanation, but in each case it has been the discovery by psychoanalysis of the new factor and its causal powers that has resulted in the form's ceasing to be marginal and becoming canonical. Here then we move beyond Freud's *deepening* of everyday or traditional psychological explanation, and we are now concerned with ways in which he *elaborated,* or *provided variants upon,* it. I now turn to three such variants, which increasingly diverge from the original proforma. It becomes progressively less plausible to see the behaviour at issue as the outcome of a practical syllogism, and correspondingly less and less convincing to think of it as an action.

(b) In the first place, then, someone does something, and what he does is explained by appeal to an unconscious desire and a belief (or perhaps phantasy) *and* a chain of association operative in the person's mind. In such cases there is an action that the desire and the belief would rationalize, but this action is not what the person actually does and hence is not what is to be explained. What the person does, and is indeed caused to do by the desire and the belief, is something that is connected with the original or rationalized action along the operative chain of association. In such a situation the background is provided by the fact that the person is for some internal reason prevented from doing the original action, but nothing inhibits him from doing the associated action. For those things which persons do and that have this causation and that consequently receive this new form of explanation, I use the term 'displaced action'—though this term is to be understood so as to leave it open whether such things are, strictly speaking, actions. What this further question turns on is whether what is done inherits—associatively—enough rationality from the action for which it is substituted. To what degree, in other words, do the desire and belief that cause the agent to do what he does also rationalize it?

An example of this first variant, or of a *displaced action,* would be this: The Rat Man, while on holiday in the mountains, in the company of what the translators call "his lady," suddenly embarked on a harsh and, as things turned out, near-fatal weight-losing regime. Before lunch was over, he would get up from the table and tear along the road in the blazing August sun and then would rush up a mountain at a run until, dripping with sweat, he was forced to stop.[8] This regime is explained, first, by appeal to the Rat Man's intense but unconscious jealousy of his lady's cousin Richard, who was staying with her at the same resort, and his instrumental belief that, with Richard out of the way, the situation would improve and his jealousy disappear. However what this desire and this belief rationalize is the Rat Man's murdering Richard, which it was out of the question that he should do. So the explanation of the Rat Man's curious regime further appeals to a chain of association, operative in his head, which runs from murdering Richard to getting rid of his own fat, the intermediate links being supplied by Richard's nickname, "Dick," and the German word for "fat," that is, *dick*. The desire and the belief, which in the case of a different type of person might have caused him to kill his rival, cause the Rat Man to lose weight in this ferocious fashion: something which has a further appositeness, in that, as Freud suggests, what the Rat Man does is over-determined, for it is additionally caused by the Rat Man's desire to punish himself for having entertained murderous impulses, even if only to reject them.

This first variant form of explanation applies to most of what Freud discusses as symptomatic actions. It also applies to an important subclass of neurotic symptoms: it applies to those symptoms which Freud refers to as in effect constituting "the patient's sexual activity."[9] They are all displaced actions.

Now, to the second variant form of psychological explanation.

Someone does something, and this is explained by appeal to an unconscious desire on the part of the person, which however is not paired, as it is in the two forms of psychological explanation we have so far considered, with an instrumental belief (or even a phantasy). Instead of the belief there is what may be thought of as a mechanism or an instinct. I shall use the term 'instinct'—though not, I should perhaps point out, in the conative sense, which is also well-entrenched. The instinct, which enters into the new explanatory form, is sensitive to circumstances, and it is usually triggered by anxiety, which is, in Freud's mature thinking, a 'signal' of danger.[10] The desire and the instinct cause the person to do what he does, but, since instinct has replaced instrumental belief, what is done is not rationalized, even in the limited sense in which at any rate *some* displaced actions may be thought of as rationalized. For this reason it seems to me dubious that the things we do that have this particular causal history should be regarded as actions. Of course, the notion of 'rational' is far broader than that of 'rationalized', and I do not want to deny that some things we do that originate in this way are rational: the sensitivity of the relevant instinct to circumstances may ensure this.

Things that we do that are appropriate for this kind of explanation I shall call cases of 'activity' rather than action, and now I give two examples of this second variant, of *activity,* both drawn from Freud. The first is this: A little boy, proud of his penis and led to believe that all living creatures, perhaps all things animate and inanimate, possess a genital like his own, one day, by chance, catches sight of a little girl naked. He notices that she is without a penis: this induces in him fears for his own: and what he does is that he 'disavows' his perception. In consequence he comes to believe that he has seen her with a penis.[11] What the boy does, the disavowal, is explained by the boy's desire that his penis should be completely safe and free from all hazards, and by an instinct which serves to protect that desire from the thought of anything that runs counter to it. Note that the little boy behaves just as if he had the instrumental belief that disavowing the perception will safeguard the desire, but it would be quite implausible to credit the boy with any such belief about the resources of his mind.

The second example of activity comes from the history of the same little boy, slightly older, say around six. Now the boy overwhelmingly desires his mother's love. He desires it exclusively for himself, and indeed he phantasizes himself enjoying it. Then he recognizes that his father stands in his way: he becomes fearful of his father: and his fear takes the form of dreading that his father will castrate him. Under the impact of this great fear, the boy represses his love for his mother.[12] This is, of course, the classic Oedipal scenario, and what the boy does in this situation, the repression of his childhood love, is explained by his desire—the negative desire, which is triggered by the fear that he feels, that his penis should not be mutilated—plus an instinct which serves to remove the offending passion which might bring down retaliation upon him. Once again, it would be far-fetched to ascribe to the boy an instrumental belief which, paired with the desire, would have rationalized what he did, but he might be thought to have behaved as if he had such a belief.

One thing that these two examples bring out is that the characteristic instance of an activity is something that we do internally: disavowal of a perception, repression of a desire. However, not all activities of ours are internal. When the young Wolf Man, aged one and a half, saw his parents copulating, he—according to Freud's reconstruction of the scene, which his patient endorsed—defaecated on the floor.[13] This is surely an instance of an external activity: if, that is to say, Freud was right in hypothesizing that the boy's incontinence was not, as he put it, "purely accidental." However the central instances of activity are provided by the mechanisms of defence, so called because we use them to fend off unwanted desires, but which also have constitutive roles to play in the build-up of our personalities: repression, reaction-formation, introjection, projection, projective identification, splitting, disavowal. And these, of course, are all internal.

The third variant of explanation that Freud hit upon is close to the second, but I have, comparatively recently, come to think that it needs to be distinguished. Someone does something, and this is explained by appeal to an unconscious desire plus some precipitating or facilitating factor which allows the desire to find an outlet. There is no instrumental belief, and there seems to be nothing deserving the name "instinct" at work. Further, unlike both displaced actions and activities, what the person does in these cases has no connection with an objective function. With displaced actions, what the person does is a substitute for an action that would have had an objective function: with activities, what the person does is objectively functional, but that this is so is no part of the person's reason for doing it. With what I shall now call 'expression' what the person does has no objective function, but often enough the person, under the influence of a primitive way of thinking, believes that it has. What is done produces an imagined or hallucinated satisfaction of the desire, which the person momentarily confuses with the real thing. This confusion is transient, but its transience does not stand in the way of its constant reiteration: it is repeated, Freud tells us, over and over again.

Expression is a very broad category, and a lot of what Freud discussed falls within it. The form of explanation that goes along with it—in terms of unconscious desire and precipitating factor—applies to dreams, to those neurotic symptoms which are not to be thought of as displaced actions, and to those errors which are not to be thought of as actions with an unconscious motivation. A very special and therapeutically very important case of expression is provided by what Freud called 'acting-out', or the way in which in the course of the analysis, when the transference is fully in place, the patient will simply enact the phantasies that he has recreated around the analyst and the analyst's environment. He enacts them so as to avoid 'working-through' or understanding them. An example: Having placed Freud in the role of the castigating father, the Rat Man would frequently walk around the room, as if he were trying to avoid being beaten, or, if he stayed on the couch, he would bury his head in his hands, cover his face with his arm, and then suddenly jump up and rush away, his face distorted with pain.[14]

(c) So far we have been considering the different ways in which Freud first *deepened,* and secondly *elaborated upon,* commonsense or ordinary psychological explanation. The next task is to consider how, as I put it, Freud *contextualized* psychological explanation. But before I do so, I want to go back and make good a claim I advanced earlier: that every move that Freud made to develop—that is, to deepen and to elaborate upon—commonsense explanation was enabled by the discovery of some fresh aspect of the mind that has a causal influence on how we behave. Such a claim is, of course, indispensable to my overall strategy, which is that of trying to show that Freud basically accepted the traditional conception of the mind and that, in so far as he ultimately departed from it, this was the cumulative result of successive responses to new information which he felt he could accommodate within the old model. Freud's innovations in explanation may be paired with his discoveries about the mind in the following ways: The deepening of the desire/belief schema is a response to the discovery of non-conscious desires and beliefs and (up to a point) phantasies: the explanation of displaced actions is a response to the discovery of associative thinking which is active under repression and under other forms of defence: the explanation of activities is a response to the discovery of the mechanisms of defence and of how they operate: and the explanation of expression is a response to the discovery of the pervasive power of wish-fulfillment and 'omnipotent' thinking.

So now I move forward to the third thing that Freud did to commonsense explanation: he *contextualized* it. Since this term itself is not perspicuous, I shall do my best to explain the idea. The cultural value of psychoanalysis and many of its applications to daily life depend upon contextualization, but what this involves is not well understood. It is certainly not well understood by many of Freud's critics, who regularly confuse what is central and what is peripheral to his style of explanation.

We may think of Freud as initially engaged in two seemingly independent projects. On the one hand, he produced a large number of psychological explanations: in each case, what was to be explained, the *explicandum,* is a pathological piece of behaviour, and the explanation, the *explicans,* is a psychological factor always including a desire and, additionally, a belief, or a phantasy, or a chain of association, or a mechanism of defence, or some combination of these factors. On the other hand, Freud was constructing a developmental account for the individual, in which the different stages were identified through successive organizations of the libido. Each organization corresponded to the dominance of one part of the body—mouth, anus, phallus, genital—which was not merely, for the duration of this organization, the main source of pleasure but also the ideal, the model, for what pleasure is. The organizations were passed through in the order I have set them out, but regression, or return to an earlier organization, was, in the case of all but the strongest characters, an ever-present danger.[15]

These two projects became linked as soon as Freud recognized two things: The first was that certain desires, and other psychological factors (phantasies, chains of association, mechanisms of defence), recurred with great frequency in the explanations that he found himself giving of pieces of behaviour that were clinically significant. The second was that these recurrent factors were redolent of particular sexual organizations. They were firmly grounded in certain phases of the developmental account. They were pronounced phase-specific. To give examples: Introjection as a mechanism of defence, embedded in phantasies of incorporation through the mouth, could be associated with the oral phase; both reaction-formation as a mechanism of defence, inspired as it is by disgust, and phantasies of beating, which are substitutes for the desire to be penetrated through the anus, could be associated with the anal phase; strong sexual desires for the parent of the opposite sex could (at least in the case of the male) be associated with the genital phase.

Now, once these two projects of Freud's—explanation by reference to psychological factors, and the construction of a developmental narrative which reveals certain psychological constellations as successively salient—had been brought together in this way, the stage is set, the materials are ready for the contextualization of explanation. For contextualization occurs when, in the explanation of a piece of behaviour, advantage is taken of the association that holds between the factors that explain this behaviour and some developmental phase to which they are specific, and the result is that the explaining factors are dropped and the behaviour is characterized as oral, anal, phallic, genital—*and* these labels are taken as explanatory. What makes these labels explanatory is the understanding that they stand in for particular desires, particular chains of association, particular mechanisms of defence, specific phantasies, associated with the developmental phase that the label picks out. The developmental phase as such explains nothing because it causes nothing except through the various psychological factors that flourish under its aegis and that therefore provide the necessary infilling to contextualized explanation.

4. I turn now to Adolf Grünbaum and to his study of Freud entitled *The Foundations of Psychoanalysis: A Philosophical Critique*, published in 1984.[16] Grünbaum's work is securely within the fold of the philosophy of science, though the title of the book does not give us a fair picture of its contents. Grünbaum, who is certainly no verificationist, distinguishes between the content of a hypothesis, which is a timeless matter, and the issue of what tests have been designed for it and how it meets these tests, which are questions to be answered only relative to the time of asking them. It requires, after all, real intellectual ingenuity, not just powers of semantic analysis, to construct and conduct testing procedures. As Grünbaum puts it, "I reject the hubristic expectation that, if high-level psychoanalytic hypotheses are testable at all, then almost any intellectually gifted academic ought to be able to devise potentially falsifying test designs for them."[17] Having made this distinction, Grünbaum then proceeds to concentrate entirely on the testability, the here-and-now testability, of Freudian theory.

In point of fact Grünbaum's scope is more restricted than even this suggests. For in *The Foundations of Psychoanalysis* he confines himself to clinical testability—or, as he puts it, testing psychoanalysis "on the couch"—leaving extra-clinical testability as an independent topic, to another time, another book. Furthermore he spends about a third of the space allocated to clinical testability on a reconstruction, which I, and a number of other readers, find unconvincing and ill-supported by Freud's text,[18] of how *Freud* thought his hypotheses were clinically tested. The view attributed to Freud is the so-called Tally argument, according to which the truth-value of a hypothesis—or, as it would be called in the clinical setting, an interpretation—is determined by its therapeutic consequences. Freud believed this because (according to Grünbaum) he held that only true psychoanalytic interpretations can give the patient insight into his neurosis, and only insight can cause remission of the neurosis: in consequence, if there is remission, the interpretation in whose wake it follows has been tested and confirmed.[19]

I shall return later to the first of these two restrictions, or Grünbaum's exclusive attention to clinical testability: I shall maintain that the distinction between clinical and extra-clinical testability is ultimately untenable, as well as insensitive to Freud's overall project. On the second restriction, or why Grünbaum spends so much time on how the founder of psychoanalytic theory thought that his theory could be tested, a word now. The explanation of this tactic seems to lie largely in a very local consideration: Grünbaum *versus* Popper—to adapt the subtitle of one of Grünbaum's first salvos against psychoanalytic theory, or "Popper *versus* Freud." For, whereas Popper had claimed that Freudian theory is untestable and that Freud himself was indifferent to this, Grünbaum, by eliciting the Tally argument from Freud's text, believed himself to have established beyond dispute the superficiality of Popper's critique. Freud *did* care about testing. In this Grünbaum is surely right, if for the wrong reason. But does this by itself justify the attention he pays to Freud's views about testing?

There are more far-reaching expectations that Grünbaum's tactic might seem to encourage, only ultimately to disappoint. Granted the distinction between the empirical content of a theory and its test-conditions, it is nevertheless often profitable to investigate what the author of a certain theory took to be its test-conditions. For this can throw light on how *he* understood his theory, that is, on what he took to be its content, which can in turn help us in deciding what its content is. But I do not think that this is how we can account for the time Grünbaum spends on Freud's views about testing, if only for this reason: that, in a closely related context, Grünbaum fails to draw the appropriate inferences from a study of how Freud came to think of certain evidence as good. There he does not use this fact in order to learn, as he so readily might have, something about how Freud understood that which this evidence is evidence for.

The context I am thinking of is Freud's reliance upon free association and what Grünbaum makes of this reliance. Freud, as we know, frequently used a patient's free associations to a symptom or to a dream in order to confirm its cause, when he had located this in some strong but unconscious desire. Freud would encourage the patient to say whatever came into his head, and he would conclude that where the chain of association stopped was, or was one step short of, the effective desire. Grünbaum rejects Freud's reliance on this evidence as based "on nothing but a glaring causal fallacy."[20] But what Grünbaum fails to appreciate is the reason why Freud did set such evidential store by the patient's associations. He does not recognize that for Freud the evidential value of these associations is directly connected with the nature of the symptom or of the dream as psychoanalysis had come to conceive of them. For Freud held that it is intrinsic to the symptom and the dream that they are invariably formed, formed by the patient, along an associative pathway, which, setting off from a desire that the patient is no longer able to act upon in any straightforward fashion, terminates upon the symptom or the dream. Freud's expectation was that in his free associations the patient would retread, if not this path, then one sufficiently related to it, though now in the opposite direction, so as to direct patient and analyst towards the pathogenic desire.[21] However this whole dimension to Freud's evidential preferences goes in effect unacknowledged in Grünbaum's argument. Grünbaum cites Freud, but then counters him by declaring that belief in free association as an evidential tool is totally dependent on the therapeutic efficacy of free association. He writes, "*The attribution of therapeutic success to the removal of repressions not only was but remains to this day the sole epistemic underwriter of the purported ability of the patient's free-associations to certify causes.*"[22] Under guise of making a methodological point, Grünbaum is surely simply denying a substantive point Freud made about the mind. In other words, why Freud believed that free association provides valuable evidence for the causes of symptoms and dreams is because of what he simultaneously believed about how symptoms and dreams are formed and the residue that this leaves behind in the mind. If he was in error about the associative workings of the mind in symptom- and in dream-formation, then his confidence in the evidence provided by free association was misplaced. What is at stake is not the validity of an inference (as Grünbaum asserts), but a belief about the mind that, if anything does, underwrites this inference.

It is then Grünbaum's failure in the context of free association to pursue Freud's evidential preferences that makes the time he spends on how Freud thought his theory in general should be tested so puzzling.

So I return to clinical testability, but by now clinical testability *as such*, not clinical testability as Freud conceived of it, or is thought to have conceived of it, and see how Grünbaum thinks that Freudian theory fares under it. The short answer is that Grünbaum holds that Freudian theory fares very badly, and a reader might be forgiven for thinking that ultimately there is not all that much difference between Grünbaum's final judgment and Popper's. But in this essay I am less interested in Grünbaum's verdict, and more concerned to indicate how, along the way, Grünbaum misconceives Freud.

I start with this question: When Grünbaum asks whether Freud's findings can be tested, alternatively confirmed, on the couch, and answers, No, they can't be, what are the "they"? What are the Freudian findings whose testability is at stake?

Grünbaum uses interchangeably for what he has in mind words that are themselves far from interchangeable: 'findings', 'interpretations', 'theories', 'fundamental tenets', 'the psychoanalytic theory of personality', and finally 'psychoanalysis' *tout court*. However an actual example that Grünbaum provides may put us on track. The example comes from the Rat Man case, and the proposition to be tested is that punishment by the father for a sexual offence, for example, masturbation, causes (is a necessary condition of) obsessional neurosis.[23]

Now this is a pure example of what I have been calling a 'contextualized' explanation: that is to say, an explanation where what is to be explained, or the *explicandum,* is a pathological manifestation, but the *explicans,* the explanatory factor, is not a psychological condition at all, say a desire, but an event or phase in the person's life. I have maintained that what licenses contextualized explanations and what brings them (if provisionally) within the fold of psychoanalysis is the developmental aspect of psychoanalytical theory, which correlates certain phases in the life-history of the individual with certain desires, certain phantasies, certain mechanisms of defence. If however we neglect this infra-structure on which contextualized explanations rest, and simply see these explanations as what on the surface they are, conjunctions of external phase and pathological manifestation, we have nothing of specifically psychoanalytical concern. Whether such conjunctions can or cannot be tested clinically, and, if they can be, how they emerge from these tests, are matters of no real interest as far as the status of psychoanalytical theory is concerned. If such correlations hold, this would confirm psychoanalytical theory to no higher degree than some theory that behaviourism might have inspired. If they are found not to hold, this may turn out to be explicable in terms of, say, some mechanism of defence whose intervention had not been anticipated: in other words, the failure of the correlation might itself have a psychoanalytic explanation. Now in his consideration of the Rat Man case as an instance of the aetiology of obsessional neurosis, Grünbaum confines himself to the correlation. He finds the correlation disconfirmed by Freud's own case-history. And that for him is the end of the matter.

It is not my claim that the only kind of Freudian "finding" that Grünbaum considers, or whose clinical testability he probes, is a contextualized explanation. That would be to ignore the attention he pays to a hypothesis in which not only is the *explicandum* a pathological manifestation but the *explicans* is also a psychological, indeed a deep psychological, factor and not a mere phase in the person's life: that is, the clearly psychoanalytic hypothesis that repressed homosexual love causes paranoia.[24] But, after attending to what is wrong, or what is psychoanalytically irrelevant, in the way Grünbaum treats the explanation of obsessional neurosis, we shall the more readily be able to see a similar error at work in his consideration of this new hypothesis. For once again, Grünbaum treats the hypothesis as though it asserted a mere correlation, whereas what was actually of interest to Freud was the infilling between *explicans* and *explicandum*.

Freud's views about the detail of the infilling upon which the correlation of repressed homosexual love and paranoia rests are given in his famous case-history of someone whom he never met: the so called Schreber case, entitled "Psychoanalytic Notes upon an Autobiographical Account of a Case of Paranoia (Dementia Paranoides)."[25] Grünbaum shows himself to be familiar with the case-history, and with the infilling it proposes: but he doesn't grasp its methodological import or its relevance to the polemic of his book.[26]

Senatspräsident Schreber, a judge of appeal and local politician of some eminence in the affairs of Saxony, fell ill of a mental disorder ultimately to culminate in paranoid delusions and florid religious mania, when, after several years of happy marriage, it became clear to him that he would have no children. The final stage of his illness was the conviction that, as a result of the sun's rays, he was being very painfully transformed by God, working through his doctor, into a woman, from whom a new race of men would spring. Eventually these delusions led to his being removed from public office, and he confided their content to his *Memoirs,* from which Freud reconstructed their genesis. The path that led Schreber from homosexuality to paranoia Freud subdivided into three stages. To each stage he allocated a judgment made by the subject. This judgment was naturally the core of powerful feelings and phantasies that the subject experienced. This turmoil then precipitated, through a mechanism of defence, the next stage, sign-posted with its distinctive judgment. The judgments are, successively, (one) "I love him," *disavowal* of which leads to (two) "I hate him," *projection* of which leads to (three) "He hates me." The correlation of paranoia with repressed homosexuality is irrelevant to psychoanalysis unless that correlation is the outer shell of this inner core, which is its infilling.

Grünbaum, I have been suggesting, has an inadequate view of what it is that must be clinically tested if anything properly called psychoanalysis or psychoanalytic findings can be said to have been tested on the couch. He has this inadequate view because he fails to do justice to the structure that Freud attributed to the mind and that, according to his theory, mediates the correlations upon which Grünbaum concentrates. But, if we enrich in this way what is to be clinically tested, is there any possibility of thinking that it *can be* tested, and tested *clinically*? I think that the answer can be Yes only if we correspondingly enrich the notion of the clinical. The question that then arises is whether we have to enrich it to bursting point. Certainly clinical testing as Grünbaum understands it won't do.

There is in existence a summary of Grünbaum's book which he provided for the special issue of *Behavioral and Brain Sciences* dedicated to it.[27] At the end of this summary Grünbaum offers what he calls a "technical" definition of clinical testing. Clinical testing is testing through clinical data, and clinical data, we are told, "are data obtained from the psychoanalytic treatment-setting and the analyst's observation of what the patient says and does."[28]

Technical or not, this definition certainly trivializes the issue. For instance, at one point Grünbaum points out that, in the Rat Man case, though the hypothesis that obsessional neurosis is caused by parental punishment for early sexuality was tested (and falsified), it was not tested clinically. Not clinically: because what Grünbaum thinks of as the crucial evidence was provided not by the Rat Man in the session but by his mother between sessions.[29] Suppose then that the mother had written down her observations and her son had read them out to Freud during a session, would that have constituted, for Grünbaum, clinical testing? The

"technical" definition suggests Yes. This gives us a distinction without—
at any rate for all that Grünbaum has told us—a significant difference.

It is obviously correct to insist that what is crucial to clinical testing is
what the patient says and does in the session. But we don't begin to understand what clinical testing is until we recognize two further things.
The first is what kind of thing it is that a patient characteristically does
say and do in an analytic session. Grünbaum is in the dark here, and
seems to believe that all that a patient does or can do is (one) retrieve
memories; (two) free-associate; and (three) say yes or no to interpretations. Of what it is that the transference facilitates—in the way either of
particular material that the patient produces or of particular motives that
are likely to lead him to produce particular material—there is not a word
in *The Foundations of Psychoanalysis*. The second thing to recognize is
that, if what the patient says or does is to be brought to bear upon the
hypothesis under consideration so that it, the hypothesis, can then be said
to have been tested on the couch, the patient's material will in most circumstances have to be subsumed under categories deriving from psychoanalysis. It cannot be left in a "raw" state, otherwise the two will not
match up: what the patient says or does will neither confirm nor discon-
firm the hypothesis except in marginal cases. In saying or doing what he
does, the patient has to be identified as, say, presenting *anal material* on
a massive scale; resorting to *phantasies of omnipotence; assaulting,* or
fragmenting, or *idealizing,* the analyst's interpretation; *acting out;* and
so on. In other words, the patient's material must be subsumed under
transference categories: that is, categories which capture what the person
is doing *vis-à-vis* the analytic situation as he phantasizes it. In all this
there is, of course, no circularity so long as that part of psychoanalytic
theory which furnishes the categories under which the patient's material
is subsumed is not identical with that part of the theory which is under
test. Psychoanalytic theory, though an interlocking whole, is not monistic, and to believe that it is is, interestingly enough, an error that Grünbaum attributes to Popper.[30]

The point that I have been trying to make might be put in the following
way: that, just as, if the hypotheses that clinical testing tests are to be
restored to anything like a recognizably Freudian character, they have to
have a great deal more psychological structure restored to them or built
back into them, so, equally, if clinical testing is going to be adequate to
testing such hypotheses, then it must in its procedures give fuller recog-

nition to such structure. Forget about structure, and Grünbaum's understanding of clinical testing is appropriate: that it is a matter of testing
mere correlations in isolation from any background, and doing so on the
basis of evidence that is hopelessly impoverished from a psychoanalytic
point of view. Put structure in, and then clinical testing has to become
ingenious enough in its procedures to tell us not only whether, given an
initial condition, a further condition comes about, but how it does so or
along what route.

If it now appears, as a consequence of what I am saying, that clinical
and extra-clinical testing are entwined, my response is, So much the better, So much the more realistic. Indeed there seem to be three distinct ways
in which the two forms of testing are interconnected. I cannot see that
any of them get full recognition in *The Foundations of Psychoanalysis*.

In the first place, if psychoanalytic hypotheses are to be clinically
tested, then we must assume, at least for the duration of the test, certain
more general psychological principles for which the hope must be that
eventually tests will be devised, presumably of an extra-clinical kind, that
will establish them. These principles will include such things as symptom formation, the mechanisms of defence, primary process or concrete
thinking, regression under anxiety, types of character-structure such as
the narcissistic or the paranoid-schizoid, and the stages of libidinal organization. How credible we find these principles will decide for us how
rational it is to assume them in advance of well-designed, extra-clinical
tests.

Secondly, though these principles will largely be tested extra-clinically,
nevertheless, if the correlations that assume them actually hold, then this
fact will to some degree confirm them—though, of course, to no higher
degree than any other set of credible principles that might have been
assumed for this purpose. To sum up these first two points: Clinical and
extra-clinical testing are distinguished from one another not so much by
what hypotheses they test, as by reference to which hypotheses they fore-
ground and which, for the time being, they relegate to the background.

Thirdly, though all clinical testing is testing in the session, certain
things said, perhaps certain things done, on the couch may also be used
in extra-clinical testing. Everything depends on how it seems reasonable
to take what the patient says and does. If it seems reasonable to take
them solely as expressive of the transference, then they will be used only
in clinical testing. But if they can also be taken historically or as literal

evidence for the actual life-history of the patient, then they can be used as part of some extra-clinical test in that the evidence they provide for some genetic hypothesis is completely independent of the fact that they were collected from the session. In this case an extra-clinical test will have been carried out in the very setting that serves to define the clinical test. From his case-histories we can see that Freud often used material that repeatedly came up in sessions as providing straightforward historical evidence.

I conclude my consideration of Grünbaum on a coda. I have already said that I do not intend to address myself to Grünbaum's verdict on the clinical testability of Freudian theory, which he makes the centrepiece of his book. (If the first half of this essay is correct, and psychoanalytic theory is an extension of commonsense psychology, perhaps we should begin by asking, How is commonsense psychology tested?) I am expressly confining myself to what I think is the more interesting issue: the conception, more specifically the misconception, of Freudian theory that underlies Grünbaum's inquiry. The crucial feature of this misconception is that it leaves out the psychological structure that Freud was at such pains to reconstruct. Furthermore Grünbaum leaves it out as though it were the obvious thing to do, or as though there were no need for structure within a science of the mind.

Now this attenuated view of psychology reasserts itself, within Grünbaum's overall assessment of Freudian theory, at a totally different point from any I have been considering, and I want to point out where this occurs. This is my coda.

One of the key reasons that Grünbaum has for thinking that Freudian theory is clinically unconfirmable is that it is impossible to free the evidence from the taint of suggestion by the analyst.[31] Suggestion, or suggestibility, remains in as a possible explanation of—and note the different areas in which this hypothesis is entertained—why the patient recalls his past as he does, why he free-associates as he does, why he recounts his dreams as he does, indeed why he dreams as he does, and, most sobering of all, why he gets well if he does. According to Grünbaum, the clinical setting is completely unable to keep itself free of such contamination, which threatens every aspect of what occurs within it. Now, as Arthur Fine and Mickey Forbes pointed out in the issue of *Behavioral and Brain Sciences* dedicated to Grünbaum, in a brief note, which is the best single thing I have read on the book,[32] suggestibility starts off rather like Descartes' demon, or as a mere place-holder for sceptical doubt. But gradually it escalates. Its claims upon our credence grow: its content is inflated. Soon it appears as an alternative theory to psychoanalysis, replete with its own hypotheses. It is, for instance, asserted as a fact that, on balance, we are more suggestible when our positive feelings toward the analyst have been aroused, though, once we have fallen victim to suggestion, we carry our susceptibility to it to any other analyst should we happen to transfer.[33] Indeed so powerful is this alternative theory, and so grotesque are the workings of the mind that it postulates, that Grünbaum readily slips from the term 'suggestion' to what he treats as by now its synonyms: 'indoctrination' and 'brainwashing'.[34]

But what is interesting is that, for all the serious attention that Grünbaum asks *us* to give to this alternative theory, he never for a moment thinks that its plausibility requires *him* to give an account of how suggestion by the analyst would engage with the patient's psychological structure. He never proposes, nor feels the need for, any infilling when he invokes the possibility, indeed the likelihood, of suggestion as the real explanation for what the patient does or says. In the absence of such infilling, the situation is envisaged in the following way: (one) the analyst makes his wishes known; (two) the patient complies. It is a sign of just how far apart Grünbaum and Freud are in their conceptions of how psychological theory gains plausibility, that Freud, who also thought that suggestion could not be conclusively dismissed as the explanation of why the patient got better, never ceased to chip away at the problem of what the underlying mechanisms could be on which suggestion depended. Freud thought that, if suggestibility was to be an alternative theory to his own, it must be a theory, a psychological theory. It must, in other words, attribute a genuine mind to the mind.

VII Crime, Punishment, and "Pale Criminality"

1. In his essay "Murder and the Principles of Punishment"[1] H. L. A. Hart refers at two different places, in two distinct contexts, to the mental or subjective factors that operate in the mind of the criminal. This essay was written in 1957, or during the great British debate on capital punishment, which terminated in 1965 in abolition, and the essay is touched by a subdued eloquence that the solemn occasion fired and chastened.

The first of these references occurs when, breaking off from a consideration of the statistics of murder, punishment, and deterrence, Hart asks what the principles are to which men appeal when they argue about the death penalty. Hart has already had something to say, in this and earlier essays, notably the "Prolegomenon to the Principles of Punishment," about how we should segment the issues involved in any such discussion, and let me first remind the reader of his proposals, for I do not believe that there is anyone who has tried seriously in the intervening years to resolve these problems and who does not owe Hart a massive debt for the framework he constructed.

Penology abounds in answers, but to recognize the differences between them gets us nowhere until, Hart points out, we recognize that penology also abounds in questions and that many different answers are often answers to different questions. So we may ask, (one) What is punishment? (two) What justifies a system of punishment?, (three) Whom may we punish?, and (four) How severely may we punish? There is the question of *definition,* there is the question of *general justifying aim,* there is the question of *liability,* and there is the question of *amount:* the two latter questions, those of liability and amount, the Who? and the How much? questions, being conflatable into one question, or that of *distribution.*

A further point that Hart makes suggests an elaboration of the framework. Any tolerable answer to the first question, or any adequate definition of punishment, must, he contends, include a clause to this effect:

that in standard cases punishment is for an offence against legal rules, or for a crime. Why the clause? And, for that matter, why the proviso it contains? The point of the proviso, or of inserting "in standard cases" into the clause, is to prevent the definitional stop being applied to such discussions as whether it is permissible to punish hostages or the relations of offenders. To say in such cases "But that wouldn't be *punishment*" blocks legitimate consideration of what is objectionable in such practices. However, the point of the clause itself is to bring out, to make clear, that in general a penal system, or a system that allots punishment to certain kinds of behaviour, presupposes a criminal system or a system that denounces certain kinds of behaviour as offences. Penal system and criminal system are two different kinds of system, and the elaboration I had in mind is that presumably we can ask of the criminal system some of the questions already asked of the penal system. So we can ask for the definition of a crime and, more significantly, we can ask for the general justifying aim of a criminal system.

I return to penology and the questions we can ask of a penal system. How are they to be answered? The definition of punishment—the point I have just been making, or the clause it must contain, apart—need not detain us, but a broad condition that Hart lays down upon how the remaining three questions—general justifying aim, liability, and amount—are to be answered is of real concern to us. It is this: that, if the general justifying aim of a penal system can be constructed out of purely utilitarian or consequentialist materials, the issues of liability and amount cannot be settled in this way. They cannot be settled consequentially without grave insult to our ethical intuitions. More precisely, the upper limits of distribution—that is, of liability and amount compounded—may be fixed by appeal to consequences: for punishment that is in excess of efficacy is clearly unwarranted: but any precise determination of punishment that falls below this ceiling requires us to invoke another social value. Hart calls this value Justice or Fairness. It is Justice or Fairness that requires us, in determining what precise penalty should be imposed upon an offender, to take account, either at the point of conviction or at the point of sentencing, of such questions as whether he was ignorant of what he was doing or of the circumstances that he was in, whether he was under duress, whether he was mentally abnormal, or whether he had peculiar difficulty in keeping the law. Justice requires us to take account of these factors and to temper punishment accordingly, even if from a utilitarian point of view the adjustments they lead us to make bring about a less desirable result. For a possibility we must face is that they will weaken the consequentialist or deterrent value of the law. The factors that Justice asks us to consider are in effect the mental or subjective factors operative within the criminal mind, and it is in this context, of the competing claims of Utilitarianism and Justice, that Hart makes the first of his two references to them.

The second reference occurs later, at the end of a substantive examination of the case for capital punishment as a deterrence. Hart divides the case into two parts. There is the statistical argument, whose findings prove singularly inconclusive, and there is the argument provided by common sense. Hart considers them in turn, very judiciously, and he then turns and directs our attention to this somber disquieting thought:

> Those who base their advocacy of the death penalty on this rough 'commonsense' psychology must seriously consider psychological theories that run in the other direction. For at present theories that the death penalty may operate as a stimulant to murder, consciously or unconsciously, have some evidence behind them. The use of the death penalty may lower, not sustain, the respect for life. Very large numbers of murderers are mentally unstable, and in them at least the bare thought of execution, the drama and notoriety of a trial, the gladiatorial element of the murderer fighting for his life, may operate as an attractive force, not as a repulsive one.[2]

2. In 1916 Sigmund Freud collected under the general title "Some Character-Types Met with in Psychoanalytic Theory" three essays wide-ranging in scope, of which the third is called "Criminals from a Sense of Guilt."[3] I do not know whether Hart had this essay in mind when he wrote the passage I have quoted, but in it Freud tells us how he was led on from accounts that patients regularly gave him of youthful misdeeds to ponder the criminal activities that some carried out while they were actually in treatment with him. Analysis revealed two things: first, that these forbidden actions were done largely because they were forbidden, and, secondly, that doing them, or being detected doing them, brought mental relief.

How could this be? And Freud sought to restore intelligibility to these actions by proposing that the agent already, independently, suffered, consciously or unconsciously, from a heavy burden of guilt, and it was in order to lighten this burden that he embarked on his course of criminal action. The action served the guilt in two distinct ways. In the first place, it gave the guilt, which up till then appeared to float free, something on which to suspend itself: it rationalized the guilt. Secondly, by bringing punishment in train, the action offered the guilt a way of dissipating itself: the guilt could not only be rationalized, it could be purged. What secured this explanation was the independent evidence for the pre-existent guilt provided by (I quote Freud) "a whole set of other manifestations and effects." And as to the origin of that sense of guilt which is now the motivating force, Freud had no difficulty in tracing it back to the incestuous and murderous wishes omnipotently entertained at the height of the Oedipal phase. That these wishes were omnipotently entertained is significant for the explanation that Freud offered in that it means that for the adult agent there would be no subjective register, there would be at most bare knowledge, of the fact that the objects of his wishes were things that he had merely desired to do as opposed to things that he had actually done. And, given the enormity of these things—sexual intercourse with the mother, dismemberment and destruction of the father—it is barely surprising that the aspirant criminal could feel that any crime he contemplated was barely a match for the guilt that already tormented him.

For these criminals from a sense of guilt Freud appropriated a phrase of Nietzsche's, which serves as one of the chapter-headings of *Thus Spake Zarathustra:* it has come to be translated as 'pale criminal'. Criminals from a sense of guilt are pale criminals. With them guilt precedes and explains, rather than, as we like to think is usually the case, follows on and is explained by, the crime they commit.

Freud combined, as ever, boldness of speculation with modesty in the face of the facts. He ends his essay characteristically: "Let us leave it to future research to decide how many criminals are to be reckoned among these 'pale' ones."[4]

3. In pointing out how in "Murder and the Principles of Punishment" Hart makes a dual reference to the subjective factors in the criminal mind, once in so far as they function as excusing conditions, and once in so far as they contribute to what we can now think of as pale criminality, I was not suggesting that in Hart's eyes pale criminality is an excusing condition.

However, the question must raise itself: *Is* pale criminality an excusing condition? And one thing that Hart does is to make clear what kind of question this is, and how it is to be answered. It is a matter of whether pale criminality amounts to non-voluntariness, and whether it amounts to non-voluntariness in turn is a matter of what are the mental facts of the case. And it is, I believe, worth emphasizing that, in arguing that the issue whether, when certain conditions obtain, they make an action done under them non-voluntary, or excuse it, is a matter of mental fact, or a matter of the difference that these conditions make subjectively, Hart was in effect dissociating himself from two views of excusing conditions, both of which were philosophically influential at the time he was writing and may still be. These two views would settle the question whether a condition is or isn't exculpatory on a very different basis.

The first view makes the issue a linguistic issue. It is to be settled by reference to what the words in which the law formulates the offence mean. The issue is a matter of whether, when the condition obtains, the agent's act still falls within the extension of terms such as 'voluntary', or 'responsible', or 'free'. The second view makes the issue a legal issue. It is to be settled by reference to what pleas the law permits an accused person to enter. The issue is a matter of whether, when the condition obtains, the prima facie offender is legally entitled to cite the condition in order to get his action condoned or mitigated. It is not hard to see what Hart would have objected to in these two views. Both views invoke some agency outside the mind—language in one case, the law in the other—to arbitrate the issue of responsibility, and on neither view is it intelligible how we could come to criticize or to transcend (on one view) what ordinary language requires us to say or (on the other) what positive law recognizes as due process.

Hart then psychologizes—more precisely, he repsychologizes—*mens rea,* but, in returning to this tradition, Hart evidently thinks that it is no part of the philosophy of law to propose a general framework of the mind within which this fragment can be embedded. I wish to take a few steps beyond the point at which Hart thinks it wise to stop.

4. Any convincing account of what non-voluntary action is—more specifically, any account that is convincing and provides the materials for determining whether particular types of action are or are not voluntary—must cohere with general motivational theory. It must exhibit non-voluntary action as a mutant, as a motivational mutant, of voluntary

action. This is because the non-voluntariness of an action must be a characteristic of how it came to be performed, and it is implausible that the motivation of non-voluntary action should be not just different from but discontinuous with that of voluntary action. Accordingly we must ask: What is different about the motivation of an action when it is performed under conditions that in special circumstances the law will, or at any rate should, recognize as excusing?

In future I shall call such conditions excusing conditions, but a word on the circumlocution: "conditions that in special circumstances the law will, should, recognize as excusing conditions." The circumlocution makes the unabstruse point that the law calls certain conditions excusing only when they lead to an action that would otherwise be a crime—that is, when there is indeed something to excuse. But there is no reason to believe that those very same conditions cannot also lead to actions where there is nothing to excuse. Nor is it mere pedantry that makes me make this last point. There is a real danger that the motivation of non-voluntary action might elude our grasp because we take too narrow a view of the scope of the phenomenon we are trying to understand. Prejudice blinds us to its full range. For I believe it to be more than a merely theoretical possibility that there should be non-voluntary action where there is nothing to excuse. It strikes me that a great deal of action that is done, say, out of conscientiousness, or out of loyalty, is less than voluntary.

And now I have another explanatory point to make before I return to the principal argument. In discussing the conditions, the psychological conditions, that make actions done under them non-voluntary, I am using the term 'action' in a full-blooded sense: I mean, what might be called 'acts of commission'. I exclude 'acts of omission', though, of course, the law is also concerned with them and recognizes a way of deciding when they are or are not voluntary. Whether my account can be extended to cover them is therefore an important point, but is not one which I consider in this lecture.[5]

I return from this parenthesis to the question how non-voluntary action is to be accommodated within general motivational theory, and my first observation is that motivational theory allows itself to be formulated to different degrees of elaboration. At the top level it can be formulated schematically. Then it merely identifies the different motivational factors and specifies how they must interrelate to be jointly effective. An example of this schematic formulation is the desire-belief theory, which tells us that actions are caused by paired desires and beliefs so related that the agent believes of the action that it is a good means, perhaps the best means available, towards the satisfaction of the desire. It is relevant for me to say at this stage that I subscribe to the desire-belief theory. However, what the schematic formulation fails to tell us is how, or the mechanism by which, the motivational factors prove effective. The desire-belief theory, for instance, doesn't tell us how suitably interrelated desire and belief prod the agent into action. However just this is what we should expect motivational theory to tell us when it is elaborated at the bottom level: at any rate this is the degree of elaboration in which I shall be interested in this lecture. And it is my conviction, which I shall illustrate rather than argue for, that what this requires, or what is needed in order to achieve this degree of elaboration, is that the phenomenology should be filled in. Motivational theory, elaborated so as to provide the mechanism of motivation, has to tell us what it is like, subjectively, for the agent when the factors that have been identified for us by the theory schematically formulated lead to action.

Now once it is recognized that motivational theory admits of different degrees of elaboration, once it is recognized that there are at least these two degrees of elaboration, the question must arise: On what level should we formulate it if we want to exhibit what is distinctive about the motivation of non-voluntary action? Will the schematic formulation suffice to capture what is so special about excusing conditions, or do we have to introduce the phenomenology?

At this point the excusing conditions fall conveniently into two broad groups. If we want labels for them, we may call them the cognitive conditions and the conative conditions, without attaching great theoretical weight to the nomenclature. Typical of the cognitive conditions is whatever brings it about that the agent's action was a mistake. Typical of the conative conditions is whatever brings it about that the agent's action was done under duress or was something that he couldn't stop himself from doing. And this division of excusing conditions into these two groups is of present relevance in the following way: that to show why the cognitive conditions excuse can be managed within motivational theory at the top or schematic level, whereas to do the same thing for the conative conditions requires the further elaboration of motivational theory; we must call upon the phenomenology of motivation.

5. The claim, just made, that schematic motivational theory provides an adequate framework within which to show why the cognitive conditions excuse I shall substantiate within the specific context of desire-belief theory. We can see the competence of desire-belief theory to account for the exculpatory character of cognitive conditions once we bear in mind the three following facts: (one) that desire-belief theory yields for every particular action what we might call the agent's desire-belief schedule, which lists the motivating factors, (two) that each desire-belief schedule lists the relevant desires and beliefs in an opaque fashion or intensionally, and (three) that the voluntariness or non-voluntariness of an action is always relative to a certain description true of it. Now it is a consequence of these three facts that the desire-belief schedule for a given action is more informative than we might initially expect it to be. *Ex hypothesi* it will tell us what motivated the action: it will tell us which desires and which beliefs, opaquely characterized, were effective. But it will also circumscribe the descriptions under which the action is voluntary. For an action can be voluntary under a certain description only if two conditions are fulfilled: the description is true of the action *and* the description occurs on the desire-belief schedule in the characterization of one of the effective beliefs. It works like this: Imagine that a particular drug is administered to an old woman and it kills her outright. Now the administration of the drug cannot be viewed as a case of voluntarily killing the old woman if on the agent's desire-belief schedule there is no belief to the effect that the drug might have a lethal character—and the agent's beliefs have been formed with adequate conscientiousness. It is only if the agent had some inkling of what the drug could do that he is a candidate for murdering her.

Now the cognitive conditions are defined as those which result from a mismatch of the following sort: There is a description true of a certain action which an agent has done; in the standard case it is a description in which the law takes a punitive interest; but at the same time there is not to be found in the agent's mind any belief to the effect that the action, or the outcome of the action, falls under this description. This is common to the cognitive conditions, and they then differ amongst themselves in the actual causation they invoke for this mismatch. If this is right, then it is evident that desire-belief theory, or (to put it more generally) schematic motivational theory, can fully exhibit how the cognitive conditions excuse, for such a theory can readily show how the satisfaction of these conditions ensures the non-voluntariness of the action under the description at issue. To exculpate the agent we do not have to consult anything outside his desire-belief schedule.

6. But all this changes radically when we turn from the cognitive to the conative conditions. For, when the conative conditions hold, it is not, as we might at first think, simply a matter of our turning from the agent's beliefs to the agent's desires in order to understand why his action is non-voluntary. To grasp the non-voluntariness of the action, we need more information than turns up on the agent's desire-belief schedule. This articulates a familiar intuition that, when an agent does something which he couldn't help doing or which he had to do, what is at stake is not just the desires that he had, it is the hold that these desires had over him. It is not to the desires, it is to their imperiousness, that we should look, though it may well be the case that certain desires, or certain kinds of desire, desires with certain histories, have a tendency to acquire the required imperiousness.

To understand the conative conditions, to see how they exculpate, and to do this within general motivational theory, we must go on to motivational theory in its elaborated form. We must be able to exhibit the imperiousness with which certain desires demand satisfaction as a mutant of the way in which desires ordinarily achieve outlet, and this means that we need motivational theory not simply in the form of an inventory of motivational factors: it must tell us how they become efficacious. If I am right about this requirement, we need a filling of phenomenology. We must drop a level.

At this point, in proposing a shift of level for motivational theory, I also intend to introduce another shift: a shift that is terminological, but also more than terminological.

So far in talking about desire as a motivational factor, I have followed current philosophical practice and used the term in a very broad sense, which is required if desire and belief between them are to exhaust the motivational inventory. There is no harm in this usage provided it is taken for the artificiality that it is: in moral theory, where this provision seems ignored, the usage is, I suspect, harmful. However, in the rest of this lecture I shall use desire in a narrower sense, which approximates to the ordinary usage. In this narrower sense, desire contrasts itself, on the one hand, with merely wanting to do or be something, which falls short of desire proper, and, on the other hand, with an emotion or mood, which is likely to generate a number of desires proper. What makes this terminological shift opportune is that, if we are to say anything informative about how motivational force is achieved, we need to look at the motivational factors closer up, in finer detail, than the broad sense of desire permits. At the same time the shift can be effected without any loss of generality that we might come to regret. This is because, when the conative conditions hold, it is desires in the narrow sense, not desires in the broad sense, that are likely to be involved. They are the things that gain undue power.

So: How do they do so? In proposing an answer to this question I shall abridge some arguments that I have elsewhere elaborated.[6]

The first point to be noted, and it is a very general point, and fatal to behaviourism, is that most of the dispositions that persons have—and this includes desires—lead to action, when they do so, not directly but indirectly. Directly they lead to mental states. By mental states I mean transient events occurring in the mind, of a sort that are held to make up the life of the mind, or the stream of consciousness, and which are endowed with phenomenology. It is then in response to the phenomenology of his mental states that the person acts. More specifically, mental dispositions manifest themselves in appropriate mental states, and appropriateness here means that the mental states have a phenomenology such that when the person acts in response to it he furthers the role of the disposition. The role of the disposition I shall take as primitive. The normal course of motivational flow is then from dispositions through mental states to action.

Phenomenology, the distinctive attribute of mental states, is in fact a complex attribute, the two constituents of which are (in my terminology) intentionality and subjectivity. The intentionality of a mental state is its thought-content, and the subjectivity of a mental state is its experiential character, or 'feel' as philosophers used to say, or, as they now say, what it is like for the subject to be in that state, and the relevance of this distinction for the present discussion is that the motivational flow that passes from disposition to action has, as it passes through the mental state, two pathways open to it. It can pass solely through the thought-content of the mental state: it can activate just its intentionality, and ignore its subjectivity. But it is a distinctive feature of our psychology, doing as much as anything else to separate us from the lower animals (whoever they may be) and from intelligent machines (whatever they might be), that the flow from disposition to action can also pass through the subjectivity of the mental state: it can exploit the experiential feel of the state, getting that to move the person to action.

Let me illustrate the two pathways. I take as my example not a desire but an emotion: say, the fear of snakes. Now let us assume that the behaviour in which the fear of snakes issues, that which furthers its role, is flight. Now the two pathways along which fear of snakes will lead to flight, given the appearance of snakes, are these: On the one hand, fear will give rise to a mental state whose intentionality consists of recurrent thoughts amounting to the drumroll of, This is no place to be, This is terrible, I must get out of here, If I don't get out of here something worse will happen. And in response to these thoughts and to nothing else, the person starts running. On the other hand, fear might give rise to a mental state whose subjectivity warrants us in thinking of it as a state of terror. In addition to the drumroll of thoughts, the person experiences sudden weakness, a dryness of the throat, utter incertitude, quivering in the chest, visions of pain and destruction, and it is in response to these further aspects of the mental state as well as to the thoughts that it contains that the person starts running. When this second pathway is followed, I shall say that the mental state lures the person to action. To allay doubts, let me say that 'lure' is also a causal notion.

Of these two pathways, the second, besides the general significance that it has for psychology, possesses a very special efficacy, and it is no accident that many of our more exigent dispositions regularly have resort to it in initiating action. They exploit lure. And, amongst our most exigent dispositions are, of course, those of our desires which attain imperiousness and cause involuntary actions.

Is there anything to be said about the distinctive phenomenology, that is, intentionality plus subjectivity, of those mental states which desire induces when it motivates action along the second pathway? I believe there is, at any rate in rough general terms. Generally, roughly, we may say that, when desires motivate action along this second pathway, they lead us to imagine what we desire to do or be. It is the envisagement of these events or states of affairs that work upon us as lure, and the force that combined intentionality and subjectivity bring to bear upon us, as opposed to the force of intentionality uncombined, becomes more in evidence as we move into the realm of the imperious desires.

Just one amplification: When we imagine outcomes under the influence of desiring them, we do not imagine these outcomes neutrally. We conjure them up as desirable or as offering pleasure, and this colouring partly accounts for the way in which the imagination lures. It is indeed I believe here, in the motivational force of imagination, that we find such truth as there is to the ancient doctrine of psychological hedonism. It is not the case that everything we desire we desire for the pleasure it will bring, nor is it the case that when we act on our desires we necessarily believe that our actions will achieve pleasure for us. But what I believe to be the case is that, when we desire something and in consequence imagine it, desire also leads us to imagine it as pleasurable, and it is this that precipitates us into action.

We are now, I believe, on the brink of understanding what is distinctive about the motivation of non-voluntary action when the non-voluntariness can be ascribed to the fact that the conative conditions hold. For the conative conditions coincide with an intensification of the way in which we imagine the outcome of our desires. By intensification I mean an increase in the vivacity, or an increase in the persistence, with which these imaginings crowd in upon us. Lure escalates to seduction or to intimidation.

This suggestion is grounded in introspection, though it exceeds introspection. For I am not contending that every such case of intensified imagination is conscious or even preconscious. It will often be unconscious. Then it will be based on self-interpretation.

However, one decided merit of the suggestion is that it allows us to make sense of two distinctions which independently recommended themselves. This is a further argument in its favour.

The first distinction, which is one that moral philosophy habitually elides, is that between, on the one hand, how we evaluate something that we desire, or the importance of the desire, and, on the other, how forceful the desire is, or the irresistibility of the desire. Under the blanket term 'strength of desire' these two issues are often run together. But this must be wrong. The tragedy of much crime is that the criminal sacrifices satisfactions that are very dear to him, or upon which he sets a high value, for the sake of satisfactions that may very well mean nothing to him, but to which he cannot say No. In this lecture I have nothing to say about the importance of desire; I am concerned only with the force of desire; and mostly I want to make the point that the two are not the same.

The second distinction, a related distinction, which my suggestion makes it easier for us to recognize, is that between understanding why an agent desires something and understanding why an agent acts on his desires. For one way of coming to appreciate this second distinction is to see that, though there will certainly not be a single answer to the question why we desire something, for that depends on what we desire, there very well might be a single answer to the question why we act on our desires. For there very well might be a single mechanism that impels us into action, and just what my suggestion does is to offer such an answer.

The second distinction is one that we manipulate in thinking about criminality. We manipulate it in order to distance ourselves from criminality. And, by talking of manipulating it, I mean that we conflate the distinction, and yet we recognize it. For instance, we say of the criminal, "I don't see how anyone could do such a thing"—as though that were the unbridgeable gap between him and us. But, if I am right, it requires no great leap of the imagination to see this, given that he has the desires that he has. What we are very unlikely to be able to see is why he has those desires, why he desires what he desires. But then the criminal himself is likely to be in exactly the same position. When the serial murderer Dennis Nilsen recounts how, as he casually got up and went out to the kitchen to fetch some string or a tie out of which to make a noose for the young man with whom he had been drinking and listening to music, the thought entered his mind, "Oh Stephen here I go again,"[7] he is thereby revealing something which the psychology of the criminal law tries to disavow. His murderousness surprises him as much as us.

One plausible response to this last point is worth considering. Someone might grant me that the criminal could fail to understand why he had a certain desire and simultaneously be so haunted by images of its satisfaction that he was driven to acting on the desire: yet, the objector would go on, this co-existence must be short-lived. For surely the criminal's incomprehension of his desire must have the effect of diminishing the pleasure that attaches to the images of its satisfaction, with the result that intimidation or seduction will be attenuated to lure, and then lure to indifference.

But the response is narrow-minded. If there is any diminution of the pleasure with which the outcome of the criminal's desire is invested, it is this diminution that it is likeliest to be short-lived. And the reason is that, within our psychology, an incomprehensible desire glamourizes its object in a way that is not true of a comprehensible desire. By 'glamourize' I mean that the desire suffuses its object with an aura that is not subject to testing either in reality or in imagination. For a point I have not had time to mention is this: if it is ordinarily the case that a desire in motivating action first causes the person to imagine the desire fulfilled, and this image of fulfilment lures him to act, there is also a danger to this mechanism. It may misfire. Imagining what he desires may cause the person to reconsider his desire: the image of fulfilment can come to serve as a test of the desire, and the person may respond to what he has imagined in such a way that there is a change of desire. This, I repeat, is something that readily happens in ordinary circumstances, and for these purposes the line between the ordinary and the extraordinary is drawn by whether the desire is comprehensible or incomprehensible. Accordingly, so long as the desire remains incomprehensible, then, should for a moment the person be able to imagine the outcome of this desire as no more pleasurable than it is likely to prove in reality, the next moment this will alter, the effect of judgment will prove unstable, and pleasure will flow back in and reinvest the object. Glamour will be restored, and lure consolidated.

7. I pause at this point because I may have given the impression that the conative conditions and their claim to have exculpatory force can be understood entirely in terms of the intensification of lure. Incomprehensible desires are at work leading the person to imagine their outcome with such vivacity or such persistence that he is intimidated or seduced into acting upon them. I believe that this account is highly promising for many of the conative conditions, but, if pale criminality is to be reckoned amongst them, pale criminality is certainly a pathological phenomenon, and pathological motivation requires us to take account of a new factor.

To retrieve this factor I propose that we return to pale criminality.

Freud's 1916 discussion of pale criminality is manifestly inadequate for a rather obvious reason. It is broken-backed. The central insight of Freud's essay is that there is a certain type of criminal in whom conscience is not, as wiseacres assume, too weak. On the contrary, conscience is too strong, and criminality is inspired by its strength. I am sure that this is a brilliant insight, and it is appealing for the neat way in which it offends common sense. But it is from this point onwards that the inadequacy of Freud's account manifests itself. For the account now shifts character, and becomes purely energic. Guilt here, like sexuality in certain other places, is treated purely as a quantity pressing for discharge, and both the crime that the guilt motivates and the punishment that the crime secures are assigned no special significance. But it is a notorious fact that, unless such energic accounts are supplemented by some story couched in psychological, not in energic, terms, indicating what the crime and what the punishment mean to the pale criminal, they are useless. They encourage error in explanation. If, for instance, a masochist falls down in the street and sprains his ankle, we cannot explain this as a case of his satisfying his erotic desires: however pent up his sexuality, however painful the injury, there is no explanation unless and until we can establish that he effected a connection between the suffering he seeks and the suffering he receives. For his masochism to be satisfied he must, by some association, have eroticized the accident.

If we ask how the nexus can be formed in the case of the pale criminal, the likeliest story is that the criminal, in finding the punishment purgative, thinks of those from whom it comes as continuous with, or as persisting versions of, those against whom the original, the Oedipal, wishes were directed. He must, in other words, identify the authors or the agents of the penal authority with the internalized parental figures. Thus can the punishment seem to the criminal not a mere contingent misfortune: like the masochist's accident. However, once we have taken this first step in reconstructing the pale criminal's perception of things, it is natural to go on to believe that he will identify the crime he commits with the early wishful assaults upon the parents' bodies.[8]

But, it might now be objected, this reconstruction of the pale criminal's perspective has been achieved at too high a price. For the most original, indeed the most arresting, feature of Freud's 1916 proposal has now been abandoned. The crime is no longer motivated solely by the desire for punishment, it is now motivated also by whatever it was that found expression in the early Oedipal wishes. The neat reversal of common sense, so that guilt explains crime, has been ironed out.

But this objection is not just. For if, on the new integrated account, crime is not motivated solely by the desire for punishment, if the perceived nature of the crime also adds to its appeal, there is this to be noted: that one crucial reason why a breach of the law is identified with a renewed attack upon the parents is because the law and the parents are both, in the criminal's perspective, punishing forces. In attacking, in re-attacking, the parents, the criminal *is* seeking punishment.

8. I have however taken the revised account of pale criminality thus far, not so much for its substance, as to indicate the structural alterations that it requires in motivational theory. The key to these alterations lies in the term 'phantasy', and they are alterations necessitated by any pathological condition if the motivation it supplies is to be theoretically understood.

The pale criminal has desires: we have seen that. He has beliefs: we have seen that. But, in so far as his mind lies under the influence of phantasy, these beliefs and desires do not co-exist in comparative autonomy: the desires seeking satisfaction and using beliefs only as a means to attaining it, the beliefs seeking confirmation. Rather in his mind desires and beliefs are interlocked, so that desires reinforce the very beliefs on which we might expect them to be conditional, and beliefs in turn are the products of desires whose fulfilment they anticipate. So, if we find it plausible to think that underlying the pale criminal's behaviour is a phantasy which unites (one) his continuing aggression against his parents, (two) a belief that they are consummately punitive, and (three) the desire for punishment, then the phantasy will entwine them in the following way: hostility to the parents reinforces the belief that they are punitive, and this belief in turn arises in response to the desire for punishment.

Phantasies offer their own gratifications, and this is one reason why they are formed, but they also press for outlet. When they do, and are efficacious, two things happen. First, if the subject has not already done so, he projects the phantasy on to the world: he sees the world through it, and the points of contact between the phantasy and the world are given by the subject's identifications. Secondly, the subject acts out the phantasy: he acts upon the world in such a way that would be rational only if the world conformed to it.

There are many interesting ways in which acting out a phantasy differs from acting on a desire. These differences correspond to ways in which motivational theory needs to be adjusted if, or when, it is to accommodate phantasy as a motivational factor. I want to consider just two differences between acting-out and acting on. I select them because of their relevance to the question which we are inexorably approaching but which I shall leave unanswered: that is, whether pale criminality is, and so should be recognized as, an excusing condition.

Of course, before we turn to the differences between acting and acting-out, there is this similarity: that a phantasy, like a desire, can obliterate voluntariness through the way in which mental states appropriate to it invasively occupy the mind. In the case of phantasy this invasion of the mind will invariably be unconscious.

And now for the differences. In the first place, phantasy has a tendency, unremarked of desire, to draw into its orbit emotions, feelings, desires that might ordinarily be expected to run counter to it. A criminal phantasy, for instance, will recruit solicitude: solicitude (it may be) for the victim, or for the victim's victims. But the upshot will be, not that the crime is arrested or impeded, but that it is more certain: solicitude, somehow or other, insists that the crime is perpetrated. Secondly, when the subject acts out his phantasy, the effect that what he does has upon him is that it appears to confirm or to cement what was antecedently the case. Nothing seems new. For this reason he is denied satisfaction or pleasure, and for this very same reason he has no sense that the desires or the beliefs that the phantasy imprisons have in any way been put to the test. All he can do is, when the occasion seems opportune, when the appropriate identifications have been established, to re-enact the phantasy. The pale criminal, if he cannot break the mould of the phantasy, must repeat his crime.[9]

This last point brings us back to Professor Hart. For, though Hart does not undertake to provide us with a list of excusing conditions, nor does he attempt an account, which is what I have been offering, of how conditions amount to non-voluntariness, what he does do is to offer a rationale why non-voluntariness should exculpate. He shows what is superior about a system of social control that moves only against voluntary actions. And one of the points that he makes is that only under such a system does the citizen trade off actions against satisfactions. It may very well be that Hart, in making this point, had particularly the cognitive conditions in mind. I don't know. But my claim is that it also works for the conative conditions. They excuse those actions in which the subject is deprived of a plus, which would be pleasure, to set beside the law's minus, which would be punishment.

9. I want to end on a speculative note. Speculation consorts with the thinker this lecture honours.

It is certainly true that, if pale criminality is indeed an excusing condition, this confronts penal systems with a severe challenge: How is it within the forensic capacity to detect such a condition? But this is an epistemic or practical challenge, and the challenge that I wish to pose in conclusion is, if it is to be taken seriously at all, a more profound challenge. It transcends practical difficulties, and it confronts any penal system: even one which has recognized the exculpatory force of pale criminality. It is a challenge to any system of the kind whose virtues Hart has laid out for us: any system which attaches penalties to voluntarily committed offences.

The challenge that I have in mind presupposes one assumption about human nature and one view about social institutions. Dismiss either, and the challenge needn't trouble us. But can we dismiss them? The assumption about human nature is to the broad effect that pale criminality enjoys, in some way to be made clear, a centrality in our psychology. It is not an assumption about the distribution of a certain form of behaviour, it is an assumption about motivation, and it holds that *in foro interno* we have a disposition, which is bound up with what is deepest in us, to do what is forbidden, and to do it for that reason. The view of social institutions is that, if not all, many of them imply a particular psychology, and, if the particular psychology that they imply is in point of fact false of human nature, then the institution is at fault because instead of facilitating, it impedes, self-knowledge.

Now, if it is true of any institution that it has inscribed into it a psychology, this is likeliest to be the law: particularly the criminal law. And, though the details of this psychology must be very complex, what it cannot, what it must not, include, surely, is the thesis that we are motivated to do what we are enjoined not to do. The law would be, I suggest, a very grim institution if it embraced the conclusion that it made it more difficult for us to do whatever its injunctions asked of us. Accordingly, if pale criminality is central, the law is an institution that misrepresents us to ourselves. It abets self-deception or self-disavowal.

One way of bringing the present challenge into focus, one way of appreciating its radicalism, is to ask what system of social control those who present it would prefer. The answer, of course, might be, None, for it might be that there was no conceivable system that did not have a false psychology, a psychology that denied pale criminality, built into it. But if there were, by the standards of the challenge, a preferable system, it seems that it would be one that did not wait for an offence to be committed and whose operation consisted in something like an educative process. We can envisage systems of this sort, ranging from the repressively preventitive to the benignly therapeutic, but any such system would have to abandon totally not just the term 'punishment' but the phenomenon. I barely have to point out the relevance of this last remark. For no one has argued more incisively than Hart against those hybrid systems of social control which first borrow from a penal system the crucial condition of an offence that has been committed, and then, rejecting the claims of Justice, distribute, according to the criteria of social hygiene, punishment, which they and the system of social control they are likely to sponsor, prefer to call 'treatment'. The challenge that I am considering does not lead towards, in fact it leads away from, the ideas of, say, Lady Wootton and now Professor Stern.

We do not however take this challenge seriously unless we are prepared to raise the further question, How much security from criminal behaviour are we entitled to expect? How much protection can we rightly claim from those with whom we share our psychology? If, not criminality, but the seeds of criminality, are, in some identifiable way which the science of mind can make clear, present in all of us, how far are we right to distance it from us?

We know how politicians would answer this question. They would say that we are entitled to as much protection as is consistent with the demands of justice, *and a bit more*. But politicians have constituencies, philosophers do not, and yet social philosophers have often written as if tomorrow they might wake up and find themselves in elected office. I think that such a heavy assumption of civic responsibility is inimical to free inquiry.

And let me make it clear that the question that I have in mind is this: How far, if the need arose, should we be prepared to sacrifice security for self-knowledge? It is not: How far should we be prepared to sacrifice security for the greater expression of aggression? After all, our society, our world, tolerates aggression on a massive scale. It not merely tolerates it, it idealizes it. And, to compound the matter, it tolerates it in ways that perpetuate self-ignorance, self-error, and self-disavowal. For the ways in which it tolerates aggression are labelled with distinctions, and, though they are not distinctions that correspond to no differences whatsoever, they are distinctions that grossly exaggerate the differences they register. The distinctions that I am thinking of are retaliation *versus* attack, deterrence *versus* intimidation, defence forces *versus* terrorists. In each case the arsenals of violence that the nation-state has at its disposal are approved of, and the ruses to which desperate men are driven are thought of as unspeakable. Such rhetoric does not advance self-knowledge, even if the powerful sleep better for it.

But to return to the profound challenge itself: Should we listen to it, even if the only outcome is to leave us dissatisfied with the only institutions we can conceive ourselves as having? Or is there nothing to it? I have no means of evaluating it: though I must confess that—to re-use a term I have appropriated as a term of art—I experience its lure.[10]

VIII Art, Interpretation, and Perception

1. I shall start with a thesis about the correct method of criticism in the arts. I call it the Scrutiny thesis, and it can be seen as an attempt to make practical criticism conform to certain broad philosophical constraints. Those constraints may initially seem to be those of Kantian aesthetics, but I shall be arguing that this is true only on one reading, or one version, of the Scrutiny thesis. The thesis asserts that

—in criticizing a poem we should confine ourselves to what we can come to know through reading the sequence of words ordered on the page:
—in criticizing a piece of music we should confine ourselves to what we can come to know through listening to the sequence of notes and chords and rests that comply with the score:
—in criticizing a painting we should confine ourselves to what we can come to know through looking at the marked surface of the painting:

and so on through the various arts.

The Scrutiny thesis combines itself with the view that, before a work of art is scrutinized, it should be restored, either in reality or in the critic's mind, to its best condition. This is generally, though not invariably, equated with its pristine condition. So the overall view of criticism to which the Scrutiny thesis belongs defines criticism as Restoration followed by Scrutiny.

2. The Scrutiny thesis has obvious appeal, but is it correct? As it stands, the thesis is indeterminate in a crucial respect, and therefore the question doesn't allow of an answer. So the thesis requires supplementation. Supplement the thesis in the way that coheres with its natural appeal and that its proponents assume, and it is incorrect. If however we supplement it in the way required for it to achieve even plausibility, then it ceases to have the character from which its initial appeal derives: in effect it ceases to be a Scrutiny thesis. The plausibility of the thesis and the appropriate-

ness of its title vary inversely. This is the central claim of this essay. But in pressing it I hope to show that the natural appeal of the Scrutiny thesis rests on an erroneous view of the role of perception in criticism: supplementation of the thesis to the point at which it becomes at once plausible and unrecognizable as a Scrutiny thesis permits us to relocate perception within the critical task.

3. Let me briefly refer to one argument in favour of the Scrutiny thesis only to put it to one side. It is an argument that once commanded attention. It was the ideology of the New Criticism.

The argument starts from the fact that every inquiry, or at any rate every inquiry in the humanities, has its distinctive method. Accordingly criticism has its distinctive method, and its distinctive method is Scrutiny. It is only by clinging to Scrutiny that criticism can preserve its autonomy and not decline into psychology, sociology, biography, and so forth. But there are three assumptions to this argument that need stronger support than seems forthcoming. Why should the various humane inquiries be disjoint, and why shouldn't there be overlap? If however they are disjoint, why should this be effected through disjointness of method? Finally, if the different inquiries are disjoint and this is effected through method, why should the distinctive method of criticism be Scrutiny—apart from the clearly inadequate reason that no other inquiry has claimed it as its distinctive method? Anyone who wishes to revive this *a priori* argument for the Scrutiny thesis must ponder these questions harder than was the practice sixty years ago or so when it was current.

4. But the interest of this last argument—or its interest in the present context—is that it brings out how arbitrary it is to assign a method to a particular inquiry in the absence of any reference to the end or aim of that inquiry. The appropriateness of a method must at least in part relate to its capacity to advance that end more effectively than its rivals in the field.

For the purposes of this essay I shall assume what I in fact take to be beyond question: that the aim of criticism in the arts is, in the broad sense of those terms, to *understand,* or to grasp the *meaning* of, the work of art; an aim that receives within critical theory two very different interpretations, which divide theorists.

On one interpretation meaning is conceived of as something that is to be discovered, on the other it is something that is to be constructed and then imposed by the critic. On the first interpretation meaning may be connected primarily with some set of rules or conventions within which the work of art was formed, alternatively with what the artist meant: it derives from the creative process. On the second interpretation the meaning of the work is what permits it, in Croce's phrase, to mean most to us 'here today': it derives from a self-motivating critical process. Conceptually the two interpretations are sharply contrasted, but epistemologically, or in the matter of the evidence upon which understanding of the work depends or of how its meaning is actually arrived at, the difference between the two interpretations is highly problematic: just as the analogous difference in ethics between subjectivism and objectivism, which seems clear enough in itself, shows up obscurely in the epistemology of morals. In neither case does the metaphysical distinction have a clear-cut operational equivalent—a point which, at any rate in the domain of critical theory, is frequently lost. I shall call the two conceptions of the critical aim that are generated by these two interpretations of meaning or understanding Retrieval and Revision respectively. Where meaning is thought of as something to be discovered, the critical aim is Retrieval: where meaning is something to be constructed and imposed and (presumably) done so afresh from age to age, the critical aim is Revision.

My own instincts go in the direction of Retrieval, and the crucial consideration as far as I can see is that Retrieval is, and Revision isn't, an appropriate response to the central fact about art: that it is an intentional manifestation of mind.

5. That (as I have claimed) the Scrutiny thesis is indeterminate as it stands comes from the way it ignores the interlock between perception and cognition. It recognizes that perception gives rise to cognition— indeed it makes explicit use of this fact—but it overlooks just how perception depends upon cognition. To see this let us think that on any given occasion what I perceive is given by the most expanded version of that sentence which, inserted into the opaque context "I perceive that . . . ," produces a true perceptual judgment. Now what the Scrutiny thesis overlooks is that, when I scrutinize something, what I actually perceive will vary not just with the visual stimuli that I receive but also with the knowledge, belief, and conceptual holding—what I shall call the cognitive stock—that I bring to bear on the visual stimuli. (This thesis does not apply on the lowest level, where modularity holds.)

The truth of this thesis is readily apparent from cases outside the perception of art. Suppose that I look at a row of trees, and the trees are elms, then I shall be able to perceive that there is a row of elms in front of me only if I possess the concept 'elm' in addition to the concept 'tree'. But in point of fact I shall not perceive that there is a row of elms in front of me if, possessing the concept 'elm', I fail to bring it to bear on the visual stimuli, and this I might do for a variety of reasons. Momentarily I might not have it at my disposal: or a previous expectation on my part that the trees would be oaks has led me to believe, falsely, that there is a row of oaks in front of me, and I bring this belief to bear upon the visual stimuli.

Now, that the Scrutiny thesis overlooks this interlock of perception and cognition is clear from the fact that, in insisting that the critic who is concerned to grasp the meaning of the work of art should utilize only what he has come to know through scrutinizing the work, it omits to say anything about what cognitive stock the critic may draw upon when he scrutinizes the work. This would be all right only if the cognitive stock did not affect the critic's perceptual findings. But, as we have seen, it does, and so the thesis is indeterminate. For the thesis to gain determinacy the cognitive stock must be specified, and we may therefore think of each such specification—for there are clearly many ways in which the stock may be defined—as giving us its own version of the Scrutiny thesis. This being so, the central point of this essay might now be re-expressed by saying that the versions of the Scrutiny thesis that most naturally suggest themselves, which are those which specify the cognitive stock very parsimoniously, are those in which the thesis ultimately lacks plausibility: whereas the versions in which the thesis starts to gain plausibility, which is when the cognitive stock is specified more generously, have a diminishing right to be called versions of a Scrutiny thesis. Indeed they ultimately require that the role of perception in criticism be reconsidered.

Let us look at this:

(a) The most parsimonious specification of the critic's cognitive stock derives from Kant: though, it should be pointed out, not from Kant's views about our proper attitude to art and its adherent beauty, but from what he required of our attitude to the free beauty of nature and ornament. On this version of the Scrutiny thesis the legitimate cognitive stock for the critic is the zero-stock. Nothing in the way of knowledge, belief, or conceptual holding should be brought to bear upon the critical perception of a work of art.

The attractions of the Scrutiny thesis in this version are not hard to find. Scrutiny as the method of criticism guarantees autonomy not just for criticism—as an earlier argument would have it—but for the work of art itself: a far more important gain. The meaning of the work of art speaks for itself: it is not in need of any ancillary amplification to make itself heard.

However, the question that has to be asked is whether this autonomy is purchased at too heavy a price. How circumscribed will the meaning of a work of art turn out to be if the only properties of the work relevant for its ascription are those which are perceptible without benefit of cognitive stock?

It is interesting that a number of theorists who have agreed in subscribing to the zero-stock version of the Scrutiny thesis have also subscribed to Formalism or the view that the meaning of a work of art is to be found within its formal properties—and here again the influence of Kant has been important. What is the connection between these two commitments? Two beliefs seem to be at work here. The first is the belief that no properties of a work of art other than formal properties can be discerned without benefit of cognitive stock. To discover expressive properties, representational properties, rhetorical properties, cognitive stock is needed. The second is the belief that formal properties can be discerned with less in the way of cognitive stock than any of those other properties.

However, even if both these beliefs were true, the connection between Formalism and the zero-cognitive stock clearly would not be established. At best Formalism would be the least unacceptable account of the meaning of the work of art, but for it to be acceptable more has to be shown than that the cognitive requirements it lays upon the critic are lower than those of any rival candidate. In point of fact I think that even this—the second belief—is false, and in the work of the more perceptive Formalists it is out in the open that, to grasp even the formal properties of a work of art, the work must be perceived in its diachronic setting or as part of an aesthetic tradition, and any such perception calls for an evidently replete cognitive stock. This insight is implicit in the great art historian Heinrich Wölfflin—witness his attachment to the comparative method—and explicit in the contemporary critic Clement Greenberg. However, even if there is available a non-historicist account of formal properties, the Formalist critic requires at least the concepts under which to subsume these properties, and so his cognitive stock cannot be empty.

This discussion can now be generalized so as to exhibit the fundamental flaw in the zero-stock version of the Scrutiny thesis, and this might be put by saying that it constrains criticism to the point of totally inhibiting it. For, while the thesis in its present version recognizes that perception varies with cognitive stock, it fails to take account of the further fact that perception requires some cognitive stock.

(b) Once it is recognized that any viable version of the Scrutiny thesis must specify the cognitive stock as higher than zero, a wide variety of knowledge, belief, and conceptualization will press its claims for inclusion, each combination of such items determining its own version of a revised Scrutiny thesis. For instance, it seems hard to deny that general truths about the world have a right to serve as background for the critic's perception of the work of art—something that we are more likely to see when we start to appreciate how extensively such rights are in fact exercised in the normal course of criticism. Just what truths about life does the ordinary reader have to bring to bear upon his reading if he is to grasp the meaning of *Le Père Goriot* or *Lord Jim?* Again there are the claims of general artistic conventions to be included in the critic's cognitive stock—claims which can be rejected, it seems, only at the risk of absurd misperception. Erwin Panofsky has amusingly illustrated the point when he observes how readily the right wing of Rogier van der Weyden's Blaedelin altarpiece could be misread if the critic ignored the convention that a figure represented as if standing in the sky is in fact an apparition to those represented as kneeling on the ground.

Once any such truths are admitted, it is hard to see where the line is to be drawn—so long as the determination of meaning is in each and every case permitted to determine the issue.

But to anyone who has once felt the attraction of the Scrutiny thesis the really hard cases arise when we shift from truths seemingly external to the particular work of art to truths seemingly internal to the work. Which of these latter truths can enter into the cognitive stock of the critic so that he can draw on them in scrutinizing the work of art?

One reaction would be to deny right of entry to all truths internal to the work of art, and the thinking behind it would be as follows: The artist in making the work of art inevitably makes it against a certain background. This background may very well affect how the artist expresses himself and would therefore be evidential for understanding the work. However there is no reason why, if the artist exploits the background, he should also have to incorporate it into the work—therefore it is condonable that knowledge of these relevant parts of the background should have to be independently acquired by the critic. But (the argument continues) when we turn from the background to the work itself, the same leniency seems out of place. Either some fact internal to a work of art is critically irrelevant or it is something that the critic can gain from perception of the work. The English language in which Hamlet is written and the understanding of which is crucial to the play may have to be learnt prior to reading the play, but the same thing cannot hold true for the nature of Hamlet's revenge or his attitude to Ophelia. If it did, then certainly the autonomy of the work of art would be in jeopardy.

It should be apparent that the preceding consideration does not in point of fact deny entry into the critic's cognitive stock to truths internal to the work of art. At most it restricts the way in which entry into the cognitive stock is effected: it must be effected through perception. So any truth about a work of art may be drawn upon in later perception of the work if and only if it was the object of some earlier perception.

But this way of framing the restriction is too powerful. The aim of the restriction is to ensure that every item in the critic's cognitive stock should itself be perceptible. But, if this is the aim, it is a further and unwarranted demand that the item should actually have been gained in perception. For the fact is that there are truths about works of art that are perceptible but which even a highly developed critic may be able to perceive only if he knows that the corresponding thing is there to perceive in the work. The truth may be confirmed in perception but, for it to be so, it must already have found a place in the perceiver's cognitive stock. Such a situation, which may initially seem paradoxical, is in point of fact familiar to us from early experience: consider, for instance, those line-drawings made for the amusement of children in which representations of animals are masked in the contours of trees and vegetation, and often so effectively that they cannot be made out by the child until their existence is pointed out to him—and then they can be. The child who watches the finger of a grown-up trace the outline of some animal may thereupon be in a position not just to *say* but also to *see* that there is a squirrel underneath the tree. A counterpart that suggests itself in the domain of art occurs with attributions, though also elsewhere: once we have been told whom a work of art is by, we can often see that this is so, though we might not have been able to see it without first being prompted. Everyone can now see that the Dresden *Sleeping Venus* is by Giorgione though, before Morelli pointed this out, no-one could.

(c) However, if my argument as a whole has been cogent thus far, it should also be apparent that this is no stopping-point. Any version of the Scrutiny thesis that specifies the critic's cognitive stock as consisting of all truths external to the work and those truths internal to the work which are perceptible must be unsatisfactory. It must be unsatisfactory because it restores indeterminacy to the thesis. For we must now ask of those truths internal to the work which are said to be admissible—admissible because they are perceptible—"Perceptible on the basis of what cognitive stock?" In other words, the thesis again needs supplementation. If we are right to insist that truths about the work of art cannot enter the critic's cognitive stock unless they are perceptible, we need to ask about the cognitive stock on the basis of which the cognitive stock was (or could have been) acquired in perception. Now on the assumption that such insistence is right, it seems to me that there is no non-arbitrary limit that can be placed on the secondary cognitive stock. So long as we remain committed to understanding, or grasping the meaning of, the work as the end of criticism, there seems no reason why we should not draw upon any perceptible truth about the work of art, no matter how it was acquired, no matter what cognitive stock its perception called for, if it helps us in this aim.

(d) But are we right to insist that every truth about the work of art that is entitled to be in the critic's cognitive stock must be perceptible? Why shouldn't the critic draw upon truths about the work of art that, no matter what cognitive stock is drawn upon, just are not perceptible?

Several kinds of non-perceptible truth suggest themselves for inclusion, but a crucial case, often cited, is that of truths about the intention of the artist. On the artist's intention and its critical relevance there is a prevailing thesis. It makes a good starting point for discussion, and it is this: An artist in making a work of art will form certain intentions. These intentions are either fulfilled, wholly or partly, or they are unfulfilled. If, or in so far as, they are fulfilled, they are of critical relevance. If, or in so far as, they are unfulfilled, they are of no critical relevance. But to the extent to which they are fulfilled, they can be recovered from the work of art by scrutiny, and the only circumstances in which they aren't recoverable from the work of art is when they are unfulfilled and hence critically irrelevant. So the relevance (in certain circumstances) of the artist's intention does nothing to upset the requirement of perceptibility.

But this thesis has grave difficulties.

Now it is true that, in so far as the artist's intention is fulfilled in the work of art, it is perceptible there. But it may very well not be recoverable from the work of art unless we already know what it is—in this respect it will resemble the animals in the children's drawings. And this is because the work provides evidence for fulfilled intention only in so far as we know how much of the work to concentrate upon as intentional and how much of it to pass over as unintentional or accidental.

But, more crucially, if intentions are critically relevant at all, they are not irrelevant just because they are unfulfilled. For they can still influence our perception of the work. Consider the case of *The Idiot*. In this work Dostoievsky set out to portray a perfectly good man: he failed: but knowledge of this intention is essential to our reading of the book in that vital aspects of Prince Myshkin's character become observable when we recognize it but would pass unnoticed if we didn't. Similarly it can be crucial to know of an intention that was not merely unfulfilled but actually abandoned: the artist switched from one intention to another, but the intention changed-from as well as the intention changed-to may provide insight into the work. An example is Rodin's statue of Balzac, which was originally conceived of and worked on as a male nude and ended as a heavily draped figure. Knowledge of the original intention, which could not be perceptual knowledge, is bound to modify, and appropriately, our perception of the work. It helps us to grasp Rodin's notion of the monumental.

The conclusion of this argument and the way it was phrased—"and appropriately"—introduces two considerations that at this stage need to be taken into account. First of all, the sole requirement that is now placed upon the cognitive stock—namely, that it should allow the critic to perceive something that he might otherwise have overlooked—is to be understood in a way that falls within the aim of retrieval. In other words, it must be taken to mean that any information is legitimate if it allows the critic to perceive something *that is there* in the work of art. Secondly, "to perceive something in the work of art"—hence "to perceive something that is there in the work of art"—is susceptible of two interpretations, and it is important to see that the reformulated requirement upon the cognitive stock holds under both interpretations. For the ancillary information might be utilized by the critic to perceive *some fact* about the work of art that he would otherwise have overlooked, or it might be utilized to perceive the work of art *in some way* that would otherwise have eluded him. An example of the first would be the perspectival information that leads a viewer to see the anamorphic skull in Holbein's *Ambassadors* as a skull: an example of the second would be certain facts about Monet's life that allow a viewer to see the great paintings of the ice-flows on the Seine in thaw as expressive of bereavement, mourning, and recovery. Once we appreciate that the requirement upon the cognitive stock is geared to the second as well as to the first kind of perceptual gain, it becomes evident how generously furnished the critic's cognitive stock may very well need to be.

6. It is at this point, when the Scrutiny thesis has been adequately supplemented, that my most general remark about the thesis can be assessed: that is, that by the time the thesis becomes plausible as a thesis about criticism, it loses its right to be called a *Scrutiny* thesis. For, if the thesis still insists that criticism should be grounded in perception, the restriction that this imposes has become considerably attenuated from what was initially suggested. However this is not all—nor even perhaps the most important thing—that has happened to the Scrutiny thesis in the course of this discussion, and we should look at the total transformation that it has undergone.

The Scrutiny thesis was originally introduced as a thesis about what is acceptable evidence for understanding, or grasping the meaning of, a work of art. Any such evidence (the thesis claimed) must be based on perception, but, in leaving the matter like this, the thesis overlooked the fact that perception is in turn based on cognition. For it failed to say anything about the cognitive stock upon which the critic's perception of the work may draw, and for this reason it lapsed into indeterminacy.

This indeterminacy I have tried to rectify by specifying—as it turns out, very broadly—what in the way of cognitive stock the critic may draw upon, and the question is whether in doing this I have been engaged solely in redefining the evidence that may legitimately be used in understanding the work of art. And the answer is that I do not see it like this, for it seems to me that the Scrutiny thesis is wrong not only in what it says implicitly about the nature of perception but also in what it says explicitly about the role of perception in criticism. For I cannot accept the view that perception of the work of art is primarily an evidence-gathering activity, the evidence thus gathered then being utilized in discovering the meaning of the work of art, where this is some kind of non-experiential activity. On the contrary, I think that perception of the work of art *is*, in favoured circumstances, or when all the relevant information is in use, the process of understanding the work of art, and, in trying to fix the cognitive stock, I have had in mind that it should be adequate to allow perception based on it to fulfill just this role.

That the process of understanding a work of art—and here the natural contrast is with understanding an utterance or an inscription—is essentially experiential is clearly recognized when we think that to change one's mind about the meaning of a work of art simply on the basis of retailed evidence without perceptual return to the work itself is illegitimate. Reinterpretation of Cézanne's early work requires that we go back and look at it again. Understanding a work of art is—I am saying—understanding by acquaintance. Why is this fact not merely unacknowledged but actually denied in most critical theory? How is the denial to be explained?

One explanation is that theory has given undue or one-sided attention to literary works of art. For it is *prima facie* plausible to identify the understanding of a literary work of art with the non-experiential grasp of meaning. Understanding Eliot is understanding the words Eliot wrote, and this isn't, though it may be accompanied by, an experience. Or so it might seem. In fact I think that this view of what it is to understand a literary work is wrong, and it might even be that the very best antidote to the misconception I have in mind would be to study just how we do come to understand a literary work. For reflection shows that understanding a literary work cannot be equated with, or must transcend, grasping the linguistic meaning of the text—no matter how we elaborate the process of linguistic interpretation, in the current literary theoretic style, by conjoining semantics with pragmatics or speech act theory. The simplest way of making this point is to deny that the literary work of art literally *is*, or is identical with, its text. There are, in support of this non-identity, innumerable discrepancies in property between the two: for instance, a literary work may be innovatory, full of hidden presences, ephemeral, cautious, cautionary—none of which things (and they have been cited at random) a text could be.

I have emphasized that understanding a work of art is experiential because in the light of this view the attenuation of the Scrutiny thesis which this essay advances takes on a different colouring. The natural advocate of the Scrutiny thesis takes a parsimonious view of the critic's cognitive stock just because he wishes to constrain heavily the evidence that will be used in forming the critical judgment in which the meaning of the work is articulated. He does so for this reason: that, if the evidence is allowed to outrun our experience of the work, the critical judgment will be arbitrary. But such qualms, understandable enough on one view of the critical process, give me no cause for fear; and that is because on my view of the matter the critic's cognitive stock has a further check placed on it. For what is required of it is that it should contribute substantively to the critic's understanding, or grasping the meaning of, the work of art, and this process is itself an experiential matter. No matter how the cognitive stock has been accumulated, it is, in the very critical act, subjected to a process of perceptual recycling, and it is the second time around that its experiential character is put to the ultimate test: Can the cognitive stock— or can it not—so modify our perception that it allows us to perceive something in the work that we might otherwise overlook? That for me is the question. A way in which I might express my disagreement with my running opponent in this discussion is to say that, whereas he basically looks backwards—that is, to its source in perception—in order to warrant the evidence that criticism gathers, I look forwards—that is, to their role in understanding—in order to justify the truths that criticism employs, and in consequence I can afford to be indifferent whether these truths do or do not have a perceptual origin.[1]

IX Correspondence, Projective Properties, and Expression in the Arts

1. I start with a phenomenon that is familiar to us all.[1] I illustrate it from my own experience, but the phenomenon itself, or that which the illustrations exemplify, is of wider significance. It has a lot to tell us about expression in the arts. It lies at its core. Or such is the claim of this essay. In point of fact, though I believe this claim is true for all the arts, in this essay I shall develop it solely for the visual arts.

So for the examples.

> Autumn rain has been falling throughout the early afternoon. It stops abruptly, and the sun breaks through. Drops of water sparkle on the leaves and on the grey slates, and they drip down on to the pavement, which glistens with a hard sheen. There is a smell of wall-flowers and sodden lawn. The sky is blue, but streaked with black, suggesting distant rain. This is a melancholy scene.

> The narrow road rises and falls. Along the verge on either side there are apple-trees in blossom. The fields as they slope away from the road are a brilliant green, dotted with the blue, yellow, and white of wild flowers. A few miles away the mountains rise up sharply from the rolling landscape. They are grey tipped with blue, cut by the silver lines of mountain torrents. Patches of snow persist on the rock face. The air is fresh, and there is the sound of cowbells. At the foot of the mountains, beyond the rich orchards, there are large half-timbered farmhouses forming villages. It is a happy countryside.

What each of these passages has to tell us can be recorded in one or other of two ways. We can, in Carnap's distinction, use the material mode of speech or the formal mode of speech. Using the material mode of speech, we would say that sunlight after rain is melancholy, that the Bavarian landscape is happy. Using the formal model of speech, we would say that the sunlit scene is called 'melancholy', or that the predicate 'happy' is applied to the landscape. We can say how certain things are, or we can say how they are described.

There are philosophers who on metaphysical grounds would hold that the formal mode of speech is invariably more fundamental: it shows what is basic. But there are other philosophers, who don't have such general views, but who nevertheless maintain that, in the sort of case I have just cited, resort to the formal mode of speech is better. It is more perspicuous. Their reasoning would go as follows: Neither the suburban scene nor the Bavarian landscape has a psychology. In consequence neither can have a psychological property. Neither can actually be melancholy or happy. That being so, we can't in cases like this explain our saying that the suburban scene is melancholy or that the landscape is happy by appealing to the fact that this is how they are. In consequence explanation has to go the other way round, and we must explain our thinking that the suburban scene is melancholy (which it couldn't be), or that the landscape is happy (which it couldn't be), by appeal to the practice of calling the suburban scene 'melancholy' or calling the landscape 'happy'. In these particular cases, the reasoning runs, the formal mode of speech does indeed reveal what is basic.

Let me call the phenomenon that my examples illustrate 'correspondence': a word that derives from the visionary Swedenborg, and that was made familiar by a poem of Baudelaire's. In my examples the suburban scene *corresponds to* melancholy, the landscape *corresponds to* happiness, and correspondence is, it must be recognized, one way, just one way, in which we can correlate parts of nature with psychological phenomena. I shall call the view that we can explain correspondence by reference to a special use of psychological predicates the Predication view. The Predication view holds that, when we think that some part of nature corresponds to a psychological phenomenon, this is because we have the habit of applying to that part of nature the predicate that we normally reserve for persons who are in the grip of that phenomenon. Of course, it might be thought that, for the Predication view to be cogent, it has to go on and give an account of the otherwise mysterious predications that it takes as basic. Without such a further account its diagnosis of correspondence seems incomplete.[2] With this further account, correspondence is explained away.

2. In this section I want to argue against the Predication view. It can, I believe, be faulted on two counts. There are two assumptions it makes,

neither of which is well-founded. The effect of these assumptions is to obscure from us the real nature of correspondence, and so the real nature of expression in the arts. It makes us look in the wrong direction.

The first assumption is that, in each case of correspondence, or whenever we think that some part of nature corresponds to a psychological phenomenon, the predicate that is ordinarily applied to persons exhibiting this phenomenon can, as a matter of current usage, be correctly applied to this part of nature. If there is no such widespread practice, the Predication view lapses. That which it cites in order to explain what it wishes to explain is a myth. Let us call the practice whereby a psychological predicate has this dual application—to persons in a certain condition and to nature in so far as it corresponds to this condition—the 'doubling-up' of the predicate, and it seems to me clear that correspondence does not universally correlate with doubling-up of the predicate. There are cases where the two—correspondence and doubling-up—go together and cases where there is one without the other, and as important as this fact is the further fact that there seems no principled way of accounting for the two kinds of case.[3] For instance, nature can be found to correspond to depression and to terror as well as to melancholy and to happiness: but, though we can call nature 'melancholy' and 'happy', we cannot call it 'depressed' or 'terrified'—or, more precisely, we cannot call it 'depressed' or 'terrified' for the reason that it corresponds to depression or terror: and there is no apparent explanation why this should be so. Of course, once we do think that some part of nature corresponds to depression or terror, we can cobble up some predicate that will do the work that the unavailable predicate cannot take on. But it is obvious that any such improvisation cannot give the Predication view any support. Once improvisation is called for, it must be the case that what we say follows on from what we think, not vice versa.

The second assumption that the Predication view makes, also erroneously, is that, when we apply to corresponding nature a psychological predicate, there is no property of the object to which we thereby refer. What is given as a reason for this, and what is undoubtedly true, is surely irrelevant. This is that there is no *psychological* property of the object to which we thereby refer: we do not, in this kind of predication, refer to a property that could be possessed only by the possessor of a psychology. That is true, but it is irrelevant, because it is perfectly possible that the psychological predicates that we apply to corresponding nature refer to properties, but not to the properties that they refer to in their standard use. In other words, we could hold the view that there is what philosophers call 'a fact of the matter' to correspondence without believing in animism or committing the Pathetic Fallacy. In fact I believe that such a view is right, even though it does require invoking a notion that I believe we should in general try to avoid: ambiguity. Psychological predicates that double up *are* ambiguous.

Let us consider for a moment an alternative strategy to which a supporter of the Predication view might incline, since it would allow him to deny that psychological predicates, applied to corresponding nature, pick out properties. The strategy also has an independent plausibility. This strategy consists in maintaining that such predicates are used metaphorically.[4] The supporter of the Predication view would claim, in other words, that it is metaphorical to say of the suburban scene that it is melancholy, or of the Bavarian landscape that it is happy.

Let me add that, when I credit this view of the matter to an upholder of the Predication view, I am for the purposes of the present argument assuming him also to hold a certain recently espoused view of metaphor.[5] This is a view which *I* find wholly plausible, though I dare say not everyone does, and it makes the following sense of his claim: When the suburban scene is called 'melancholy' or the landscape 'happy', and the two predicates are used metaphorically, they retain their standard meaning, even though this often results in the sentences to which they contribute being false; but the speaker is indifferent to their truth value, for the point of metaphor is not to convey information, but to get the hearer to see what is being talked about in a new light; and this effect can be achieved variously by banalities, implausibilities, and arrant falsehoods. Such a view of metaphor makes metaphor a genuine alternative to ambiguity in explaining our thoughts about correspondence. Is it a convincing alternative?

Metaphorical assertions about nature may be thought of as falling into two rough groups. There are those metaphors which try to capture a transient aspect of nature, or an aspect that is dependent upon the mood we are in. And there are those metaphors which try to capture aspects of nature that are independent of our mood and that endure until nature itself changes. Now it is only the second kind of metaphorical assertion that could be relevant to correspondence. Correspondence is not dependent on mood, although, where correspondence is with a certain mood, being in that mood may help us discern it. However I contend that it would be wrong to identify attributions of correspondence with any kind of metaphorical assertion: with the second kind no less than with the first. Metaphor and attribution of correspondence are different, in that they do different things. The difference between them may be brought out like this: What attributions of correspondence do is that they refer to, or pick out, those properties of nature of which related metaphorical assertions are intended to heighten our awareness. Attributions of correspondence do what some advocates of the theory of metaphor I have been supporting tell us is impossible: they give us directly what metaphor aims at by indirection. (In claiming that the direct approach is impossible, such philosophers, I should claim, overlook attributions of correspondence.)

If I am right, a grasp of the real difference between metaphorical assertion and attribution of correspondence supports the view that correspondence is a matter of the properties that nature possesses, and in this regard it undercuts the attempt to explain—or, as we might say, to explain away—correspondence by appeal to certain things that in certain circumstances we say about nature. In other words, it undercuts the Predication view. But, once we reverse the direction of explanation and we attempt to explain the practice we have of, say, calling the landscape 'happy' by appeal to its being so, the issue arises of what kind of property this involves. If correspondence does rest on the properties of nature, they are certainly not ordinary properties: they are properties of an unusual kind. Thinking about what they must be like can drive us back, in desperation, into the Predication view. It can convince us, if against the grain, that the phenomenon of correspondence is, after all, best characterized in the formal mode of speech. This is a temptation to resist.

If the Predication view is misguided, then correspondence survives as a genuine phenomenon, which, as we shall see, can play its part in a broad account of expression in the arts. But, first, some refinements, and then a deepening of the topic.

3. I have already implied that psychological predicates can be applied to parts of nature for various reasons: correspondence to psychological phenomena is only one such reason. When I say that a slope is gentle, or that a province of the empire is peaceful, or that the lake is treacherous, that has nothing to do with correspondence. In the first case, I am saying something about how easy the slope is to negotiate: in the second case, I

am transferring to a tract of land the character of the people who inhabit it: in the third case, which is not an uncommon kind of case, I am thinking of the lake as some faceless creature and attributing to it a make-believe personality. However, when psychological predicates are applied to nature for reasons of correspondence, what they refer to I call *projective properties*. (It follows from what I said earlier that some projective properties cannot be referred to by psychological predicates. In these cases, we have to resort to some improvised locution.)

What then are projective properties?

In the first place, projective properties are properties that we identify through experiences that we have: experiences that are both caused by those properties and of them. In this regard projective properties resemble secondary properties, such as colour.[6]

If however we ask what is distinctive about projective properties, the answer lies with the nature of the experience through which we identify them. The experience has a special complexity: a complexity we don't find in the experience of secondary properties.

There are two aspects to this experience that account for its complexity. For, on the one hand, though the experience is a percpetual experience, it is not a wholly perceptual experience. It is a partly affective experience, but the affect that attaches to the experience is not affect directed towards the property itself, or, at any rate, not exclusively directed towards it. It is affect directed partly towards older or more dominant objects. When a fearful object strikes fear into an observer, as it does, it is not solely fear of that object. On the other hand, the experience reveals or intimates a history. It is not so much that each individual experience intimates narrowly *its own* history: that is true only of the formative experiences in the life-history of the person. What later experiences do is to intimate how the sort of experience they exemplify comes about. Such experiences occur originally in the aftermath of projection, and the fact that later experiences intimate this origin, and do so even when they do not themselves originate in this way, is the reason why I call them experiences of 'projective' properties.

The nature of projection apart, this last claim may still seem obscure. An experience can be of its history, certainly, but how can it reveal or intimate either its history or the history of experiences of the sort to which it belongs?

A comparison may help. Let us take experiential memory, or the capacity we have not just of remembering that certain events occurred in our life but of remembering those very events.⁷ Now any particular experience of this kind that a person has is always of an event in his life. But there is a further feature of experiential memory: and this feature might be characterized by saying that the memory intimates that it originated in the event that it is of. This is a further feature, for we might have had experiences which carried true beliefs about past events in our lives but, just because they didn't intimate that they originated in these events, would be experiences which played a different role in our lives. For instance, we would not instinctively trust them.

However, if this comparison with experiential memory does something to illuminate the notion of intimation, it doesn't fully light it up. For it does little to make plausible the broader claim that I made about experiences of projective properties. This broader claim was that, when such experiences do not—and most do not—intimate how *they* came about, they do intimate how experiences of the sort that they exemplify come about in general. A different comparison may help to clarify this claim. The comparison is with pain. Most experiences of bodily pain intimate specifically how *they* originate: that is, in damage to that part of the body where they are felt. But there are some individual pains that do not arise in this way: the part of the body where they are felt is undamaged or has been amputated. But such pains, which are in the minority, nevertheless intimate how pain in general arises. Experiences of the sort that they exemplify arise, they tell us, from damage to the body.

The next question to ask is, What is projection, and how can it have this afterlife?

4. Projection is an internal act that we carry out under instinctual guidance, when there is either a mental condition of ours that we value (like love or curiosity) and that we find threatened, or one that we dread (like cruelty or melancholy) and by which we find ourselves threatened. Anxiety alerts us to this situation, and projection alters it. I shall not in this essay investigate the nature of projection itself, except to suggest that it is bound up with phantasies that we entertain and that represent mental processes as bodily processes. I have elaborated this elsewhere.⁸ Instead I shall concentrate on the consequences of projection. The only danger to this tactic is that an unwary reader might identify projection itself with what are just the consequences of projection. I can only warn against that.

In order to spell out the consequences of projection, I must first distinguish, as the literature on the topic tends not to, between two forms of projection. I shall call them simple projection and complex projection, though the differences between them are greater than this might suggest.

I start with somewhat schematic examples.

For the sake of both examples we assume a person who is melancholy, but who can no longer tolerate his melancholy. Instinct compels him to project it. If this is a case of simple projection, the upshot will be this: (one) the person will now believe that some figure in the environment other than himself is melancholy, and (two) there will be some remission in his own interior condition. However, if this is a case of complex projection, the upshot will be this: (one) the person will come to look upon, and respond to, some part of the environment as melancholy, and (two) there will be a change for the better in his interior condition.

These schematic examples allow us to see straight off certain differences between the two forms of projection. Three differences need detain us.

In the first place, in the case of simple projection, projection is on to a figure in the environment, or something which possesses a psychology: or, at any rate on to something which is treated as though it had a psychology. With complex projection, projection is on to some natural part of the environment, or something which does not, and is not held to, possess a psychology.

Secondly, in the case of simple projection, it is basically the person's beliefs that are changed as the result of the internal act, whereas with complex projection, though the person's beliefs will certainly change, what is fundamental is a new attitude towards the environment, a new way of experiencing it, which is then cemented by whatever new beliefs he acquires.

Thirdly, in the case of simple projection, the property that the figure in the environment is believed to have is the very same property as the person himself originally had. The figure is held now to be what the person was: melancholy. With complex projection, the property that some natural part of the environment is experienced as having is not the same as the property that the person originally had. How could it be, given that nature has no psychology? A blanket-phrase, a made-up locution, for saying how the two properties are related would be this: that nature, in its relevant parts, is felt to be, not actually melancholy, but *of a piece with* the person's melancholy. A deceptive feature, which could misguidedly be seized on as an instructive feature, is that, although, in the case of complex projection, the two properties involved are different, in certain circumstances someone might use the same predicate to pick out both: as indeed I did, a few moments ago in introducing complex projection. This is a practice of which the doubling-up in correspondence is a special case.

We can now put simple projection out of our minds, for, of the two forms of projection, only complex projection could be capable of generating new properties, let alone properties of a new kind. But does complex projection have such a capacity? Can it alter the world? Does it have the afterlife I attributed to it? There are deep metaphysical issues which I shall bracket. But I shall try to set out the situation as I see it.

5. I start a little way back with a point on which so far I have said nothing: and that is whether, when complex projection is activated, there must be an affinity between the inner condition of the person that is projected and the part of nature that it is projected on to. Must nature have features that encourage and sustain the projection? Or is this unnecessary? What seems certain is that, unless there is some such substrate, there can be no justification for saying that what the person experiences in the aftermath of projection is a *property* of nature.

This question cannot be answered without taking stock of the inherently developmental nature of projection. At the beginning of life, projection most likely occurs in a totally haphazard fashion. The infant projects feelings, welcome and unwelcome, on to random parts of the environment, without any concern for, or interest in, what the environment is like. But, as a corollary, projection at this stage of development has only a transient effect. It may momentarily relieve anxiety, but it has no enduring influence upon the way in which the infant continues to perceive the environment. However, as the psychology matures, projection becomes more orderly, and those parts of the environment upon which feelings are projected are now selected because of their affinity to these feelings. And in consequence they can continue to be experienced as of a piece with those feelings. What I called the formative experiences or instances of projection can occur only after this developmental stage has been reached.

The next question to ask is, Granted that some affinity between (one) the internal condition that is projected on to nature and (two) the part of nature on to which it is projected is necessary if the latter is to be perceived in some enduring fashion as of a piece with the former, why is this affinity not sufficient for the perception to occur? It obviously isn't: otherwise projection itself would not make any real contribution to our perception of projective properties, or (for that matter) to projective properties themselves.

But why is this so, and what is required over and above affinity?

To see what the requirement is, let us return to the claim that I made in introducing projective properties and how they are experienced. That claim, it will be recalled, fell into two parts. Both parts of the claim are currently relevant.

The first part of the claim was that a number of such experiences intimate their own actual history: they intimate, in other words, that they derive from an instance of projection. Consider then the case of someone who has just projected his feelings on to the environment: say, melancholy. Now if this person perceives the relevant part of nature as of a piece with his melancholy, what will lead him to do this is, in addition to the affinity of one to the other, a memory of the projection. This memory will organize or structure the perception in a way that should be familiar to us from analogous cases. So, for instance, a person's pain in his thumb might well be stabilized by the memory that he has just grazed his thumb in the course of paring a carrot.

However, as things stand, this account of projective properties and our perception of them is uselessly narrow. For it confines that which can be explained to those perceptions which occur in the immediate aftermath of projection. That is evidently too restrictive, for we can and do perceive nature as of a piece with our feelings in cases where we can no longer recall having projected those feelings on to it, and, indeed, in innumerable cases where we have not done so.

This brings us to the second part of the claim I made about our experience of projective properties. This was that those experiences of projective properties which do not intimate their own history nevertheless intimate how experiences of such a sort originate: they intimate that such experiences originate in projection. But how does this intimation make itself felt?

A natural suggestion is that this intimation takes the form of a recognitional capacity we have. In other words, we recognize parts of nature as those on which we might have, or could have, projected this or that kind of feeling. Indeed we might think that such a recognitional capacity is part and parcel of the ability to project. If, then, we do have such a capacity, this capacity seems fully competent to extend the explanation of our perception of projective properties beyond the narrow base provided by what I have called the aftermath of projection.

It might seem a lacuna in this account that I have said nothing informative about the affinity between psychological conditions and parts of nature on to which we are inclined to project them. But what more is wanted?[9] If what is wanted is information about how exactly nature has to look in particular cases if it is to be apt for the projection of this rather than that feeling, then this demand must surely go unsatisfied. For how could we convincingly describe what it is about some aspect of nature that makes it suitable for the projection of some particular feeling without upgrading the mere affinity into the projective properties of which it is—at any rate, on my view—the mere substrate?

I hope I have said enough to suggest how the phenomenon of correspondence fits within the framework provided by projection and projective properties. The idea briefly is this: When some part of nature is held to correspond to a psychological phenomenon, this is because it is perceptible as being of a piece with that state or as something on to which we might have or could have projected the state. That it is perceptible in this way comes about through two factors which make their independent contributions to this result: an affinity in nature, and our capacity to project internal conditions.

6. Correspondence has now received the refinement and the deepening that I promised, and I now turn to the central topic of this essay: expression in the arts. Correspondence is interesting in itself, but it is fundamental because of the contribution it makes to the concept of artistic expression.

Let me first say that I am not confident that expression, specifically artistic expression, is one of those concepts of which we have such a strong pretheoretical grasp that, when a theoretical elucidation is produced, it can be assessed by seeing how far it fits and explains what we originally took expression to be. Some of what philosophers will say on this subject must be stipulative. And I shall start by stipulating, *contra* Goodman, that artistic expression is invariably expression of an internal or psychological condition. The topic is thus returned to its tradition.

My central claim is that a work of art expresses an internal condition by corresponding to, or being of a piece with, it. Furthermore the perceptible property in virtue of which it does so is a property it has intentionally: the property is due to the intentions of the artist. The artist intended the work to have this property so that it can express some internal condition that he had in mind.

7. An initial trouble with this claim is that, as it stands, it is not merely compatible with, it seems positively to encourage, a counter-intuitive view of the matter. The counter-intuitive view comes to this: When an artist who is engaged in making a work expressive of some internal condition judges that his work is complete because it now, in virtue of how it looks, expresses that condition, he arrives at this judgment in just the same way as a spectator would when he judges that some part of nature, in virtue of how it looks, corresponds to a particular internal condition; exactly the same evidence counts in the two cases. Now I certainly believe that the judgment in the two cases has the same content, but how the judgment is reached in the two cases is surely different. And what gives rise to the difference is the fact that, in one case, correspondence arises out of a creative act whereas, in the other case, it doesn't. In one case the correspondence is *made,* in the other case it is *found.* How what is judged comes to look as it does makes a difference.[10]

That we ordinarily recognize that history of production makes a difference comes out clearly if we adopt for a moment the epistemological perspective: that is, if we consider how we come to the conclusion that a work of art expresses this emotion or that feeling. (In certain respects accounts of expression go astray just because they overemphasize the epistemological perspective. Consider, for instance, Gombrich's account.[11] But this is not one of those respects.) When we assign expressive value to a work of art, we invariably draw upon our knowledge of, or our beliefs about, the artistic processes involved. For instance, within the oeuvre of a given painter, we are likely to make different expressive assignments as we move from passages with broken brushstrokes to passages with long fluent strokes. Knowledge of the technique influences our judgment about what it is that the work expresses. Such a judgment has still to do with the look of the picture, but it is an essential fact that the look that a picture has comes about through the processes of art.

One striking way of putting the counter-intuitive view that my account of artistic expression appears to foster would be to say that it denies the creative act. It denies the creative act in that it refuses to discriminate between the process of making an object, on the one hand, and, on the other, a process of selecting an object out of a large, perhaps an indefinite, range of pre-made objects. It assimilates the act of making to an act of choosing.[12]

But I must emphasize that, though there is this crucial difference between the way in which correspondence is established outside, and the way in which it is achieved inside, art, this does not mean—as a number of theorists have claimed—that in the domain of art correspondence is less dependent upon perception than it is in the domain of nature. It does not mean that correspondence in art is conventional. In both domains, correspondence, being concerned with projective properties, is concerned with properties that are identified through our experience of them. The difference is that, in the case of art, the experience that is evidential for the projective property is based on a larger body of background knowledge, a larger cognitive stock, than is required for the perception of correspondence in nature. The background knowledge must include beliefs about a work's history of production and the specific processes of art that went into its making.

That expression in art, though it derives from a creative act, is nevertheless borne by strictly perceptible properties receives confirmation from an impeccable source: that is, the nature of the creative act itself, regarded as a piece of behaviour.[13] For across the visual arts the creative act always finds physical realization in a posture that allows, that encourages, the artist to attend to his work even as he makes it. It ensures that the artist is the original spectator of his work. But, if this is what he is, it is important to see why. He is so, not just in order to discover what he has made, but, crucially, in order to make it. The painter paints (partly) with his eyes: the sculptor carves or models (partly) with his eyes: the draughtsman draws (partly) with his eyes. In other words, if, as I have contended, correspondence in art derives from the artistic process, the process itself anticipates this dependence through its physical or behavioural realization. For, by compelling the artist to take stock of the work as it comes into being, the posture that he assumes permits him to see whether the work corresponds to the inner condition that he all the while has had in mind. He can, while making the work, note the experience that it causes in him, and he can then regulate, by what he does to the work, the experience it may be expected to cause in others. And there are two other things that can be hoped for from the conventional posture. In the first place, by repeating the process of what Gombrich calls 'making and matching' over and over again, not merely within the making of one work, but across the making of different works, the artist can refine his sense of what it is for a work to correspond to a particular psychological condition. Secondly, as the artist makes the various works, he can expect to acquire a better, a sharper, sense of just what psychological condition it is that he has in mind and is endeavouring to express.

8. There are two well-entrenched or traditional theories of expression in the arts, which, just because I have not mentioned them, I might be thought to be out of sympathy with. This is not the case.[14] And, if I have delayed mentioning them, this is because I believe that my own account of artistic expression, couched in terms of intentional correspondence, can do better justice to the considerable truth that each theory, once it is properly amplified and articulated, can be seen to embody. Amplification is not the usual fate of either theory.[15]

According to the first theory, a work of art expresses a certain psychological condition just in case it was that psychological condition which caused the artist to make the work. According to the second theory, a work of art expresses a certain psychological condition just in case it is that psychological condition which perception of the work causes in the mind of the spectator.

Each theory as it stands, or as it is usually formulated, suffers from two faults. Each theory has one feature too many, and one too few, and the features are the same in both theories. The adjustments needed to rectify the two faults are minor. They are not surgical.

As for the feature too many, both theories go wrong in requiring that the emotion that the work of art expresses is actually *felt*, whether this be (as our theory claims) by the artist or (as the other theory claims) by the spectator. That the emotion is felt is not a sustainable requirement. What is enough is that (as I have been putting it) the emotion is something that the artist or spectator has in mind, or (perhaps better) it is something with which they are put in touch, or (perhaps best) it is something upon which, or upon memory of which, they can draw. These are not easy ideas—there is more to be said about them—but none of this will require us to revive what Nelson Goodman has named the Tingle-Immersion theory.[16]

As for the other fault, or the feature too few, both theories go wrong in failing to require that a work of art expressive of a certain emotion should *look* any one particular way. Yet surely it must. Expressiveness cannot be independent of appearance. What is necessary can however readily be introduced by insisting that the causal chain that runs from the artist to the work of art, alternatively from the work of art to the spectator, should pass through a perception of the work, in the one case in the head of the artist, in the other case in the head of the spectator, as corresponding to the emotion that is expressed. This perception should, either way round, have its special causal weight to pull.

The two theories thus amplified, thus rectified, seem to me to fit in well with, perhaps to be constitutive parts of, the theory I have been urging.

Let me in conclusion refer to yet another traditional theory. It is often called the Local Quality theory, because it equates the expressiveness of a work with some sensible property that the work has.[17] If that is what the theory says, then I am, as far as I can see, in favour of it. But, traditionally, this traditional theory has been presented in such a sparse fashion, without the genetic psychology that I regard as crucial, that it lacks any clear claim upon our support. The greater part of what I have been saying in this essay may be regarded as an attempt to put this right.[18]

X Representation:
The Philosophical Contribution
to Psychology

1. It is now, I hope, accepted as the outmoded view that it is that philosophy and psychology are totally independent disciplines. It seems to me that there are many philosophical questions that cannot be answered unless we know the relevant psychology, and there are many psychological questions whose answers await the relevant philosophy. I think that one of the many reasons why the topic of representation is so interesting is that it illustrates extremely well the interdependence of the two disciplines. I shall be content if in this essay, which is necessarily schematic, I can make this view seem worth taking seriously.

2. The first and most basic fact to be noted about representation is that every representation is a representation of something or other. The Of-ness thesis—as I shall call the thesis that to be of something or other is an essential feature of representation—can also be expressed by saying that necessarily every representation has an object.

The Of-ness thesis lays itself open to three misinterpretations, all of which are serious. The first and second misinterpretations are quite distinct, but the second and the third are connected. Each misinterpretation involves, initially, a distortion of the nature of the concept of representation and, derivatively, a contraction (so it turns out) in its extension.

The first misinterpretation, which I call, for a reason presently to emerge, the Figurative thesis,[1] insists that, for every representation, the something or other that it is of, or its object, can always be brought under some nonabstract concept. The Figurative thesis denies the possibility of there being representations whose objects cannot be brought under any concepts, and it also denies the possibility of there being representations whose objects can be brought only under abstract concepts. Whatever can be represented can also be described (according to this thesis) and, moreover, can be described in figurative terms.

The Figurative thesis puts as the central cases of representation those where what is represented is, for example, a warrior, a bowl of apples, a garden, or some complex of such things. It displaces from the class of representations geometrical illustrations, such as the drawing of a cube, as well as the whole range of designs and 'abstractions' for which no verbal classification exists or is likely to exist. We might hope to capture the Figurative thesis if for a moment we narrow our attention upon the domain of art, for we might then say that the impact of the thesis is to exclude from representational art anything except figurative art—hence the name I have given it.

As a corrective to the Figurative thesis, and as a way of getting right both the nature and the extension of the concept of representation, I suggest the following rule of thumb:[2] that, confronted with a configuration on a two-dimensional surface, we should think of representation whenever we assign spatiality or a third dimension to what is in front of us—in so far, that is, as this assignment does not derive directly from the spatial properties of the stuffs of which the configuration is constituted.

The second misinterpretation to which the Of-ness thesis is exposed I call the Existential thesis, and it insists that for every representation there must exist an instance of the kind that the something or other represented belongs to. This formulation of the thesis is, even for the roughest purposes, too slack, and the thesis cannot be satisfactorily formulated without introducing the idea, which is not unobvious, that the something or other represented is always represented *as* something. So what I have talked of so far loosely as a representation of a warrior or a garden may now be thought of as a representation of something or other as a warrior or as a garden. (Of course, there are or may be representations of a warrior or a garden that do not represent them as warriors or gardens—the warrior, say, is shown undressed and asleep, or still in his cradle. But these cases need not concern us.) The Existential thesis may now be reformulated thus: For every representation, there must exist an instance of the kind that the something or other represented is represented as belonging to. So there can be, according to this thesis, representations of cardinals—that is, representations in which something or other is represented as a cardinal—just because there are cardinals: but there cannot be representations of unicorns—that is, representations in which something or other is represented as a unicorn—since there are no unicorns.

The Existential thesis, unlike the Figurative thesis, has few intrinsic attractions—though there may very well be philosophical positions from which it appears difficult, if not impossible, to resist. However, the principal interest of the thesis lies in the distinction that it embodies—that is to say, the distinction between representation as indifferent to existence and representation as entailing existence—rather than in the stand that it actually takes upon this distinction. And much the same can be said for the third misinterpretation.[3] The third misinterpretation, which I call the Portrayal thesis, holds that, for every representation, not only must there exist instances of the kind that the something or other represented is represented as belonging to, but the question can always be legitimately raised, Which something or other, which instance of the kind, is it that is represented? Of course, the Portrayal thesis allows that anyone of whom the question is asked may in fact be unable to answer it: indeed the evidence required for answering it may, for contingent reasons, no longer be available. But the point is that there is an answer to it. For every representation there is a particular something or other that is represented: every representation is, according to this thesis, a portrait.

If the Of-ness thesis is formulated as, If R is a representation, then there is some property f such that R is a representation of an f, then the Existential thesis may be formulated as, If R is a representation of an f, then there must exist fs, and the Portrayal thesis as, If R is a representation of an f, then there must be some particular f such that R represents it.

3. Once the Of-ness thesis is granted, two problems immediately suggest themselves as questions whose answers would go a very long way towards providing a general theory of representation. The questions are: (one) What is it that is of whatever is represented?, or, What (in the narrower sense of the term) is a representation?; and (two) What is the relation between the representation (in this narrower sense of the term) and the something or other that it is of?, or, What is it to represent?

If it is true that, in order to provide a general theory of representation, it is necessary (if not sufficient) to answer these two questions, a promising approach to existing theories would be to look at the answers that they actually give. However, we find not only that some theories only laboriously divide themselves in this way, but some appear to concentrate exclusively on one of these two questions.

But this is not necessarily damaging. For certain answers given to one or other of these two questions virtually determine the answer to the other. So, for instance, if we are told that to represent is to deliver to the eye of an observer the same bundle of light-rays as would be received from whatever is represented (the Arousal of Sensation theory), we cannot be in much doubt what sort of thing a representation is. Or, if we are told that a representation is an illusion (the Illusion theory), that pretty well decides the nature of the representational relation.

Of course, there will be theories of representation within which the answers to the two questions are quite independent one of another. And there will be theories that constitute intervening cases. And this in turn suggests one way in which theories of representation might be classified. Theories of representation can be classified according to the degree of dependence or independence between the answers they provide to the two questions.

However I should like to draw attention to another, though clearly related, way of classifying theories of representation.

Armed with a theory of representation, we might imagine ourselves approaching a possible representation and asking of it, Is it a representation?, and then, on the assumption that the answer is Yes, going on to ask of it, What does it represent? Now, the answers that such questions receive might be called the applied answers of the theory that we are armed with. It is in terms of this notion that we may introduce the second way of classifying theories of representation. Theories of representation can be classified according to the degree of dependence or independence between the applied answers they provide.

It is not hard to see that these two possible ways of classifying theories of representation are not just different but very different. For the first way depends on considering the relations between the two applied answers themselves; whereas the second way depends on considering the relations between the two bodies of information that the theory says are at once necessary and sufficient for reaching these answers. In the case of any given representation, different theories of representation may very well deliver up precisely the same applied answers. Indeed, if the theories attain to a minimal adequacy—what might be called material adequacy— they can be relied on to do just this. But the theories will differ amongst themselves as far as the information on which they prescribe that these answers are based. The second way of classifying theories of representation amounts to this: that one should first consider the information that each theory stipulates as necessary and sufficient for determining whether something is a representation, and then should see how far this information goes towards determining what, according to the theory, is represented. The assumption to this way of classifying theories of representation is that there will be real differences in such reckonings: that with some theories there will be a considerable overlap between the two pieces of information, and with other theories virtually none or indeed none at all.

Let us look at some examples of this second way of classifying theories of representation, and start with the Illusion theory. The information that the Illusion theory stipulates as necessary and sufficient for answering whether something is a representation goes a long way towards answering what it represents. This is because we discover that something is an illusion only by noticing what it tends to get us to believe. What it tends to get us to believe is what it represents. If we turn to the Semiotic theory of representation, we get a very different result. For the information that such a theory stipulates as necessary and sufficient for answering whether something is a representation gets us virtually nowhere at all towards answering what it represents. For, according to this theory, to know that something is a representation we have to know only that it is a character in *some* symbol system that satisfies certain formal requirements, whereas to know what it represents we need to know *what* actual symbol system it belongs to *and* we need to know the lexicon as well as the formal rules of the system.

I shall now say of this second way of classifying theories of representation that it classifies them according to the *naturalness* that they assign to the representational relation. The smaller the increment of information that a theory insists on if we are to be able to move from knowing that something is a representation to knowing what it represents, the more "natural" account it gives of representation. By contrast, the larger the increment of information that it specifies as requisite, the more conventionalist account the theory gives of representation.

My claim would be that this captures a central part, though certainly not all, of our intuitive understanding of the dispute whether representation is grounded in nature or rests on convention.[4] It might, for instance, be said that the dispute also concerns what counts as a representation, and therefore concerns the information, absolutely reckoned, on which we have to draw in order to determine whether something is a representation.

If it were claimed, against me, that the notion of information, as I have used it, is *ultimately* untenable, I would not be unduly worried, for my suspicion is that the distinction between a natural and a conventionalist account of representation is ultimately untenable. And, if it were claimed that the notion of information, as I have used it, is tenable but ultimately only inside some larger theory of cognition, I should be delighted because what I am most inclined to think is that the same is true of the distinction between the two kinds of account of representation.

4. It should now be possible to assemble, out of these philosophical ideas, some requirements on any adequate theory of representation. I propose two.

The first requirement comes out of the immediately preceding discussion. It is that an adequate theory of representation should assign to representation the degree of naturalness, conversely the degree of conventionality, that it actually has. It should neither underestimate the difficulty nor fail to appreciate the facility with which we can move from recognizing that something is a representation to identifying what it is a representation of. Presumably an adequate theory of representation will not locate the phenomenon at, or perhaps even very close to, either of the two ends of the natural-conventional spectrum.

The second requirement goes back to an earlier point. Granted that it would be an error to think that all representations are portraits, it is nevertheless true that some are. The requirement is, then, that an adequate theory of representation should indicate how portraiture is accommodated within representation. It must indicate the differential conditions of when we are, and when we are not, permitted to ask of a representation of an *f*, which *f* it represents, and it must also indicate how this question is to be answered consistently with the rest of what it says about representation.[5]

The choice of a theory of representation lies, as the current discussion stands, between about five or six alternative theories, depending on how precisely we individuate them. I have mentioned already *(a)* the *Illusion theory*,[6] *(b)* the *Arousal of Sensation theory*,[7] and *(c)* the *Semiotic theory*.[8] To these we could add *(d)* the *Resemblance theory*,[9] according to which a representation is of what it resembles, or looks like, a theory generally very unforthcoming, perhaps because it is altogether permissive, about what (in the narrow sense of the term) a representation actually is; and *(e)* the *Information theory*,[10] according to which a representation—which once again is generally left unspecified—is of something or other if and only if it delivers to the observer an experience containing the same information as is found in the experience of that something or other. All these theories seem to me to be not implausible candidates, though I think that there are fatal objections to all.[11]

5. I cannot hope in this essay to substantiate these last remarks, which are bound to seem dismissive, and I shall rest my case on arguments that have been produced elsewhere by myself and others. I shall simply offer, in a necessarily crude version, what seems to me the best available theory of representation. It comes out well by the criteria of adequacy that I have proposed, and it also seems to me to have other things to recommend it.

The theory is stated in terms of 'seeing-in'. For at least central cases of representation, a necessary condition of R representing x is that R is a configuration in which something or other can be seen and furthermore one in which x can be seen. This gives necessity but not sufficiency for the simple reason that it covers such cases as the cloud that is very like a whale or the photograph of Charlie Chaplin that anyone might mistake for a photograph of Hitler. Sufficiency (or something close enough to it for our purposes) is reached only when we add the further condition that R was intended by whoever made it to be a configuration in which x could be seen. And this condition must be understood in such a way that whoever made the representation was in a position or had the required competence to form and act on this intention, and did so.[12] The representation does not simply conform to the intention: it fulfills it.

6. Perhaps the most natural way of demarcating philosophical and psychological inquiry about representation is to think of philosophy as characteristically interested in the nature of representation and psychology as characteristically interested in the various representational skills.

What I have said so far, if accepted, should challenge the view that the two forms of inquiry, thus demarcated, can be carried on with any real degree of autonomy. If I am right about the nature of representation, and the best available theory of the matter is in terms of 'seeing-in', it is at least an open question whether philosophical inquiry does not run out into psychological inquiry. For to see something or other in a configuration is a representational skill—I shall call it 'representational seeing'—

and the question is open how much of the substantive psychological findings about representational seeing the philosophical analysis of representation in its final state will need to incorporate. But however this turns out, it should already be clear that even in its early state the philosophical analysis has constraints to lay down to which relevant psychological findings must conform.

I shall specify some of these constraints, and in each case I shall, by referring back to something said in discussing the nature of representation, locate the source of the constraint.

The first constraint is this: that the skill that psychology studies *should have the appropriate scope*—that is to say, it should be in operation whenever anything three-dimensional is seen in a two-dimensional configuration. This constraint connects with the error involved in what I called the Figurative thesis. For that thesis in effect limited what can be represented, hence what can be representationally seen, to those things which can be brought under a non-abstract concept.

It is the failure to respect this first constraint that vitiates, for instance, the well-known cross-cultural studies of W. Hudson and later workers on the perception of representations amongst various non-European populations of South Africa.[13] For the kind of experimental situation in which a subject is shown a drawing of a huntsman, an antelope, and a mountain that is represented as being in the background but that configurationally lies between the other two, and is then asked whether the huntsman can hit the stag, does not test, by the answer he gives, whether he possesses the skill of representational seeing. For, in so far as the subject understands the question in relation to the drawing, he shows himself possessed of the requisite skill. For to see the huntsman, to see the antelope, to see what does or does not lie between them, suffice to show that he has the skill.[14] (Of course, it is right to point out that it is no easy matter to determine whether the subject, as I have put it, understands the question in relation to the drawing, and whether he tries to answer it by looking at the drawing and reporting on what he sees in it. For there could be specific cues from which the subject might infer that a certain configuration must be a drawing of a huntsman or an antelope, and he could do this without seeing, without being able to see, the huntsman or the antelope in the drawing. He might be able to answer the question in relation to the drawing, though not to understand it in relation to the drawing. The difference would be, of course, accessible to further experiment.)[15]

The second constraint upon psychological findings about representational seeing is this: that the skill that psychology studies *should have the appropriate consequences*—that is to say (and now we have a weak and a strong version of these consequences), weakly, that representational seeing should be regarded as in operation only when the observer is not necessarily led to believe that what he sees is actually there, and, strongly, that representational seeing should be regarded as in operation only when the observer is led away from believing that what he sees is actually there.

The source of this constraint lies in something that has been more implicit than explicit in what I said about the nature of representation. In enumerating the different theories of representation, I distinguished between the theory that I favour and the Illusion theory. Now the difference is that, whereas the Illusion theory defines, partially, a representation in terms of the observer's being led to have an existential belief about what he sees, my theory does not additionally require that he should have an existential belief about what he sees. My own view is that what representational seeing does additionally require of the observer is that, as well as seeing something or other in the configuration, he should, and as part of the same perceptual experience, be aware of the configuration itself[16]—a possibility which, of course, an adherent of the Illusion theory is intent to deny. In other words, the observer is led *away* from believing that what he sees is actually there.

I am not in a good position to say whether this second constraint is or is not likely to be respected by psychologists. Historically there is a disturbing omen in the tendency, widespread in classical psychology and persisting well into our own day, of appealing to situations in which representational seeing is in operation as though they were cases, indeed as though they were paradigms, of three-dimensional or nonrepresentational seeing. Experiments in which our perception of solid objects is tested for its conditions on the basis of subjects' being shown *drawings* of solid objects, or experiments in which the influence of shadow on perception of concave or convex surfaces is tested for its conditions on the basis of *photographs* of shadow, are cases in point. Such experiments seem to me misconceived in two related and important ways. In the first place, the phenomenon whose conditions they test for is not what it is purported to be—that is, three-dimensional seeing—it is rather representational seeing. (Sometimes, it is a different thing again: it is illusion—which must have its own distinct conditions.) And, secondly, the conditions that they purport to establish are not the conditions that they actually test: for the conditions they test are the representations of those conditions. (In the case of many conditions of perception, or perceptual cues, the distinction between conditions and represented conditions is an elusive one to make, but none the less vital. For instance, it is at first difficult to realize that in a drawing there is no such thing as over-lap—there is only representation of overlap.)

Of course, the classical experiments that I have in mind do not violate the constraint under consideration. They do not assimilate representa-tional seeing to three-dimensional seeing. They commit the converse er-ror: they assimilate three-dimensional seeing to representational seeing. But what error and converse error have in common is a seeming indiffer-ence to whether what is tested is a form of perception that does, or a form of perception that does not, generate an existential belief: and either way round, the only thing that could justify the indifference is the theo-retical conviction that, from the point of view of psychology, there is no difference between the two forms of perception.[17]

The third constraint upon psychological findings about representa-tional seeing is this: that the skill that psychology studies *should have the appropriate degree of flexibility*—that is to say, it must be capable of occurring within different systems or rules of representation. This derives from what I said about whereabouts on the spectrum that runs from the natural to the conventional an adequate theory of representation should locate representation. My conclusion was that it should not be located at, or, for that matter, too near, either of the two ends of the spectrum: more particularly, that it should not be located at, or too near, the natural end. The significance of this for psychology is, however, best brought out in a somewhat broader context than that of mere representational *seeing*.

7. I have suggested that the proper topic of psychological inquiry into representation is the various representational skills. One such skill is rep-resentational seeing. Another such skill is the skill of producing represen-tations, or drawing skill as I shall call it.

Initially it might seem that drawing skill and representational seeing are linked rather like a speaker's capacity and hearer's capacity in the domain of language. But a fatal objection to this analogy is that someone might have the capacity to see but no capacity to produce representa-tions: a possibility for which we do not allow even theoretical room in the domain of language—except in evidently degenerate cases. Nevertheless, the analogy is valuable in suggesting a dependence of drawing skill on representational seeing that is closer than might otherwise be surmised.

If the correct analysis of representation involves a reference not only to what can be seen in a configuration but also to what is intended to be seen in it, it is evident that anyone who has the capacity to produce representations has also the capacity to see things in them: for how else could he produce configurations intending this rather than that to be seen in them? So in a general way drawing skill requires representational seeing.

However, the more interesting dependence of the productive skill on the receptive skill occurs on a less general level. It follows from the fact that there are different systems or rules of representation that not only are there different modes of representational seeing but that there are different modes of drawing skill. Now to claim that someone is capable of a certain mode of drawing skill is also to make a claim about the mode of representational seeing of which he is capable: it is to claim that the representational seeing of which he is capable is in a mode that integrates with the kind of representation that he produces. In so far as this is not so, his capacity to produce representations that conform to a certain system or fit certain rules is not a sufficient index of his drawing skill and its mode. The conformity might be accidental. This shows something highly significant about the nature of the skill that drawing skill is: it shows something about the kind of internal mechanism that psychology needs to posit in order to account for it.

An example of this last point: Someone draws representations in—that is, in conformity with—ordinary oblique projection. If he also in each instance sees in the configuration that which the representation is of, and moreover does so with at least as great a facility as he would with representations in some other projective system, then there would be little doubt about the mode of drawing skill that we should assign to him. This is so because in this case the mode of representational seeing integrates with the kind of representation that he produces. But imagine another case in which someone produces similar representations but either he has with each drawing some difficulty in seeing in the configuration that which the representation is of, or (a more realistic alternative) he has much greater facility at seeing things in configurations made in some other projective system, for example, linear perspective. In such a case we surely would not think that the kind of representation that he draws was a clear index of his drawing skill and its mode. The way he draws does not integrate with his mode of representational seeing. He not only recognizes that there are better, that is, representationally better, drawings than those which he does, but he also thinks that there are better—once again, representationally better—kinds of drawing than those which he does.

Once it is realized that an individual's drawing skill is invariably within some mode, it is tempting to go on and try to order the various modes in which drawing skill can be exemplified into a hierarchy, so that some are more advanced than others. This temptation is only strengthened when it is further recognized that there is a standard temporal sequence in which the individual as a child passes through these various modes—a sequence which can be correlated with cognitive progress.

Nevertheless it would be misguided to give way too readily to the temptation, as some ability tests do. For, even if the passage through the different modes of drawing skill can be broadly correlated with cognitive progress, it does not follow that this passage is itself cognitive progress.

Obviously any later mode of the drawing skill will serve cognitive interests that are more advanced than those served by earlier modes. For instance, linear perspective can tell us how objects look from a certain point of view, and not only how they are. However, this gain will be at a price, and we need to know to what extent the less advanced cognitive interests can still be served by the later mode. It is only if they can be to a considerable extent that we are entitled to think of the transition from earlier to later mode as itself cognitive progress, and not just a concomitant of such progress. And often this condition is not met. For instance, linear perspective, in telling us how an object looks, no longer tells us how all sides of an object are. And the assumption, once widespread, that only linear perspective can coherently or consistently satisfy our cognitive interests, since only it provides a *systematic* way of representing space, cannot be invoked, for it appears to be without foundation.[18]

XI Pictorial Style: Two Views

1. In *The Principles of Art History,* his most ambitious though perhaps not his most successful work, the Swiss art historian Heinrich Wölfflin talks of the "double" or "twofold, root of style."[1] Whether we accept or reject the particular way in which Wölfflin makes the cut, we should be grateful for any reminder that, in our thinking about and talking of art, the concept of style turns up twice. Sometimes we think and talk about *general style:* sometimes we think and talk about *individual style.*

2. *General style* subdivides itself into at least three forms. First, there is *universal style,* best illustrated by examples, such as classicism, the geometrical style, naturalism. Secondly, there is *historical* or *period style,* examples of which would be neoclassicism, art nouveau, social realism. For the third form of general style I shall wait until I have first said something about individual style, by which time the reason for the brief detour will be apparent.

For *individual style* I shall give not examples—there can be no doubt what the examples are—but an explication: Individual style is what we characteristically refer to when we use the phrase 'style of *a*', where *a* is the name of a painter, to refer to *something in the work of a.* I put the point like this, because we can also use a phrase like 'the style of a' to refer to something in the work of *b, c, d,* all painters distinct from one another and different from *a*. So we use the phrase 'the style of Giotto' sometimes to refer not to something in the work of Giotto but to something in the work of, say, Taddeo Gaddi or some other Giottesque painter. And when we use the phrases 'the style of *a*', 'the style of Giotto', in this second way, we refer not to individual style but to *school style.* And school style is that third form of general style.

3. In this essay I shall talk exclusively about individual style, and I shall be concerned with two views of it. But first I must guard against a way

of taking what I have just said that would trivialize the distinction between general style and individual style, so that my essay would lose its
subject-matter. It might be thought that what I have been saying amounts
to this:

1. we use the phrase 'style of *a*' sometimes to refer to something
   in the work of *a*, sometimes to refer to something in the work of
   b, c, d:

2. we use the phrase in otherwise just the same way in the two
   kinds of case:

3. when we use it in the first kind of case, we call what the phrase
   picks out 'individual style':

4. when we use it in the second kind of case, we call what the
   phrase picks out 'school style'.

But this is an inadequate reconstruction of what I have said. For (2) is
not part of my meaning. On the contrary, I am assuming that the phrase
'style of *a*' is used significantly differently in the two kinds of case. For,
when used in the first kind of case, the phrase carries with it the implication that *a had indeed a style,* or that *he had a style of his own.* By
contrast, when the phrase is used in connection with the work of *b, c, d,*
no implication is carried that *b, c, d, had styles of their own:* at most
there is the implication that *b, c, d, worked in a style.* And the implication
that *a* had indeed a style, or had a style of his own, is not trivial.

The implication might seem trivial because of a confusion between it
and one or other of two different propositions, which are beyond doubt
trivial. One is that, unless *a* has a style of his own, there is no such thing
as the style of *a*. The other is that, if *a* has a style of his own, then the
style that he has is the style of *a*.

And now for the question, What is it to have a style? What is it to have
a style of one's own?

In answering this question, I shall consider it solely in the context of
the pictorial arts. For it seems to me that the function, and the importance—possibly even the nature—of individual style differ as we move
from one art to another. The relevant factors here, accounting for the
differences between the arts, include the role of the medium within the
art, the degree of apprenticeship required to be a practitioner of the art,
the significance of tradition, the involvement of the art with bodily or

psychomotor activity, and the character of the structural or compositional principles that it employs. It may be possible, or it may not, to arrange the arts on a spectrum according to the place occupied within them by individual style, but certainly there is no art where individual style occupies a more important or influential place than the pictorial arts. Accordingly, what I say about individual style in the pictorial arts cannot simply be transferred to some other art without grave risk of falsehood.

I shall now try to answer the question that I have set myself by enumerating three characteristics of individual style.

4. In order to present the first characteristic of style, I shall start with what I take to be a basic fact about our interest in pictorial art. That fact might be expressed thus: that, in so far as we are interested in paintings, we are interested only in the paintings of painters. Or, more precisely: in so far as we are interested in paintings as paintings, or in so far as we take an aesthetic interest in paintings, we are interested only in the paintings of painters. For it is undubitably true that at times we are interested in the paintings of schizophrenics, of art-school applicants, of chimpanzees, of world politicians, or of our own children. But, when we are interested in such paintings, we are interested in them so as (respectively) to diagnose sickness, to discover promise, to test a theory, to elicit biographical information, or because the painting is by who it is—that is to say, a sentimental interest. And, though I would claim, as against a misguided purism, that when we take an aesthetic interest in a painting, we may legitimately draw upon whatever we have learned from first approaching it with one of these other aims, it remains the case that approaching it with such an aim is not to take an aesthetic interest in it. So: Why can we (as I assert) take an aesthetic interest only in the paintings of painters?

One answer would be, Because they are better. It takes a painter to turn out a painting.

But this is not right for two reasons. In the first place we aren't interested—aesthetically interested, that is—only in good paintings. Indeed, if someone expressed indifference to all paintings except the best, we should doubt whether his interest in any painting was really aesthetic. Secondly, and this will lead us to the intuition we are after, to suggest that we are interested in the paintings only of painters because they are better would presuppose that the judgment of better or worse, the judgment of quality, passed on a painting was independent of the judgment whether that painting is by a painter or by a nonpainter. And it isn't. It is important to see how this dependence goes, and a way of doing so is to contrast this dependence with another: that is, the dependence of the judgment of better or worse, of quality, passed on a painting, with (this time) the judgment of who, or which painter, painted the painting. For, when the judgment of who painted the painting legitimately affects the judgment of quality, it does so, characteristically, by raising or lowering the judgment of quality. Learning that a painting is not by Braque but by one of those painters who turned Cubism into an academic exercise, we recognize faults that we had previously glossed over: learning that it is not by, say, Gleizes, but is indeed by Braque, we are led to see felicities to which we had been, up till then, blind.[2] By contrast, when the judgment that a painting is by a nonpainter rather than by a painter legitimately affects the judgment of quality, it does so, characteristically, not by raising or lowering that judgment, but by knocking it sideways. We lose all confidence in our power to make it. Learning that a painting, believed to be by a painter, is by a nonpainter, we are likely to feel that we don't know what to make of, or what weight to attach to, whatever shows up on the painted support.

Aided by this insight, we may now withdraw our first answer to the question why we can take an aesthetic interest only in the paintings of painters, and replace it with something more considered. A considered but still succinct answer would be that only the paintings of painters are fully comprehensible.

I have talked of painters and of nonpainters. I have talked of them rather as though they were trades or professions, and, in doing so, I have not said anything about what constitutes the distinction. And now let me substitute for the term 'painter' another with the same extension but more explanatory force: that is, 'someone with a formed style'. Then I can assert the first characteristic of individual style: *Style is a precondition of aesthetic interest.*

5. The second characteristic of individual style can be more rapidly arrived at. I said that it is when, and only when, we know that a painting is by a painter, or by someone with a formed style, that we have any confidence what to make of, or what weight to attach to, what shows up

on the canvas. Of the several valid interpretations that can be placed on the phrases 'what weight to attach to', 'what to make of', I select 'what is expressed by'. And then I can present the second characteristic of individual style: *Style is a precondition of expression.*

6. The first two characteristics of individual style are external characteristics of style: the third is an internal characteristic. The first two turn upon the consequences of style: the third characteristic relates to the nature of style. And a further difference is that, whereas the first two characteristics went unargued for, I shall give a sketch for an argument in favour of this third characteristic.

The characteristic is that *style has psychological reality*. The characteristic stands in need as much of explication as of argument.

Let me begin by introducing the notion of a *style-description*. A style-description is a description, as full a description as we can manage, of an individual style. We may contrast a style-description with a *stylistic description,* which is a description of a picture in a given style that fully describes the stylistic features present in it. For every stylistic description there is a style-description with which it complies, that is, the description of the style that the picture is in.

Now, let us imagine an art historian engaged in the study of a particular painter. He is a stylistically-minded art historian, and we may assume him to be engaged in the writing of a style-description for that artist. He completes it as best he can, and then he asks himself, Is this style-description adequate? But first he must ask himself, What are the criteria of adequacy for a style-description?

Our art historian finds two broadly plausible answers suggested in the literature. The interest of each answer is that it brings in train a certain conception of the nature of style. Indeed there is no better way of getting at these two conceptions of the nature of style than through the associated criteria of adequacy for style-descriptions.

So one answer goes: A style-description is adequate if and only if (one) it picks out all the interesting/significant/distinctive elements of a painter's work, *and* (two) it groups them in the most convenient way into stylistic features. And it is to be noted that the terms *interesting, significant, distinctive, convenient,* as they occur here, are to be understood relative to a certain point of view. The point of view envisaged is that (roughly) of the progressive art historian of the age, and it is understood that the standpoint of the progressive art historian of one age will not necessarily coincide with that of the next. For those who accept this criterion of adequacy for a style-description, it is welcome evidence of the continuing vitality of art history that style-descriptions have to be rewritten each generation.

I call this criterion of adequacy for a style-description a *taxonomic criterion of style,* and the associated conception of the nature of style the *taxonomic conception of style.* What justifies this label is that the problem of describing a style is conceived of merely as a problem in classification.[3]

The other answer goes: A style-description is adequate if and only if (one) it picks out those elements of a painter's work which are dependent upon processes or operations characteristic of his acting as a painter, *and* (two) it groups these elements into stylistic features accordingly, that is, according to the processes or operations that they are dependent upon. I call this criterion of adequacy for a style-description a *generative criterion,* and the associated conception of the nature of style the *generative conception of style,* and what justifies this label is that the problem of describing a style is conceived of as a problem in explanation.

In principle, for any given painter, art historians who subscribe to a taxonomic criterion and those who subscribe to a generative criterion of adequacy could agree on the style-description that they provide. Where they would disagree would be on the justification they gave for their description, and on the consequences that they would draw from it.

Now, to say that style has psychological reality is just to adopt a generative criterion of adequacy for a style-description or to think that the generative conception fits the nature of style. I shall present considerations in favour of the generative conception, but only after I have said something about a notion evidently central to this conception of style: that of a *style-process* or *operation.*

7. What is a *style-process?* A style-process can be divided up into three different items or aspects. First, there is a *schema* or *universal,* under which the painter brings some part of the pictorial resources available to him. Secondly, there is a *rule* or *instruction* for placing, or otherwise operating on, those pictorial resources which the schema picks out. Thirdly, there is an *acquired disposition* to act on the rule, where this disposition is, generally, not just psychological, but psychomotor.

I have preferred the terms *schema* and *universal* to the term *concept* because they do not carry the implication, which *concept* does for some, that the artist verbalizes, or has a verbal equivalent for, the way in which he segments the resources of his art. Nevertheless, of these two terms each has its characteristic drawback. *Schema* suggests something highly configurational, which is wrong. And *universal* suggests that the schemata employed by any one artist are available to, or even availed of by, all artists: in other words, that there are—to borrow a phrase from literary stylistics—'primes' of pictorial style. And this too is wrong. Indeed, sometimes what is most distinctive about a style is the way in which it segments the pictorial resources. So, for instance, in the work of one artist (Leonardo), line and shading are to be taken together as forming a single resource, whereas in the work of another (Raphael) they are separately exploited so that they come to make distinct contributions to the whole.

But in order to assess these points it would be valuable to have a sense of the variety of the schemata that style uses. The schemata that come first to mind are those which can be formally identified: line, hue, tonality, firmness of line, saturation of colour. Next, there are those schemata which cannot be identified exclusively by reference to formal considerations, because they depend upon representation: volume, depth, overlapping, movement, lighting.[4] And then there are the schemata that are exclusively representational: gaze, pose, eyes, drapery. And beyond them are the schemata which not only are representationally identified but have no isolable material or configurational counterpart in the picture: point of view, perspectival system, the space that surrounds the represented part of the space. And, finally, on a different tack, there are those schemata—a mixed bag—which refer to the condition of the support or to the use of the medium: edge, brushstroke, scumbling.

If, in light of this list, the question is raised: Under what conditions is a given schema *stylistically* employed by an artist?, the best answer would be that an artist gives stylistic employment to a schema just when the schematized resource plays a distinctive functional role in his painting. Paradoxically this does not have the implication that the schematized resource actually makes an appearance in his painting.

To see why this is so, I shall turn to the second item in a stylistic process: the *rule*, or *instruction*. These rules, as I have said, operate on the resources as schematized. Assume that an artist employs the schema *line:*

then, examples of rules would be 'prolong the line', 'avoid sharp changes of direction in line', 'do not use line for the definition of form.' Now, it should be clear that, whereas some rules will lead to the massive appearance of that upon which the rule is directed, other rules will result in the rather rare appearance of that upon which they are directed, and yet others will enjoin the complete omission of the schematized resource from the artist's work. Consider the rule 'replace line by changes of hue'. A proper description of this last case would be that the schema itself is employed by the artist but the pictorial resource it schematizes is not: the deletion is intentional, not just fortuitous. Wölfflin, for instance, talks in *Classic Art* of the way in which Fra Bartolommeo, following a current Venetian stylistic process, uses shadow instead of colour, and, if that is right, then we may think of colour as intentionally deleted from Fra Bartolommeo's work.[5] The same point is made on a broader scale when Gombrich emphasizes the distinction between a style that is nonclassical or unclassical and a style that is anticlassical.[6] The anticlassical artist employs a schema or set of schemata corresponding to classicism: the nonclassical artist does not. Neither employs the resources of classicism.

Even a brief discussion of the rule aspect of a style-process would not be adequate without referring to a most important subset of rules: integrative rules, or rules for coordinating the operation of rules of the kind I have just been talking about. Such rules are probably the most significant agent in securing something that any individual style must possess: that is, overallness or unity, where this is taken in a normative sense. A problem that confronts us is the choice of a suitable model, or models, for the expression of such rules. Indeed, even in reasonably sophisticated work on the subject,[7] the absence of a suitable model for integrative devices has resulted in a narrow concentration on the most primitive and presumably least used integrative device: that of mere conjunction.

On the third item in a style-process—a *disposition to act on the constituent rule*—it is worth remarking that it is this that distinguishes having a style from merely working in a style. Insistence on the dispositional aspect of individual style registers the point that the formation and the internalization of a style are one and the same process.

8. How are we to establish the superiority of the generative over the taxonomic conception of style? First we must refute the taxonomic conception. But this is not enough: it is also necessary to argue for the gen-

erative conception. For the two conceptions of style are contraries, not contradictories: they exclude one another, but they do not exhaust the field. The rejection of a taxonomic conception of style commits us to a realist conception of style. But the generative conception is only one of several possible realist conceptions. Distinctively it claims that style has *psychological* reality.

9. To refute the taxonomic conception of style, a strategy would be to consider certain unacceptable consequences of this conception. Two such consequences are the *description thesis* and the *strong relativization thesis*.

The *description thesis* provides an answer to the question, What is it for an artist to have a style, a style of his own? The answer it provides is this: For *a* to have a style of his own is for there to be in circulation a style-description written for his work.

Must an adherent of the taxonomic conception be committed to the description thesis? Why could he not think that whether *a* has or has not a style of his own is additionally a matter of whether something or other is true of *a* which would warrant the writing of a style-description for his work? But, if the adherent of the taxonomic conception believes in something that lies beyond or behind the writing of the style-description, this something should have had a place found for it in the criterion of adequacy for a style-description. A style-description should have been declared inadequate unless it makes reference to this factor.

What, then, is unacceptable about the description thesis? If it were true, then the attribution of a style to a painter would have no explanatory force. It would explain nothing about his work because it would not itself state a fact about his work. All it would state would be a fact about the existing condition of progressive art history. Yet we think that the possession of a formed style by an artist can explain certain things about his work. If I am right, it can explain both the aesthetic interest of his work and the expressiveness of his work.

A *relativization thesis* is a thesis concerning the proper interpretation of judgments of identity or diversity of style, and it comes in a weak and a strong version. The taxonomic conception of style has as one of its consequences a strong relativization thesis. A weak relativization thesis would hold that any true judgment of the form "the style of *m* is the same as, or is different from, the style of *n*," where *m* and *n* are paintings, can always be amplified by means of a clause containing a style-description: furthermore, this amplification is required if we are to exhibit the truth of the judgment. But a strong relativization thesis holds more than this. It holds that this amplification is necessary if we are not just to exhibit the truth but to determine the truth-value of such a judgment. For it holds that, depending on the style-description invoked, the judgment of style-identity or style-diversity may actually change in truth-value. There may be one style-description relative to which m and n are in the same style, and another, also adequate, relative to which m and n are in different styles.[8]

That the taxonomic conception leads to a strong relativization thesis is because, on this conception, the writing and rewriting of style-descriptions are dependent solely on current art-historical concerns. There is no further "fact of the matter" to the practice. In the description thesis we have come across one aspect of this: namely, that there is no good reason why a style-description should be written for one painter but not for another. In the strong relativization thesis, we now encounter another aspect of the same practice: namely, that there is no good reason why more than one style-description should not be written for the work of a single painter.

The strong relativization thesis can be shown to be unacceptable in the following way: We often make judgments of style-identity and style-diversity without making explicit the style-description. For, in arriving at such judgments, we can make implicit use of a style-description. However, if the truth-value of the judgment of style-identity or style-diversity is dependent upon what style-description is invoked, in that the truth-value can change with the style-description, then we cannot rationally believe any such judgment unless we can first retrieve the description employed in arriving at it. Until the description is retrieved, the specific content of the belief is not before us. But the truth of the matter is that we believe, and feel entitled to believe, many such judgments in the absence of the relevant style-description. Indeed, often what spurs us on to work out the style-description is our commitment to a judgment of style-identity: recognizing that a certain set of works are in the same style, we set ourselves to find out the character of that style.

Supplementary to these arguments against the taxonomic conception is the broader consideration that this conception is not, properly speaking, a conception of style at all. More precisely, since it prevents itself from distinguishing style from something quite else, it can make no better claim to be a conception of style than of this other thing. This other thing is what I call *signature,* and an intuition on which this essay is premissed is that there is a fundamental conceptual difference between style and signature.[9] *Signature* is that collection of characteristics of an artist's work that we use to assign his works to him, and the two concepts are not only different, they are not extensionally equivalent. There will be stylistic features in an artist's work that are not signature, and, more importantly, there will be signature features that are not stylistic. More importantly: for, if the reason why certain stylistic features are not also signature is that they are features too hard to discriminate (the line, for instance, of a sixteenth-century artist whose vivacity is due to multiple minute changes of direction observable only under magnification),[10] the reason why certain signature features are not also stylistic (for instance, the owl allegedly characteristic of the work of Herri met de Bles) is harder to formulate and takes us into the essence of style. Briefly I would say that what makes such features nonstylistic is that they are context-free: they inadequately interrelate with the structural or integrative principles of the artist's work. The owl has taken up its place in the painting without going the right way through the painter's mind. It should be obvious that the taxonomic conception cannot admit the distinction between style and signature without reintroducing what it has renounced. For this reason its claim to be a conception of style, rather than of signature, is baseless.

10. Any argument in favour of the generative conception of style must follow the pattern laid down for any argument in favour of a realist thesis. It must show just what we gain in explanatory power by supposing the psychological reality of style, or the superiority of this kind of explanation over its obvious rivals, and it must further show that there is no strong prior reason against the psychological reality.[11]

Reflection suggests two lines that any such argument will pursue. In the first place, it will try to make the point that the explanation of stylistic features in a painter's work has to be by reference to internal rather than to external factors. This follows from the fact that style is something formed, not learned. Indeed, just here we find a crucial difference between individual style and general style. It may well be that general style *is* learned, not formed, and, if this is so, then the general style in which a painter works is to be explained by external factors, including existing conventions.

Secondly, if the explanation of stylistic features in an artist's work is to be by reference to internal factors, then the argument will try to establish that the relevant internal factors are not neurophysiological factors but psychological factors. Attempts to correlate expressive movements with the innervation of specific neural pathways seem doomed to failure, in part because there is so much else within the mental apparatus—perceptual, affective, cognitive—with which the stylistic processes are integrated.

11. Ultimately the tenability of a generative conception of style is bound up with our capacity to produce style-descriptions of the relevant kind: style-descriptions, that is, that genuinely rest upon an account of underlying style-processes. Of course, it would be absurd to attach any significance to the lack of such descriptions unless a programme designed to produce them had been put into effect. I conclude by listing certain maxims by which a programme of the appropriate kind ought to be guided. Some of these maxims will function permissively compared with current art-historical practice, whereas others will have a constrictive effect.

The first maxim is that stylistic features should be expected to be identified on a very abstract level indeed. Different elements instantiating the same stylistic feature may exhibit gross diversities as far as their physical configuration is concerned, and comparatively minute differences in physical configuration might make broadly similar elements instantiate different stylistic features. This was something that, to the detriment of his work, the great Giovanni Morelli totally failed to recognize.[12]

The second maxim is that some stylistic features may be such that they can be detected in a work only with great difficulty. Stylistic features need not be obvious, and the possibility should always be entertained that some, so far from serving as clues to authorship, can be discerned only once authorship has already and independently been established.

A third maxim is that styles should not be multiplied within a given artist's work without good reason. One good reason would be that the artist has undergone a marked personality change, but in most cases where there is a temptation to invoke stylistic change, a better strategy would be to see whether the original style description had not been formulated on an insufficiently abstract level.

The willingness, indeed the eagerness, of most conventional art historians to multiply styles comes in part from their failure to recognize the variety of good alternative explanations that might be offered for why an artist with a formed style produced work that does not comply with a style-description that on all other counts seems well founded. So, the following possibilities should be taken seriously: The artist had not as yet formed his style, or the work is *prestylistic;* the artist had suffered a loss of style, or the work is *poststylistic;*[13] the artist did not draw upon his style, or the relevant work is *style-deficient.* These possibilities need to be kept in mind, not only if the generative conception of style is to be tested properly, but, more importantly, if proper respect is to be paid to the psychology of art.

Appendix

It is common practice to associate the concept of style with the concept of alternatives or options, and by extension with the concepts of synonymy and of choice. I have not said anything about these associations in the body of this essay, and, since I think that the associations are often ambiguously effected, I shall add a few notes on the whole topic.

I think that there are two quite different contexts in which we might attempt to associate style with alternatives, and these need to be distinguished. Moreover, in one context, but not in the other, a further association can be made between style and synonymy: whereas in the other context, and only in it, can the further association be made between style and choice. There is no context in which the triad of style, synonymy, and choice demands accommodation.

The first context is provided by the question, What is it for a work of art to be in a certain style, or to have stylistic characteristics? And a conventional answer to this question is that for a work to be in a style presupposes the articulation of the work into two aspects, something like form and content, and style can then be equated with form.[14] It is then taken to be a strict consequence of this that, for any given work in a style, there could in principle be another, an alternative, work with the same content but with a different form or in a different style. This is the first association between style and alternatives, and, since the alternatives thus introduced have the same content or meaning as the originals with which they are paired, there is also an association between style and synonymy. Those philosophers who reject synonymy therefore reject either style or this conventional view of style.[15] However, even if it is true that the notion of style requires us to believe that, for every work in an artist's style, there is in principle another work synonymous with it but not in his style, it does not follow that both works would be works he might have made and that, in making the one he did, he chose between them. On the contrary, if style is something internalized, it must follow that he could have made only one of them: that is, the work in his style. Even if (to quote an example of Gombrich's) [16] Mondrian's *Broadway Boogie-Woogie* and some painting of Severini's are synonymous, Mondrian could not have painted the Severini painting, and therefore it is wrong to think that he chose not to paint it or to attempt to say what such a painting would have meant had he chosen to do so. Accordingly in the present context there is no association between style and choice.

The second context in which style is associated with alternatives is provided by the question, What is it for an artist to have a style of his own? For one kind of answer to this question is that the possession of a style enables an artist to produce an ordered range of works, each different from the other, and, in this sense, alternatives to one another. This range is ordered in that each work may be paired off with a meaning which the artist now has, as a consequence of his style, a way of expressing. [17] This is the second association between style and alternative. Given that these works, these alternatives, are all in his style, the artist could make any one of them, so in this context there is also an association between style and choice. However there is no reason to suppose that the range of alternative works will contain redundancy or that there will be pairs of works in his style that mean the same. Hence in this context the further association between style and synonymy does not hold.

It is another matter whether in either context the association between style and alternatives is in fact well made out. I tend to think that in both contexts the association is exaggerated. But this note is too brief to set out the relevant considerations.

XII Pictures and Language

In *Painting as an Art*[1] I put forward an account of pictorial meaning, or of how pictures acquire significance or content, which has two features which we should not expect to find together. One is that the account seems to coincide with our pre-theoretical convictions on the subject: it captures those intuitions which we all tend to have when we come to the topic unrehearsed, and on which theory, we might suppose, would be based. The other is that my account runs counter to what a number of the theories on the subject that currently are in vogue have in common. The cutting-edge of my account is that it rejects the assimilation of pictorial to linguistic meaning: what unites structuralism, post-structuralism, de-construction, hermeneutics, what might be thought of as 'mainstream' semiotics, and certain versions of cognitive science is that they all insist upon, or just take for granted, this assimilation. I have no explanation why much current theory, and, following it, a great deal of current criti-cism, should tend in this counter-intuitive direction, and in this essay I want to consider the underlying issues.

To facilitate this, I propose that we imagine, lined up in front of us, the following: (1) the word 'bison', and below it the sentence, 'The bison is standing'; (2) a picture of a bison—say, a cave-painting of a bison; and (3) an actual bison.

What I shall do is, first, look at three arguments that point up the differences there are between how (1) stands to (3) and how (2) stands to (3). These arguments erode what I call the 'semiotic' account of pictorial meaning: they force apart pictorial and linguistic meaning. Then, second, I shall reinforce these arguments by producing the account of pictorial meaning that I would substitute for the semiotic account. It is what I call a 'psychological' account: it is the kind of account that Wittgenstein, quite rightly, deposed as an account of linguistic meaning. (In all these discussions, nothing should be allowed to hang on the labels that I, for convenience, attach to the different accounts.)

So, to the arguments.

In the first place, once we start to look for an explanation why the word 'bison', or why the sentence, 'The bison is standing', means what it does, we are inevitably led to the area of what might broadly be thought of as rules or conventions. By contrast, there can be no serious expectation that what makes a cave-painting a picture of a bison (if that is indeed what it is) is a rule or a convention. Rules and conventions might stretch pictorial meaning—witness the symbolism of medieval and Renaissance painting that iconography and iconology study—but they cannot ground it.

This is only a very broad characterization of the issue, and it needs to be made more specific. For, if it is right to think of language as inherently rule-bound, it needs to be observed that language is bound by rules of a very special kind. Linguistic rules are layered or hierarchical, and this we can see by now contrasting how the word 'bison', and the sentence, 'The bison is standing', gain their meaning. In both cases the appeal is to rules, but, in the first case, the rule is of a sort that ties words to the world, and, in the second case, the rule is one that ties well-formed sequences of words to the world and does so in virtue of two things: the meanings of the individual words (fixed by the first sort of rule), plus the principles governing their combination into phrases, clauses, and eventually sentences. It is the presence within language of this hierarchy of rules that ensures that linguistic meaning is essentially combinatory, and it is the combinatory nature of linguistic meaning that permits us to learn a language, and places the grasp of an infinite number of sentences within the capacity of a finite mind. If sentences had to be mastered like words, each time from scratch, language would lie outside our reach.[2]

A slogan for catching this last point is, "Semantics rests on syntax." Linguistic meaning presupposes the analyzability of language in terms of structure and components. And here we come to a crucial disanalogy between language and pictures. Whatever the initial temptation might be to associate pictures with rules, the rules envisaged are not, cannot be, of the sort essential to language, and the assimilation of pictorial to linguistic meaning cannot survive recognition of this point. Pictures are not analyzable in the way sentences are: they are not, for instance, *exhaustively* analyzable, or analyzable *without remainder*. (To think that they are would be like thinking that tastes are capable of mathematical analysis because we can sometimes say with reason things like "The soup would be better with less garlic and more tomato," or "This tastes very much better than that.")

Note, in this connection, that, though with (1) we can sharply distinguish between the word and the sentence, which is supremely a matter of structure, when we move to (2) we have no principled, and certainly no structural, way of saying which, the word or the sentence, better correlates with the picture. Is the cave-painting of a *thing* (like a word is) or is it of a *fact* (like a sentence is)? No amount of structural analysis of the cave-painting will yield a cogent answer. In point of fact, when we do reveal structure in a picture, this often seems to have nothing at all to do with meaning: as in the diagrammatic attempts to reveal the composition of a Raphael or a Cézanne.[3]

Secondly—and the arguments I am giving are not independent of one another—it seems appropriate to say that the relationship both of the word 'bison' to the animal and of the sentence 'The bison is standing' to the fact about the animal is arbitrary. There is no ground in nature for it: a point famously emphasized by Saussure. Another word, another sequence of words, could as well have been used for the purpose: in other languages they are. But it is inappropriate to think of the relationship of the cave-painting to the bison in the same way. The non-arbitrariness of this relationship seems quite indisputable, however we go on to account for it: and it is completely unshaken by the recognition that there is a whole variety of styles, manners, and projective systems within which a bison, or the fact that a bison is standing, can be pictured. A non-arbitrary relationship does not have to be a one-one relationship: it can be many-one, or even many-many.

Thirdly, there is the argument from transfer. Suppose that I have the capacity to recognize (2) as a picture of a bison; then, shown a picture of a dog, or a cat, or an elephant, I shall, provided only that I know what these animals look like, surely be able to recognize these other pictures for what they are. And, if I do not know what these animals look like, I may well be able (like a child) to learn this from their pictures. This is what I call 'transfer', and transfer has no place in language. Knowing the word 'bison', I shall not be able to understand the words 'dog', 'cat', 'elephant' on the basis of my original knowledge plus knowing what the animals referred to look like (or indeed anything else of a non-linguistic kind about them). I have to learn a rule afresh for each.

Of course, in learning a first language I cannot learn it simply word by word. But that does not mean there is transfer from one word to another. It means only that I learn words in groups, and contrastively they reinforce each other.

I have already said that the kind of account I wish to substitute for a semiotic account is what I call a 'psychological' account, and by that I mean an account that invokes, in addition to the visible surface of the picture, only psychological factors. It invokes two of them: one in the head of the spectator and one in the head of the artist. It invokes the visual experiences of the spectator and the fulfilled intentions of the artist.

In setting out this account I start with the spectator's experience. Now a necessary condition of the cave-painting being a painting of a bison is that it should be able to cause in a suitably sensitive, suitably informed spectator a certain sort of experience. What sort? Well not, as might at first seem required, the experience of seeing a bison, or even (since there is no bison there) an experience as of seeing a bison. That is the path to illusion, not to picturing. No, the required experience is one different from but systematically related to seeing a bison. It draws upon, not the standard capacity that we have of vision, but the subsidiary capacity that we also have of what I call 'seeing-in'. Seeing-in is a natural capacity we have—it precedes pictures, though pictures foster it—which allows us, when confronted by certain differentiated surfaces, to have experiences that possess a dual aspect, or 'twofoldness': so that, on the one hand, we are aware of the differentiation of the surface, and, on the other hand, we observe something in front of, or behind, something else. We can see things in clouds, in discoloured rocks, in wind-blown sand—and so surely could our remotest ancestors, if they had the time for such games. And we can see things—though our really remotest ancestors would not have had the opportunity to—in pictures: that is, in objects specifically made so that spectators of a qualified kind can see things in them.

In this very last point, there is a suggestion of what it is that distinguishes seeing-in when directed onto nature from seeing-in once it has been recruited by art and directed onto pictures. In the latter case, though not the former, a criterion of correctness attaches to it. With clouds, rocks, sand, it is no more correct to see one thing in them than another. With pictures, this changes. With Titian it is correct to see Venus in a particular stretch of canvas, and incorrect to see anyone or anything else there. With Rothko it is correct to see one bar of maroon in front of a blue expanse, and incorrect to see any other disposition of forms in that area of the picture.

Where does this standard of correctness come from? Why does it enjoin what it does? The criterion comes from the intentions, the fulfilled intentions, of the artist: it comes from the desires, beliefs, wishes, phantasies of the artist in so far as these guided the artist's hand and are retrievable from the work. In this way the second psychological factor (the fulfilled intentions of the artist) supplements the first (the experiences of the spectator). For, though it is a necessary condition of a picture's being of some particular thing that we can see that particular thing in its surface, a picture is not a picture of everything that we can see in it. For some of these perceptions could be the result of extravagance, of idiosyncratic projection, of downright error, on our part. A curb is needed on what we can see in a picture if what we see is to be a sufficient condition of what the picture is of. And this curb is provided by the fulfilled intentions of the artist.

One thing that I want to observe about my account of pictorial meaning is that it still leaves as the bearer of such meaning the visible surface of the picture. It does not transpose meaning either into the head of the spectator or into the head of the artist. However, what the visible surface holds for us is not, despite what Formalists would have us believe, a simple matter. What is properly visible in the surface of the picture is a matter of what experiences appropriate information allows a sensitive spectator to have in front of it, provided only that these experiences cohere with, and are due to, what the artist intended.

This account of pictorial meaning brings to the fore certain features that pictorial meaning possesses that serve to distinguish it further from linguistic meaning. I shall mention two.

First, there is the particular role of perception. In the case of pictures, perception serves us in two ways. It shows us what the picture is like, and it shows us what the picture means in virtue of what it is like. We can stare our way into understanding a picture, given that we have the right sensitivity and the right information. By contrast, in the case of language, though we may well need perception to show us what words or sentences are there, the contribution of perception stops short at this point. It cannot show us what the words or sentences mean. We cannot stare our way into understanding any fragment of language. Since, in the case of both pictures and language, finding out what is there and understanding what it means are carried out as if in one continuous unbroken process, this big difference between the two cases can get overlooked.

Second, there is a feature of pictures which directly follows from what

I have been saying about them, and for which there is not even an ana-logue, as far as I can see, in the sphere of language. All pictures display what they are of from a certain point of view, or at least from a certain direction. We cannot eliminate perspective, even if we try to combine different perspectives in one picture. There is, I repeat, no parallel to this in language.

It will be noticed that, in trying to characterize pictorial meaning in general, I have concentrated on one kind of pictorial meaning: represen-tational meaning. For all its centrality, in both figurative and nonfigura-tive or abstract picturing, representational meaning is not co-extensive with pictorial meaning. In *Painting as an Art,* I offer a checklist of the varieties of pictorial meaning: I identify expressive meaning, textual meaning, historical meaning, and metaphorical meaning. But in each case I tried to show, and think I succeeded in doing so, that the same triad of factors is at work: (a) the intentions of the artist, which cause (b) the artist to mark the surface in a certain way, which causes (c) a certain experience in a suitably sensitive, suitably informed, spectator. We all know all of this from childhood, and theory needs to go back to school.

Notes

Credits

Name Index

Subject Index

Notes

Details of the original publication of essays included in the present volume are given in the Credits.

I. The Sheep and the Ceremony

1. David Wiggins, "Truth, Invention, and the Meaning of Life," Annual Philosophical Lecture, Henriette Hertz Trust, 1976. In *Proceedings of the British Academy,* vol. LXII (1976), pp. 331–378, now reprinted in David Wiggins, *Needs, Values, and Truth: Essays in the Philosophy of Value,* 2nd ed. (Oxford: Blackwell, 1991).

2. Stuart Hampshire, "Morality and Pessimism," Leslie Stephen Lecture, 1972 (Cambridge: Cambridge University Press, 1972).

3. Nelson Goodman, *Languages of Art* (Indianapolis and New York: Bobbs-Merrill, 1968). For the issue of expressiveness, see Richard Wollheim, "Correspondence, Projective Properties, and Expression in the Arts," reprinted as Essay IX in the present volume.

4. I have argued for this in many places, but most explicitly in Richard Wollheim, *Art and Its Objects,* 2nd ed. (Cambridge and New York: Cambridge University Press, 1980), Supplementary Essay IV, "Criticism as Retrieval."

5. I here have in mind the famous anti-naturalist argument of G. E. More, *Principia Ethica* (Cambridge: Cambridge University Press, 1903).

6. For this simile I am indebted to the great monumental panel depicting the penance of Arjuna at Mahabalipuram.

7. See Richard Wollheim, "The Ends of Life and the Preliminaries of Morality: John Stuart Mill and Isaiah Berlin," reprinted as Essay II in this volume.

8. See note 10 to Essay II in this volume.

9. The relevance of this representational detail to our overall visual grasp of Manet's now dismembered painting was emphasized by Meyer Schapiro in his 1959 Columbia lectures on Impressionism, and later in conversation.

10. For the development of these ideas, see Richard Wollheim. "The Bodily Ego," reprinted as Essay IV in this volume.

11. Sir Leslie Stephen, "Dreams and Realities," reprinted in Sir Leslie Stephen, *An Agnostic's Apology, and Other Essays* (London: Smith, Elder, 1893).

II. The Ends of Life and the Preliminaries of Morality

1. *Collected Works of John Stuart Mill,* ed. V. W. Braden and J. M. Robson (Toronto: University of Toronto Press, 1963), vol. XVIII, p. 224.

2. Isaiah Berlin, "John Stuart Mill and the Ends of Life," reprinted in Isaiah Berlin, *Four Essays on Liberty* (Oxford: Oxford University Press, 1979).

3. Mill, *Works,* vol. XVIII, p. 224.

4. John Stuart Mill, *Autobiography* (London, 1873), pp. 133–134.

5. See, for example, John Stuart Mill, *Essays on Politics and Culture,* ed. G. Himmelfarb (New York: Doubleday, 1962), Introduction; and G. Himmelfarb, *On Liberty and Liberalism* (New York: Doubleday, 1974). For the refutation of this thesis, see J. C. Rees, "The Thesis of the Two Mills," *Political Studies,* 25 (1977), pp. 369–382.

6. In two early essays—the "Remarks on Bentham's Philosophy" (1833), which appeared anonymously, and "Sedgwick's Discourse" (1835)—Mill set himself against the identification of utility with selfish or self-regarding interest. In the earlier essay he used this point as a criticism of Bentham: in the later essay he used it in defence of Bentham against his critics. Both essays are to be found in Mill, *Works,* vol. X.

7. For simplicity of exposition I write throughout as though Utilitarianism is to be construed as act-Utilitarianism. I tend to believe that this is correct, but all my examples can be converted so as to accord with rule-Utilitarianism.

8. Mill, *Works,* vol. X, p. 110.

9. At two different places in the edition that he prepared of his father's *magnum opus,* for Mill a work of filial piety, he tried to ward off those who, in their efforts to criticize the view that man's evolved ends derive from the pursuit of pleasure, pointed to the fact that the two kinds of end are unresembling. Against such critics Mill argued that, when a genetic derivation is lengthy, "the resulting feeling always seems not only very unlike any one of the elements composing it, but very unlike the sum of those elements." James Mill, *Analysis of the Phenomena of the Human Mind,* ed. John Stuart Mill (London, 1869), vol. II, p. 321; cf. p. 252.

10. "Of all difficulties which impede the progress of thought, and the formation of well-grounded opinions on life and social arrangements, the greatest is now the unspeakable ignorance and inattention of mankind in respect to the influences which form human character." John Stuart Mill, *The Subjection of Women* (London, 1869), pp. 39–40. The "important but most imperfect science" of whose virtual non-existence Mill here complains he considered under the name 'Ethology, the Science of the Formation of Character,' in his *System of Logic;* see Mill, *Works,* vol. VII, book 6, chap. 5.

11. Mill, *Works,* vol. X, pp. 210–213.

12. For a discussion of these issues, see J. C. Rees, "A Re-reading of Mill on Liberty," *Political Studies,* 8 (1960), pp. 113–129; Alan Ryan, "Mr. McCloskey

on Mill's Liberalism," *Philosophical Quarterly,* 14 (July 1964), pp. 253–260; C. L. Ten, "Mill on Self-Regarding Actions," *Philosophy,* 43 (1968), pp. 29–337, and *Mill on Liberty* (Oxford: Clarendon Press, 1980); Richard Wollheim, "John Stuart Mill and the Limits of State Action," *Social Research,* 40 (1973), pp. 1–30; J. N. Gray, *John Stuart Mill's Doctrine of Liberty: A Defence* (London: Routledge and Kegan Paul, 1983); F. R. Berger, *Happiness, Justice and Freedom: The Moral and Political Philosophy of John Stuart Mill* (Berkeley and Los Angeles: University of California Press, 1984); and Jonathan Riley, *Utility in the Largest Sense: An Interpretation of J. S. Mill's Moral and Political Philosophy* (Cambridge: Cambridge University Press, 1985).

13. Mill, *Works,* vol. XVIII, p. 261.

14. Mill, *Works,* vol. XIX, p. 362. Some interesting observations on the interlock between Mill's concern with the formation of character and his political views occur in R. J. Halliday, "Some Recent Interpretations of John Stuart Mill," *Philosophy,* 43 (1968), pp. 1–17, reprinted in *Mill: A Collection of Critical Essays,* ed. J. B. Schneewind (New York: Doubleday, 1968).

III. The Good Self and the Bad Self

1. F. H. Bradley, *Ethical Studies,* 2nd ed. (Oxford: Clarendon Press, 1927), p. 214.

2. Ibid., p. 81.

3. Ibid., p. 65.

4. Ibid., p. 94.

5. Ibid., p. 144.

6. Ibid., p. 65.

7. Ibid., pp. 66, 267.

8. Ibid., p. 142.

9. Ibid., pp. 72–73.

10. Ibid., p. 71.

11. Ibid., pp. 263–268.

12. This is to be taken as the first substantive reference in this lecture to the work of Melanie Klein, with which it will later engage: and the relevant contrast here is with the work of Anna Freud and that of Margaret Mahler and her coworkers.

13. Bradley remarks wrily, "It is not pleasant to live in the public room of an inn where eating goes on all day." *Ethical Studies,* p. 268. J. L. Austin used to make a related point in his lectures when he asked his audience to consider being woken up in the middle of the night and offered a piece of plum-cake.

14. Ibid., pp. 266, 267, and 283n.

15. Ibid., p. 284.

16. Ibid., p. 284.

17. Ibid., p. 282.

18. Ibid., p. 172.

19. Ibid., p. 289.

20. Ibid., p. 276.

21. Ibid., p. 301.

22. Ibid., p. 298.

23. Ibid., p. 298.

24. Sigmund Freud, *The Standard Edition of the Complete Psychological Works of Sigmund Freud,* translated from the German under the General Editorship of James Strachey (London: Hogarth Press and the Institute of Psycho-Analysis, 1953–1974), vol. XIV, 1914c.

25. Ibid., vol. XIV, 1917e [1915].

26. Ibid., vol. XVIII, 1921c.

27. Melanie Klein, *The Writings of Melanie Klein,* ed. Roger Money-Kyrle (London: Hogarth Press, 1975, and New York: The Free Press, 1984), vol. I, p. 291.

28. See Richard Wollheim, "Identification and Imagination," in *Freud: A Collection of Critical Essays,* ed. Richard Wollheim (New York: Doubleday, 1974).

29. One of the most thorough and systematic discussions of these distinctions, though without benefit of later work, particularly of the Kleinian school, is Roy Schafer, *Aspects of Internalization* (New York: International University Press, 1968). See also Richard Wollheim, *The Thread of Life* (Cambridge, Mass.: Harvard University Press, 1984, and Cambridge: Cambridge University Press, 1985).

30. Wollheim, "Identification and Imagination."

31. This is not entirely fair. But in this lecture I have deliberately omitted whatever advantage Bradley's moral theory tries to derive from the metaphysical view that humanity is a concrete universal or that the individual self is properly seen as part of a larger whole from which it is a mere abstraction. It claims that advantage at a very high price.

32. Bradley, *Ethical Studies,* p. 269n.

33. The formulation of the depressive position and the related contrast between persecutory and depressive anxiety are first given in Melanie Klein, "A Contribution to the Psychogenesis of Manic-Depressive States," reprinted in Klein, *Writings,* vol. I.

34. Richard Wollheim, *F. H. Bradley* (Harmondsworth, Middlesex: Penguin Books, 1959).

35. Klein, *Writings,* vol. I, p. 253.

36. Ibid., vol. III, p. 186.

37. At Oxford I was fortunate enough to be amongst the very first pupils of R. M. Hare. I learnt much from him, but not always what he expressly taught. One belief that survived his teaching is that in morals philosophical psychology has precedence over the philosophy of language as a guide to the truth. Whatever substance there is to the thesis that statements affirming what we ought to do are

self-addressed commands surely comes not from the logical form of "ought"-sentences but from the phenomenology of obligation.

IV. The Bodily Ego

1. Sigmund Freud, *The Standard Edition of the Complete Psychological Works of Sigmund Freud*, translated from the German under the General Editorship of James Strachey (London: Hogarth Press and the Institute of Psycho-Analysis, 1953–1974), vol. XIX, 1923b, pp. 26 and 27.

2. Thomas Nagel, "What Is It like to be a Bat?" reprinted in Thomas Nagel, *Mortal Questions* (Cambridge and New York: Cambridge University Press, 1979), and Jennifer Hornsby, "Which Physical Events Are Mental Events?" *Proceedings of the Aristotelian Society*, 81 (1980–81), pp. 73–92.

3. Donald Davidson, "Thought and Talk," reprinted in Donald Davidson, *Inquiries into Truth and Interpretation* (Oxford: Clarendon Press, 1984).

4. Richard Wollheim, "The Mind and the Mind's Image of Itself," reprinted in Richard Wollheim, *On Art and the Mind* (London: Allen Lane, 1973, and Cambridge, Mass.: Harvard University Press, 1974), and "Identification and Imagination," in *Freud: A Collection of Critical Essays*, ed. Richard Wollheim (New York: Doubleday, 1974).

5. Freud, *Works*, vol. XIX, 1925h.

6. Ibid., vol. XIX, 1925h, p. 237.

7. Ibid., vol. XIV, 1915c, pp. 136–138; vol. XIV, 1917e (1915), pp. 243–258; vol. XVIII, 1922b, pp. 105–116 and 129–134; vol. XIX, 1923b, pp. 28–39; and vol. XIX, 1924e, pp. 167–168.

8. Karl Abraham, "A Short Study of the Development of the Libido," in Karl Abraham, *Selected Papers on Psycho-Analysis*, trans. Douglas Bryan and Alix Strachey (London: Hogarth Press, 1949); Susan Isaacs, "The Nature and Function of Phantasy," in *Developments in Psycho-Analysis*, ed. Joan Rivière (London: Hogarth Press, 1952); and various writings of Melanie Klein, of which the most important are "A Contribution to the Psychogenesis of Manic-Depressive States," reprinted in Melanie Klein, *The Writings of Melanie Klein*, ed. Roger Money-Kyrle (London: Hogarth Press, 1975, and New York: The Free Press, 1984), vol. I, *The Psychoanalysis of Children*, reprinted in ibid., vol. II, and "Some Theoretical Conclusions Regarding the Emotional Life of the Infant," reprinted in ibid., vol. III.

9. Freud, *Works*, vol. I, 1950a [1887–1902].

10. Karl Pribram and Morton Gill, *Freud's 'Project' Re-assessed* (London: Hutchinson, 1976), p. 141.

11. Freud, *Works*, vol. IV, 1900a, pp. 127–131, and vol. XV, 1916–17, pp. 126–135.

12. Ibid., vol. XIV, 1917d [1915], pp. 229–235. There is some excellent recent

work on the wish and wish-fulfillment, still unpublished, by Sebastian Gardner and Tamas Pataki.

13. Ibid., vol. X, 1909d, pp. 233–235 and 298–301; vol. XIII, 1912–13, pp. 83–90; and vol. XVII, 1917a, p. 139.

14. See Richard Wollheim, "The Sheep and the Ceremony," reprinted as Essay I in this volume.

15. See Richard Wollheim, *Freud* (London: Collins, 1971), pp. 200–202.

16. Freud, *Works,* vol. XXIII, 1940a [1938], chap. IX.

17. For example, J. Sandler and B. Rosenblatt, "The Concept of the Representational World," in *The Psychoanalytic Study of the Child,* 17 (New York: International University Press, 1963), pp. 128–145.

18. In Melanie Klein, *Narrative of a Child Analysis,* reprinted in Klein, *Writings,* vol. IV, p. 31, she writes, "I do not interpret in terms of internal objects and relationships until I have explicit material showing phantasies of internalizing the object in concrete and physical terms."

19. For example, G. E. Moore, "Imaginary Objects," reprinted in G. E. Moore, *Philosophical Papers* (London: Allen and Unwin, 1959); Robert Howell, "Fictional Objects," in *Body, Mind, and Method: Essays in Honor of Virgil C. Aldrich,* ed. D. F. Gustafson and Bangs L. Tapscott (Dordrecht, Holland: Reidel, 1979); and Kendall Walton, *Mimesis as Make-Believe* (Cambridge, Mass.: Harvard University Press, 1990).

20. Freud, *Works,* vol. VII, 1905d, p. 198; vol. XVIII, 1921c, p. 105; and vol. XXII, 1933a, p. 99.

21. Ibid., vol. XI, 1910i.

22. Melanie Klein, "The Role of the School in Libidinal Development" and "A Contribution to the Theory of Intellectual Inhibition," both reprinted in Klein, *Writings,* vol. I. See W. R. Bion, *Second Thoughts* (London: Tavistock Press, 1967), sections 8 and 9.

23. I am grateful to W. D. Hart for perceptive comments on an earlier draft and to Jonathan Sinclair-Wilson for helpful suggestions about the present version.

V. Psychology, Materialism, and the Special Case of Sexuality

1. Adolf Grünbaum, *The Foundations of Psychoanalysis: A Philosophical Critique* (Berkeley, Los Angeles, and London: University of California Press, 1984), p. 113.

2. Thomas Nagel, "What Is It like to be a Bat?" reprinted in Thomas Nagel, *Mortal Questions* (Cambridge and New York: Cambridge University Press, 1979).

3. This tripartite distinction is treated at greater length in Richard Wollheim, *The Thread of Life* (Cambridge, Mass.: Harvard University Press, 1984, and Cambridge, England: Cambridge University Press, 1985), Lecture II.

4. This is a question which Freud set himself to answer in response to the work of the Hungarian paediatrician S. Lindner: see Sigmund Freud, *The Standard Edition of the Complete Psychological Works of Sigmund Freud*, translated from the German under the General Editorship of James Strachey (London: Hogarth Press and the Institute of Psycho-Analysis, 1953–1974), vol. VII, 1905d, pp. 179–183; cf. vol. XVI, 1916–17, pp. 313–314.

5. Ibid., vol. VII, 1905d, pp. 168–169 and 212–216.

6. Ibid., vol. VII, 1905d, for example, pp. 186–187, 217, and 233.

7. See William James, "What Is an Emotion?" *Mind*, 19 (1884), pp. 188–204, reprinted in William James, *Collected Essays and Reviews* (London and New York: Longmans Green, 1920), and *Principles of Psychology* (New York: Henry Holt, 1890), chap. XXV. Freud himself inveighs against the James-Lange theory as a specific account of affect: see Freud, *Works*, vol. XVI, 1916–17, p. 396.

8. Freud, *Works*, vol. VII, 1905d, pp. 167–171, 184–188, 204–205, and 210; and vol. XVI, 1916–17, pp. 327–328.

9. Ibid., vol. VII, 1905d, pp. 183–184 and 233.

10. Ibid., vol. VII, 1905d, p. 207. But cf. pp. 213–214, where Freud warns against the complementary error, which he attributes to Krafft-Ebing, of trying to explain sexuality in terms relevant exclusively to male sexuality by identifying it with the pressure of the accumulated "sexual substances upon the walls of the vesicles."

11. Ibid., vol. VII, 1905d, p. 183.

12. Ibid., vol. VII, 1905d, p. 184.

13. Ibid., vol. VII, 1905d, pp. 201 and 202.

14. Ibid., vol. VII, 1905d, pp. 208–214.

15. Ibid., vol. I, 1950a [1887–1902], pp. 295–297; and vol. V, 1900a, pp. 565–567 and 598–601.

16. Ibid., vol. VII, 1905d, pp. 181–182, 184, and 222; cf. vol. I, 1950a [1887–1902], pp. 312 and 320–321; vol. V, 1900a, pp. 565–568; and vol. XIV, 1915c, pp. 122–124.

17. Ibid., vol. VII, 1905d, p. 148.

18. Ibid., vol. VII, 1905d, pp. 149–150, 152, and 155–160; and vol. XX, 1925d [1924], p. 35.

19. Ibid., vol. VII, 1905d, pp. 135, 162, 172, and 231–243; vol. XI, 1910, p. 46; vol. XVI, 1915–1917, pp. 238–338; vol. XX, 1925d [1924], pp. 38–39; and vol. XXXIII, 1940a [1938], p. 153.

20. See Richard Wollheim, "The Bodily Ego," reprinted as Essay IV in this volume.

21. Freud, *Works*, vol. VII, 1905d, pp. 235–240; vol. XII, 1911c, pp. 61–62, and 1912c, pp. 233–237; and vol. XVI, 1916–1917, pp. 339–375.

22. See Richard Wollheim, *The Thread of Life*, Lecture II and passim, where the issue is discussed under the description 'psychic force'.

23. See Donald Davidson, "Causal Relations," reprinted in Donald Davidson,

Essays on Actions and Events (Oxford: Clarendon Press, and New York: Oxford University Press, 1980).

24. Melanie Klein, "A Contribution to the Psychogenesis of Manic-Depressive States" and "Mourning and Its Relation to Manic-Depressive States," both reprinted in Melanie Klein, *The Writings of Melanie Klein,* ed. Roger Money-Kyrle (London: Hogarth Press, 1975, and New York: The Free Press, 1984), vol. I, and "The Mutual Influences in the Development of Ego and Id" and "Some Theoretical Conclusions regarding the Emotional Life of an Infant," both reprinted in ibid., vol. III. See also Susan Isaacs, "The Nature and Function of Phantasy," in Melanie Klein et al., *Developments in Psycho-Analysis* (London: The Hogarth Press, 1952). I have developed some of these ideas in my essay "The Good Self and the Bad Self," reprinted as Essay III in this volume.

VI. Desire, Belief, and Professor Grünbaum's Freud

1. Ludwig Wittgenstein, *The Blue and Brown Books* (Oxford: Basil Blackwell, 1958), pp. 22–23 and 57, and *Lectures and Conversations on Aesthetics, Psychology, and Religious Belief,* ed. Cyril Barrett (Oxford: Basil Blackwell, and Berkeley and Los Angeles: University of California Press, 1966), pp. 23–27 and 41–52.

2. Richard Rorty, *Contingency, Irony, and Solidarity* (Cambridge: Cambridge University Press, 1989).

3. Ibid., p. 39.

4. For this account of the explanation of action, see Donald Davidson, *Essays in Actions and Events* (Oxford: Clarendon Press, and New York: Oxford University Press, 1980), passim, especially Essays 1 and 5. That Freudian theory offers an extension of commonsense psychology is cogently argued for in an essay I saw only after writing this piece: James Hopkins, "Epistemology and Depth Psychology: Critical Notes on the *Foundations of Psychoanalysis,*" in *Psychoanalysis, Mind and Science,* ed. Peter Clark and Crispin Wright (Oxford: Basil Blackwell, 1988).

5. Sigmund Freud, *The Standard Edition of the Complete Psychological Works of Sigmund Freud,* translated from the German under the General Editorship of James Strachey (London: Hogarth Press and the Institute of Psycho-Analysis, 1953–1974), vol. VI, 1901b, pp. 227–228.

6. Ibid., vol. VI, 1901b, for example, pp. 4, 39–40, 151–162, and 167–190. See also vol. XXIII, 1940 [1938], pp. 284–285.

7. Ibid., vol. X, 1909d, pp. 204 and 303.

8. Ibid., vol. X, 1909d, pp. 188–189.

9. Ibid., vol. VII, 1905d, pp. 115 and 278; cf. vol. XVI, 1916–17, pp. 299 and 454.

10. Ibid., vol. XX, 1926 [1925], pp. 92, 129–130, 135, 138–141, 162, and 166–167; and vol. XXII, 1933 [1932], pp. 81–85 and 92–95.

11. Ibid., vol. XIX, 1923e, pp. 142–145.

12. Ibid., vol. XIX, 1924d, pp. 173–179.

13. Ibid., vol. XVII, 1918b, pp. 80–84.

14. Ibid., vol. X, 1909d, pp. 209 and 283–284.

15. See ibid., for example, vol. XVII, 1916–17, pp. 320–357.

16. Adolf Grünbaum, *The Foundations of Psychoanalysis: A Philosophical Critique* (Berkeley, Los Angeles, London: University of California Press, 1984).

17. Ibid., p. 113.

18. See, for example, Donald Levy, "Grünbaum's Freud," *Inquiry,* 31 (June 1988), pp. 193–215, and David Sachs, "In Fairness to Freud," *Philosophical Review,* 97 (July 1989), pp. 349–378, reprinted in *The Cambridge Companion to Freud,* ed. Jerome Neu (Cambridge: Cambridge University Press, 1991).

19. Grünbaum, *Foundations,* pp. 127–146.

20. Ibid., p. 186.

21. See Freud, *Works,* for example, vols. IV and V, 1900a, pp. 280–281, 311, and n. 532; and vol. XV, pp. 109–112, 170–171.

22. Grünbaum, *Foundations,* pp. 185–189 (Grünbaum's italics). For the argument see pp. 177–189; cf. pp. 221–225.

23. Ibid., pp. 251–257.

24. Ibid., pp. 38–40 and 108–111.

25. Freud, *Works,* vol. XII, 1911c.

26. Grünbaum cites what he aptly calls the "causal microstructure of paranoia" in two separate contexts. One (Grünbaum, *Foundations,* pp. 76–77 and 79–81) is in the course of his onslaught upon the hermeneutic tradition and, in particular, upon an assumption he attributes to this tradition: that all Freudian explanations of action regard action as the output of a practical syllogism. The other (ibid., pp. 110–111) is to be found in his defence of Freud against Popper's claim that Freud was indifferent to the issue of falsifiability. In neither context does Grünbaum appreciate the fundamental place that the "causal microstructure" occupies in Freud's thought, or that it is this microstructure that assures the distinctively psychoanalytic nature of Freud's hypotheses. Even the reference to repression in the correlation of repressed homosexuality and paranoia fails to alert Grünbaum to the indispensability of infilling to the hypothesis.

27. *Behavioral and Brain Sciences,* 9 (June 1986), pp. 217–228.

28. Ibid., p. 228.

29. Grünbaum, *Foundations,* p. 253.

30. Ibid., p. 281.

31. Ibid., pp. 127, 173–266, and passim.

32. *Behavioral and Brain Sciences,* 9 (June 1986), pp. 237–238.

33. Grünbaum, *Foundations,* for example, pp. 130–135, 144–145, 161, 180, 242–245, and 257.

34. Ibid., pp. 135, 144, 151, and 215 (quoting Emanuel Peterfreund).

VII. Crime, Punishment, and "Pale Criminality"

1. H. L. A. Hart, *Punishment and Responsibility: Essays in the Philosophy of Law* (Oxford: Clarendon Press, 1968).

2. Ibid., p. 88.

3. Sigmund Freud, *The Standard Edition of the Complete Psychological Works of Sigmund Freud,* translated from the German under the General Editorship of James Strachey (London: Hogarth Press and the Institute of Psycho-Analysis, 1953–1974), vol. XIV, 1916d, pp. 332–333. Hart has subsequently told me that he did not have these essays in mind, and that he was thinking of the circumstances of some much-publicized American murder of the time.

4. Ibid., vol. XIV, 1916d, p. 333.

5. The importance of making this point was brought home to me in the ensuing seminar after my lecture at Oxford.

6. Some of these topics I have considered at greater length in Richard Wollheim, *The Thread of Life* (Cambridge, Mass.: Harvard University Press, 1984, and Cambridge, England: Cambridge University Press, 1985).

7. Brian Masters, *Killing for Company: The Case of Dennis Nilsen* (London: Jonathan Cape, 1985; New York: Stein and Day, 1986), p. 300.

8. Melanie Klein, "Criminal Tendencies in Normal Children," reprinted in *The Writings of Melanie Klein,* ed. Roger Money-Kyrle (London: Hogarth Press, 1975, and New York: The Free Press, 1984), vol. I.

9. For more on acting-out and on phantasy as a kind of motivational factor, see Hanna Segal, "Acting on Phantasy and Acting on Desire," in *PsychoAnalysis, Mind, and Art: Perspectives on Richard Wollheim,* ed. Jim Hopkins and Anthony Savile (Oxford: Blackwell, 1993).

10. I am deeply grateful to those who participated in the seminar that followed my lecture. My principal thanks go to Professor H. L. A. Hart, who opened the discussion. I should also like to thank Ronald Dworkin, John McDowell, David Pears, A. W. Price, and David Wiggins. I learnt a great deal from a private correspondence with Dr. A. Hyatt Williams, who has unrivalled analytic experience with criminal patients.

VIII. Art, Interpretation, and Perception

1. I have previously discussed some of these matters in Richard Wollheim, *Art and Its Objects,* 2nd ed. (New York: Cambridge University Press, 1980), especially in Essay IV where a bibliography is to be found. However the views expressed in the latter part of the present essay represent a further development in my thinking. I am grateful to Jens Kulenkampff for his perceptive comments on this essay when it was delivered at Stuttgart.

IX. Correspondence, Projective Properties, and Expression in the Arts

1. This essay deepens the view of expression to be found in Richard Wollheim, *Painting as an Art: Andrew W. Mellon Lectures, 1984* (Princeton: Princeton University Press, 1987, and London: Thames and Hudson, 1987).

2. A philosopher who offers such a further account, though exiguous, is Nelson Goodman, *Languages of Art* (New York and Indianapolis: Bobbs-Merrill, 1968).

3. This argument derives from Anthony Savile, "Nelson Goodman's *Languages of Art*," *British Journal of Aesthetics*, 2, no. 1 (Winter 1971), pp. 3–27. See also Richard Wollheim, "The Sheep and the Ceremony," reprinted as Essay I in this volume.

4. This position is upheld in Goodman, *Languages of Art*.

5. See Donald Davidson, "What Metaphors Mean," reprinted in Donald Davidson, *Inquiries into Truth and Interpretation* (Oxford: Clarendon Press, 1984).

6. Cf. John McDowell, "Values and Secondary Qualities," in *Morality and Objectivity: A Tribute to J. L. Mackie,* ed. T. Honderich (London: Routledge and Kegan Paul, 1985).

7. This view of experiential memory is expounded at greater length in Richard Wollheim, *The Thread of Life* (Cambridge, Mass.: Harvard University Press, 1984, and Cambridge, England: Cambridge University Press, 1985), Lecture IV.

8. On projection and its two forms, see Wollheim, *The Thread of Life,* Lecture VII.

9. In trying to think about this issue, and elsewhere in writing this essay, I have benefitted, or had the opportunity to do so, from conversations with Malcolm Budd, who has an unrivalled understanding of these arguments.

10. Recognition of this point is central to the argument of John Dewey, *Art as Experience* (New York: Minton, Balch, 1934).

11. See E. H. Gombrich, *Meditations on a Hobby-Horse* (London: Phaidon Press, 1963), passim.

12. This error permeates so-called experimental aesthetics. Some writers have falsely concluded that an account of expression that appeals to correspondence is inevitably committed to this error, for example, L. D. Ettlinger, *Kandinsky's "At Rest"* (Oxford: Oxford University Press, 1961).

13. I have developed this point in Wollheim, *Painting as an Art,* Lecture I.

14. I have discussed this point in Richard Wollheim, *Art and Its Objects,* 2nd ed. (New York: Cambridge University Press, 1980), secs. 15–18.

15. For 'unamplified' versions of the first view, see Leo Tolstoy, *What Is Art?* (Moscow and London, 1898), and Harold Rosenberg, *The Tradition of the New* (Chicago: University of Chicago Press, 1960). For 'unamplified' versions of the second view, see I. A. Richards, *Principles of Literary Criticism* (London: Rout-

ledge and Kegan Paul, 1924), and Deryck Cooke, *The Language of Music* (London: Oxford University Press, 1959). At this stage it might be queried how, if the artist doesn't have to feel the emotion, the emotion can cause him to express it. There are two possible answers. It is his being put in touch with the emotion that causes the artist to make the work. Alternatively, he is caused to do what he does by the desire to express the emotion. Either way round, expression in the arts is not expression in the sense considered in Essay VI in this volume. But that should be obvious anyhow.

16. Nelson Goodman, *Problems and Projects* (Indianapolis and New York: Bobbs-Merrill, 1972), p. 94, where the theory is mockingly attributed to "Immanuel Tingle and Joseph Immersion (ca. 1800)."

17. See, for example, Monroe Beardsley, *Aesthetics: Problems in the Philosophy of Criticism* (New York: Harcourt Brace Jovanovich, 1958).

18. In writing and revising this essay, I have tried to do justice to comments from Malcolm Budd, David Hills, Kendall Walton, and David Wiggins.

X. Representation: The Philosophical Contribution to Psychology

1. For the Figurative thesis, see, for example, Monroe Beardsley, *Aesthetics: Problems in the Philosophy of Criticism* (New York: Harcourt, Brace, and Company, 1958). However the thesis is also a commonplace in thinking about twentieth-century art and in twentieth-century art-educational theory.

2. I have argued for this in Richard Wollheim, *Art and Its Objects,* 2nd ed. (Cambridge and New York: Cambridge University Press, 1980), in "On Drawing an Object," reprinted in Richard Wollheim, *On Art and the Mind* (London: Allen Lane, 1973, and Cambridge, Mass.: Harvard University Press, 1974), and in Richard Wollheim, *Painting as an Art: The Andrew W. Mellon Lectures in the Fine Arts, 1984* (Princeton, N.J.: Princeton University Press, and London: Thames and Hudson, 1987).

3. For the distinctions involved in the Existential thesis and the Portrayal thesis, see, for example, Errol Bedford, "Seeing Paintings," *Proceedings of the Aristotelian Society,* supp. vol. XL (1966), pp. 47–62; Hidé Ishiguro, "Imagination," *Proceedings of the Aristotelian Society,* supp. vol. 41 (1967), pp. 37–56; Nelson Goodman, *Languages of Art* (Indianapolis and New York: Bobbs-Merrill, 1968): David Kaplan, "Quantifying In," in *Words and Objections,* ed. D. Davidson and J. Hintikka (Dordrecht, Holland: Reidel, 1969); Robert Howell, "The Logical Structure of Pictorial Representation," *Theoria,* 40 (1974): pp. 76–109; and Kendall L. Walton, "Are Representations Symbols?" *The Monist,* 58 (1974), pp. 236–254, and *Mimesis as Make-Believe* (Cambridge, Mass.: Harvard University Press, 1990).

4. For the discussion whether representation is natural or conventional, see, for example, Rudolf Arnheim, *Art and Visual Perception* (Los Angeles and Berkeley: University of California Press, 1954); E. H. Gombrich, "The Evidence

of Images," in *Interpretation: Theory and Practice,* ed. Charles S. Singleton (Baltimore: Johns Hopkins University Press, 1969), and "The What and the How: Perspectival Representation and the Phenomenal World," in *Logic and Art: Essays in Honor of Nelson Goodman,* ed. R. Rudner and I. Scheffler (Indianapolis and New York: Bobbs-Merrill, 1972); and Flint Schier, *Deeper into Pictures: An Essay on Pictorial Representation* (Cambridge and New York: Cambridge University Press, 1986).

5. It is because of this requirement that I have not included in my list of theories of representation the Causal theory, according to which a representation is of what has played an appropriate causal role in its production. For it seems to me that, as things stand, this theory accounts exclusively for portraiture and has to account for other forms of representation independently. Some adherents of the theory (David Wiggins, private communication) hold to the belief that ultimately the Causal theory can account for all kinds of representation, nonportraiture being exhibited as derivative from portraiture. For the Causal theory, see, for example, Ishiguro, "Imagination"; and Kaplan, "Quantifying In."

6. For the Illusion theory, see, for example, Susanne K. Langer, *Feeling and Form: A Theory of Art* (London: Routledge and Kegan Paul, 1953); and E. H. Gombrich, *Art and Illusion* (London: Phaidon, 1960). *Art and Illusion* also contains other theories of representation.

7. For the Arousal of Sensation theory, see J. J. Gibson, "A Theory of Pictorial Perception," *Audio-Visual Communications Review,* 1 (1954), pp. 3–23, and "Pictures, Perspective and Perception," *Daedalus,* 89 (1960), pp. 216–227.

8. For the Semiotic theory, see, for example, Richard Rudner, "On Semiotic Aesthetics," *Journal of Art and Art Criticism,* 10 (1951), pp. 67–77; Goodman, *Languages of Art;* John G. Bennet, "Depiction and Convention," *The Monist,* 58 (1974), pp. 255–268; Umberto Eco, *A Theory of Semiotics* (Bloomington: Indiana University Press, 1975); and Jan Mukarovsky, "Art as Semiological Fact," and Louis Marin, "Towards a Theory of Reading in the Visual Arts: Poussin's *The Arcadian Shepherds,*" both reprinted in *Calligram: Essays in New Art History from France,* ed. Norman Bryson (Cambridge: Cambridge University Press, 1988).

9. For the Resemblance theory, see, for example, Beardsley, *Aesthetics;* Ruby Meager, "Seeing Paintings," *Proceedings of the Aristotelian Society,* supp. vol. 40 (1966), pp. 63–84; Jerry Fodor, *The Language of Thought* (New York: Crowell, 1975); and David Novitz, *Pictures and Their Use in Communication* (The Hague: Mouton, 1977).

10. For the Information theory, see J. J. Gibson, "The Information Available in Pictures," *Leonardo,* 4 (1971), pp. 27–35; and John M. Kennedy, *A Psychology of Picture Perception* (San Francisco: Jossey-Bass, 1974).

11. The Illusion theory is criticized in, for example, Bedford, "Seeing Paintings"; Göran Hermeren, *Representation and Meaning in the Visual Arts* (Lund: Laromedelsforlaget, 1969); and in Richard Wollheim, "Reflections on *Art and*

Illusion," reprinted in Wollheim, *On Art and the Mind.* The Arousal of Sensation theory is criticized in Goodman, *Languages of Art;* Gibson, "The Information Available in Pictures"; and Kennedy, *A Psychology of Picture Perception.* The Semiotic theory is criticized in Richard Wollheim, "Nelson Goodman's *Languages of Art,*" reprinted in Wollheim, *On Art and the Mind,* and "Pictures and Language," reprinted as Essay XII in this volume; and in Schier, *Deeper into Pictures.* The point that this theory must be incorporated in any sound overall theory is argued for in Kent Bach, "Part of What a Picture Is," *British Journal of Aesthetics,* 10 (1970), pp. 119–137; and T. G. Roupas, "Information and Pictorial Representation," in *The Arts and Cognition,* ed. David Perkins and Barbara Leondar (Baltimore: Johns Hopkins University Press, 1977). The Resemblance theory is criticized in Bedford, "Seeing Paintings"; Goodman, *Languages of Art;* Wollheim, *Art and Its Objects;* Max Black, "How Do Pictures Represent?" in E. H. Gombrich, Julian Hochberg, and Max Black, *Art, Perception, and Reality* (Baltimore: Johns Hopkins University Press, 1970); and Risto Pitkänen, "The Resemblance View of Pictorial Representation," *British Journal of Aesthetics,* 16 (1976), pp. 313–322. The Information theory is criticized in Nelson Goodman, "Professor Gibson's New Perspective," *Leonardo,* 4 (1971), pp. 359–360, and (more sympathetically) in Roupas, "Information and Pictorial Representation."

12. For this theory, see Wollheim, *Art and Its Objects.* There however the theory is stated in terms of the Wittgensteinian notion of "seeing-as" rather than in terms of "seeing-in," which I have now come to see is more perspicuous. I owe this insight largely to Richard Damann. The theory is restated in various essays in Wollheim, *On Art and the Mind,* and more recently in Wollheim, *Painting as an Art.* It is criticized in Schier, *Deeper into Pictures.*

13. For example, W. Hudson, "Pictorial Depth Perception in Sub-Cultural Groups in Africa," *Journal of Social Psychology,* 52 (1960), pp. 183–208, and "Pictorial Perception and Educational Adaptation in Africa," *Psychologia Africana,* 9 (1962), pp. 226–239; and A. C. Mundy-Castle, "Pictorial Depth Perception in Ghanaian Children," in *International Journal of Psychology,* 1 (1966), pp. 290–300, which is (in part) reprinted in *Cross-Cultural Studies,* ed. D. R. Price-Williams (Harmondsworth, Middlesex: Penguin, 1969).

14. This point seems to have been appreciated in M. Wober, "On Cross-Cultural Psychology," in *Bulletin of the British Psychological Society,* 25 (1972), pp. 203–205.

15. See, for example, Jan B. Deregowski, "Illusion and Culture," in *Illusion in Nature and Art,* ed. R. L. Gregory and E. H. Gombrich (London: Duckworth, 1973).

16. I have argued for this in Wollheim, "Reflections on *Art and Illusion.*" The point receives empirical support in M. H. Pirenne, *Optics, Painting and Photography* (Cambridge: Cambridge University Press, 1970) and is used interestingly

by Michael Polanyi in "What Is a Painting?" *British Journal of Aesthetics,* 10 (1970), pp. 225–236. The point derives from a suggestion of Albert Einstein in a letter to Pirenne. See also Michael Kubovy, *The Psychology of Perception and Renaissance Art* (Cambridge and New York: Cambridge University Press, 1986).

17. The indifference shown by many perceptual psychologists between real-scene perception and representational perception is inveighed against in R. L. Gregory, *The Intelligent Eye* (London: Weidenfeld and Nicolson, and New York: McGraw-Hill, 1970). The point is taken account of in Hochberg, "The Representation of Things and People," in Gombrich et al., *Art, Perception and Reality.*

18. Cf. Fred Dubery and John Willats, *Drawing Systems* (London: Studio Vista, and New York: Van Nostrand Reinhold, 1972). The point is disputed in Deregowski, "Illusion and Culture." See also Martin Kemp, *The Science of Art* (New Haven and London: Yale University Press, 1990). In the writing of this essay I have benefitted greatly from discussion with Patrick Maynard, Antonia Phillips, David Wiggins, and John Willats, to all of whom I owe a debt of gratitude. It was in conversation with J. W. N. Watkins that I came to appreciate how stubborn is the prejudice that mastery of linear perspective *is* cognitive progress.

XI. Pictorial Style: Two Views

1. Heinrich Wölfflin, *The Principles of Art History,* trans. M. D. Hottinger (New York: Holt, 1932), Introduction.

2. This point is examined in a subtle and penetrating way in Nelson Goodman, *The Language of Art* (Indianapolis and New York: Bobbs-Merrill, 1968), chap. 3.

3. See James S. Ackerman, "Western Art History," in *Art and Archaeology,* ed. James S. Ackerman and Rhys Carpenter (Englewood Cliffs, N.J.: Prentice-Hall, 1963), where a similar view is argued for.

4. See Richard Wollheim, *Art and Its Objects,* 2nd ed. (New York: Cambridge University Press, 1980), and *Painting as Art: Andrew W. Mellon Lectures in the Fine Arts, 1984* (Princeton, N.J.: Princeton University Press, and London: Thames and Hudson, 1987).

5. Heinrich Wölfflin, *Classic Art,* trans. Peter Murray (London: Phaidon, 1953), p. 144.

6. E. H. Gombrich, *Norm and Form* (London: Phaidon, 1966).

7. Cf. Paul Frankl, *Das System der Kunstwissenschaft* (Brunn and Leipzig: Rohrer, 1938).

8. The difference between a weak relativization thesis and a strong relativization thesis corresponds to the difference between thesis D, or the Thesis of the Sortal Dependency of Individuation, and thesis R, or the Thesis of the Relativity of Identity, as these are carefully discussed in David Wiggins, *Sameness and Substance* (Oxford: Basil Blackwell, 1980). Wiggins accepts D, and rejects R.

9. Cf. Nelson Goodman, "The Status of Style," *Critical Inquiry,* 1 (1975), pp. 799–811.

10. See J. A. Gere, *Taddeo Zuccaro: His Development Studied in His Drawings* (London: Faber, 1969).

11. Cf. Jerry A. Fodor, *Psychological Explanation* (New York: Random House, 1968), and Hilary Putnam, *Mind, Language, and Reality* (Cambridge: Cambridge University Press, 1975).

12. Giovanni Morelli, *Italian Painters: Critical Studies of Their Works,* 2 vols., trans. Constance ffoulkes (London, 1892–93). Cf. Richard Wollheim, "Giovanni Morelli and the Origins of Scientific Connoisseurship," in Richard Wollheim, *On Art and the Mind* (London: Allen Lane, 1973, and Cambridge, Mass.: Harvard University Press, 1974), pp. 177–201.

13. Such a phenomenon is brilliantly recorded in the context of Guercino's development, though described somewhat differently, in Denis Mahon, *Studies in Seicento Art and Theory* (London: University of London Press, 1947). I have illustrated these different departures from individual style in Wollheim, *Painting as an Art.*

14. For example, Stephen Ullman, *Style in the English Novel* (Cambridge: Cambridge University Press, 1957).

15. For example, Willard V. Quine, *Philosophy of Logic* (Englewood Cliffs, N.J.: Prentice-Hall, 1970); and Goodman, "The Status of Style."

16. E. H. Gombrich, *Art and Illusion* (New York: Pantheon Books, and London: Phaidon, 1960), pp. 367–370.

17. For example, E. H. Gombrich, *Meditations on a Hobby Horse* (London: Phaidon, 1963), passim, and "Style" in *International Encyclopaedia of the Social Sciences,* ed. David L. Sills (New York: Macmillan and the Free Press, 1968). I consider Gombrich's account of style and expression in Wollheim, *Art and Its Objects,* secs. 28–30.

XII. Pictures and Language

1. Richard Wollheim, *Painting as an Art: Andrew W. Mellon Lectures in the Fine Arts, 1984* (Princeton, N.J.: Princeton University Press, and London: Thames and Hudson, 1987).

2. On the requirements for the learnability of a language, see Donald Davidson, "Theories of Meaning and Learnable Languages," reprinted in Donald Davidson, *Inquiries into Truth and Interpretation* (Oxford: Clarendon Press, 1984).

3. For more on pictorial meaning and structure, see Flint Schier, *Deeper into Pictures: An Essay on Pictorial Representation* (Cambridge and New York: Cambridge University Press, 1986).

Credits

"The Sheep and the Ceremony." The Leslie Stephen Lecture, University of Cambridge, 1979 (Cambridge: Cambridge University Press, 1979).

"The Ends of Life and the Preliminaries of Morality: John Stuart Mill and Isaiah Berlin," in *The Idea of Freedom: Essays in Honour of Isaiah Berlin,* ed. Alan Ryan (Oxford: Oxford University Press, 1979). Title changed and text revised.

"The Good Self and the Bad Self: The Moral Psychology of British Idealism and the English School of Psychoanalysis Compared." The Dawes Hicks Lecture on Philosophy, 1975, in *Proceedings of the British Academy,* vol. 61 (1975), pp. 1–28. Reprinted in *Rationalism, Empiricism, and Idealism: British Academy Lectures on the History of Philosophy,* selected and introduced by Anthony Kenny (Oxford: Clarendon Press, 1986).

"The Bodily Ego," in *Essays on Freud,* ed. Richard Wollheim and James Hopkins (Cambridge: Cambridge University Press, 1982). Considerably revised.

"Psychology, Materialism, and the Special Case of Sexuality," read to the annual meeting of the American Psychoanalytic Association, 1987. Previously unpublished.

"Desire, Belief, and Professor Grünbaum's Freud." Previously unpublished.

"Crime, Punishment, and 'Pale Criminality.'" The Hart Lecture on Jurisprudence and Moral Philosophy, University of Oxford, 1985. *Oxford Journal of Legal Studies,* vol. 8, no. 1 (1988), pp. 1–16. Title changed and text revised.

"Art, Interpretation, and Perception," in *Kant oder Hegel? Uber Formen der Begrunden in der Philosophie* (Stuttgart: Ernst Klett, 1983), pp. 549–559.

"Correspondence, Projective Properties, and Expression in the Arts," in *The Language of Art History,* ed. Ivan Gaskell and Salim Kemal (Cambridge: Cambridge University Press, 1991).

"Representation: The Philosophical Contribution to Psychology." *Critical Inquiry,* vol. 3, no. 4 (Summer 1977), pp. 709–723. Copyright © 1977 by The University of Chicago. All rights reserved. A somewhat different version of this paper was presented at the Annual Conference of the Development Section of the British Psychological Society, 1976, and was published in *The Child's Representation of the World,* ed. George Butterworth (London and New York: Plenum Press, 1977). Revised.

"Pictorial Style: Two Views," reprinted from *The Concept of Style,* revised and expanded edition, ed. Berel Lang. Copyright © 1979, 1987 by Cornell University. Used by permission of the publisher, Cornell University Press. Considerably revised.

"Pictures and Language." *Art Issues,* no. 5 (Summer 1989), pp. 9–12. Revised.

Name Index

Subject Index